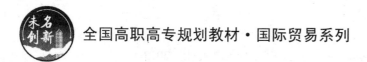
全国高职高专规划教材·国际贸易系列

商务英语函电

Business English Correspondence

主　编　周　峰　魏莉霞
副主编　陆美燕　任大力　项春媛

图书在版编目(CIP)数据

商务英语函电/周峰，魏莉霞主编． —北京：北京大学出版社，2013.1
（全国高职高专规划教材·国际贸易系列）
ISBN 978-7-301-21900-3

Ⅰ．①商… Ⅱ．①周… ②魏… Ⅲ．①国际商务－英语－电报信函－写作－高等职业教育－教材 Ⅳ．①H315

中国版本图书馆 CIP 数据核字（2013）第 002507 号

书　　　名：商务英语函电
著作责任者：周　峰　魏莉霞　主编
策 划 编 辑：胡伟晔
责 任 编 辑：胡伟晔　王慧馨
标 准 书 号：ISBN 978-7-301-21900-3/F·3470
出　版　者：北京大学出版社
地　　　址：北京市海淀区成府路 205 号　100871
网　　　址：http://www.pup.cn　　新浪官方微博：@北京大学出版社
电　　　话：邮购部 62752015　发行部 62750672　编辑部 62765126　出版部 62754962
电 子 信 箱：zyjy@pup.cn
印　刷　者：山东省高唐印刷有限责任公司
发　行　者：北京大学出版社
经　销　者：新华书店
　　　　　　787 毫米×1092 毫米　16 开本　16 印张　387 千字
　　　　　　2013 年 1 月第 1 版　2015 年 12 月第 2 次印刷
定　　　价：30.00 元

未经许可，不得以任何方式复制或抄袭本书之部分或全部内容。
版权所有，侵权必究
举报电话：010-62752024　电子信箱：fd@pup.pku.edu.cn

出版说明

自 2006 年推出《21 世纪全国高职高专国际贸易类规划教材》之后，本系列教材赢得了市场的认可，美誉度很高。不仅每年重印，有的还每年重印两三次，这自然要归功于各位参与的专家和编者，归因于他们开拓进取的精神、认真负责的态度和一切为学生着想的理念。然而，随着本学科的不断发展、各高等院校教改的不断推进，以及国际贸易形势的复杂多变，虽然每年重印都会有一些小的修订，但显然也已经有些不合时宜了。为此，我们广泛听取各方面反馈的宝贵意见和建议，汲取新鲜营养，继承原先优势，总结经验教训，共同致力打造一系列适应新形势的高品牌、高质量的优秀教材，期望在某些方面有所突破和发展，争取更上一层楼。

本系列教材的特点如下：

1. 集思广益，以学生为主体。广泛咨询采纳专家意见，研究目前教学主体（学生）的特点，站在其立场上设计相关项目，加上教师的适当点拨，不仅可以促进相关知识的内化，达到理解和巩固的目的，更有利于创新思维的形成。

2. 内容新颖，与岗位零距离。更新内容，选用新知识和新材料，运用最新的教改成果，切实结合资格考试，为学生取得"双证"、提高就业率服务。体例上突破了传统教材，采用项目化和情境式。案例与实训安排得当，与现实紧密结合，增强了实用性和应用性，最大程度地实现了与工作岗位的无缝接轨。

3. 概念明确，重点突出。考虑到国际贸易自身的特点，概念表示语言简洁凝练，表达明确，不仅标注相应的英文，而且用不同字体标出。整体教学目标明确，重点突出。

4. 配套齐全，力求立体化。配套完备，主体教材配有相应的技能训练册，且每本教材都配有相应的习题及课件或相关材料，如 PPT 等，便于教学。甚至还开发相关的网站，力图打造立体化教材。

此外，在排版上使整体风格设计更加人性化，增强可阅读性。

本系列教材不仅可供高职高专的学生使用，也可供培训机构或相关学校采用，还可供政府及企业相关人员和广大学习爱好者参考。

尽管我们尽心尽力，但仍不可能尽善尽美，敬请广大师生不吝惠予宝贵建议和意见，我们一直在追求精益求精，努力提供更好的服务。同时也热忱欢迎有志于为教学事业做贡献的您的积极参与，让我们携手，共同为打造优秀教材而努力。E-mail: huweiye73@sina.com。

北京大学出版社
2012 年 10 月

前　言

"商务英语函电"是高职高专院校对外贸易类专业的核心课程之一，其特点是要求学生能将英语语言技能与具体的外贸业务相结合，因而实际操作性很强。本教材是《国际商务函电》的修订版，所涉内容涵盖了国际商务活动中建立业务关系、询价及回复、报盘与还盘、促销、订货下单、付款、包装、保险、装运、投诉理赔、代理等业务环节，并以外贸业务员岗位典型工作任务为导向，通过业务背景知识介绍、核心句型学习、实例分析、模拟套写、考证实战、课后拓展等多种形式，使学习者科学有效地掌握处理各种外贸业务函电的技巧和方法。同时，该教材注重培养学习者对外贸英语函电的书面交际能力和实践操作能力，因而有助于满足其将来从事外贸岗位顺利完成各项实际业务的需要，同时也为在校生和外经贸从业人员参加外贸类职业证格考试提供帮助。

本教材为2012年浙江省教育厅科研项目"示范性高职院校ESP特色课程建设实证研究"成果之一（项目编号：Y201223177），"第三期全国高职高专英语类专业教学改革立项课题——基于典型工作任务的高职商务英语课程设计与教学实施"（项目编号：GZGZ7611-084）成果之一。本教材的主要特色是：

第一，科学性。从高职生实际水平和岗位要求出发，教材内容难度适中，善于激发学生学习积极性。

第二，系统性。按进出口业务流程分类，以外贸业务函电技巧为主线，运用实际案例系统编排课程内容。

第三，实用性。把握"实用、够用、能用"原则，注重实践操作技能的培养。

第四，针对性。以外贸类职业资格证书考试要求为导向，有的放矢，突出教材时效性。

本教材由周峰、魏莉霞任主编，陆美燕、任大力、项春媛任副主编。参加编写的人员有：北京工业大学通州分校魏莉霞（Unit 1、Unit 6）、丽水职业学院项春媛（Unit 2、Unit 12）、浙江广厦职业学院陈晨（Unit 3）、湖州职业学院黄笑菡（Unit 4）、湖州职业技术学院周峰（Unit 5、Unit 8）、山西旅游职业技术学院任大力（Unit 7）、山西旅游职业技术学院陈燕（Unit 9）、浙江广厦职业技术学院陆美燕（Unit 10）、山西旅游职业技术学院刘维瑛（Unit 11）。在教材编写过程中，我们得到了外贸行业专家与各兄弟院校专业教师的悉心指导和帮助，同时也借鉴了不少专家、学者的研究成果和著作，在此对他们表示衷心的感谢。

由于编者水平有限，编写过程中难免出现不当和疏漏之处，敬请各位专家、同人和读者批评指正，以便再版时进行修正，不胜感激。

编　者
2012年10月

内 容 简 介

　　本教材从高职高专院校"商务英语函电"课程的教学实际出发，遵循"实用、够用、能用"的原则，注重学习者实践操作技能的培养。全书共分 12 章，主要内容涵盖了国际商务活动中建立业务关系、询价及回复、报盘与还盘、促销、订货下单、付款、包装、保险、装运、投诉理赔、代理等业务环节，并以外贸业务员岗位典型工作任务为导向，通过业务背景知识介绍、核心句型学习、实例分析、模拟套写、考证实战、课后拓展等多种形式，使学习者科学有效地掌握处理各种外贸业务函电的技巧和方法。

　　本教材不仅可作为高职高专院校国际贸易、商务英语等涉外类专业学生课程教学使用，也可供准备参加全国外销员职业资格、全国商务英语翻译职业资格、剑桥国际商务英语等各类商务英语考试的考生复习备考以及外经贸从业人员阅读。

目 录

Unit 1　Introduction of Business Letters 1
　　Learning Aims 1
　　Background Knowledge 2
　　Writing Tips 9
　　Exercises 10
　　Supplementary Reading 11

Unit 2　Establishment of Business Relations 12
　　Learning Aims 12
　　Background Knowledge 13
　　Writing Tips 13
　　Sentence Patterns & Examples 14
　　Specimen Letters 15
　　Notes 17
　　Exercises 18
　　Supplementary Reading 21
　　After-Class Study 22
　　Chinese Version of Specimen Letters 23

Unit 3　Enquiries and Replies 25
　　Learning Aims 25
　　Background Knowledge 26
　　Writing Tips 26
　　Sentence Patterns & Examples 27
　　Specimen Letters 28
　　Notes 31
　　Exercises 33
　　Supplementary Reading 35
　　After-Class Study 37
　　Chinese Version of Specimen Letters 38

Unit 4　Offers, Counter-offers and Acceptance 41
　　Learning Aims 41
　　Background Knowledge 42
　　Writing Tips 44
　　Sentence Patterns & Examples 47

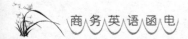

    Specimen Letters 48
    Notes 50
    Exercises 53
    Supplementary Reading 55
    After-Class Study 57
    Chinese Version of Specimen Letters 62

Unit 5   Sales Promotion 64

    Learning Aims 64
    Background Knowledge 65
    Writing Tips 66
    Sentence Patterns & Examples 66
    Specimen Letters 68
    Notes 70
    Exercises 72
    Supplementary Reading 75
    After-Class Study 76
    Chinese Version of Specimen Letters 78

Unit 6   Orders and Acknowledgements 81

    Learning Aims 81
    Background Knowledge 82
    Writing Tips 82
    Sentence Patterns & Examples 83
    Specimen Letters 84
    Notes 86
    Exercises 87
    Supplementary Reading 89
    After-Class Study 93
    Chinese Version of Specimen Letters 93

Unit 7   Terms of Payment 96

    Learning Aims 96
    Background Knowledge 97
    Writing Tips 99
    Sentence Patterns & Examples 99
    Specimen Letters 101
    Notes 105
    Exercises 111
    Supplementary Reading 114

  After-Class Study 116

  Chinese Version of Specimen Letters 126

Unit 8 Packing 130

  Learning Aims 130

  Background Knowledge 131

  Writing Tips 134

  Sentence Patterns & Examples 135

  Specimen Letters 137

  Notes 139

  Exercises 141

  Supplementary Reading 144

  After-Class Study 145

  Chinese Version of Specimen Letters 147

Unit 9 Insurance 150

  Learning Aims 150

  Background Knowledge 151

  Writing Tips 153

  Sentence Patterns & Examples 153

  Specimen Letters 154

  Notes 156

  Exercises 161

  Supplementary Reading 164

  After-Class Study 166

  Chinese Version of Specimen Letters 169

Unit 10 Shipment 171

  Learning Aims 171

  Background Knowledge 172

  Writing Tips 173

  Sentence Patterns & Examples 174

  Specimen Letters 175

  Notes 178

  Exercises 179

  Supplementary Reading 182

  After-Class Study 183

  Chinese Version of Specimen Letters 187

Unit 11 Complaints and Claims ... 189

    Learning Aims ... 189
    Background Knowledge ... 190
    Writing Tips ... 190
    Sentence Patterns & Examples ... 191
    Specimen Letters ... 193
    Notes ... 196
    Exercises ... 197
    Supplementary Reading ... 199
    After-Class Study ... 201
    Chinese Version of Specimen Letters ... 202

Unit 12 Agency ... 205

    Learning Aims ... 205
    Background Knowledge ... 206
    Writing Tips ... 206
    Sentence Patterns & Examples ... 207
    Specimen Letters ... 208
    Notes ... 210
    Exercises ... 213
    Supplementary Reading ... 216
    After-Class Study ... 223
    Chinese Version of Specimen Letters ... 225

Key to Exercises ... 227

Bibliography（参考文献）... 246

Unit 1　Introduction of Business Letters

Learning Aims

After you finish learning this unit, you are requested to:
(1) understand some basic knowledge about the layout of business letter;
(2) master the established practice to write a general business letter.

Background Knowledge

(I) *Brief Introduction to Business Letters*

Business letter has its special features, especially in format and structure. Considered in its most fundamental terms, a business letter may be defined as a message that attempts to influence its receiver to take some action or attitude desired by the sender. Thus, the ability to write an effective business letter will help those who want to represent themselves positively to their customers, competitors and employers.

(II) *Layout of Business Letters*

Usually, seven essential elements are involved in formal business letters. They are: letterhead, date, inside address, salutation, body of a letter, complimentary close and signature. Sometimes other elements may appear in the business letters such as reference number, attention line, subject line, IEC block, etc.

The general position of these elements is shown in the following sample:

```
                        Letterhead（信头）
Reference number（案号）
Date（日期）
Inside address（信内地址）
_____
Attention line（注意项）
Salutation（称呼）
Subject line（事由）
Body of the Letter（正文）
_____
Complimentary close（信尾敬语）
Signature（签名）
IEC block（缩写名、附件、分送标志）
```

✧ **Letterhead（信头）**

Letterhead should appear at the head of the first page of business letter. It includes the essential particulars about the writer—the name of his company, the full address of the company, postcode, telephone number, fax number, internet address and e-mail address.

<Sample 1>

```
            SHANGHAI FOXBORO COMPANY LTD.
       166 Caobao Road, Shanghai 200233, P. R. China
   Tel: 021-61234567    Fax: 021-61234666    E-mail: abcsale@163.com
```

Unit 1 Introduction of Business Letters

<Sample 2>

```
              SHANGHAI FOXBORO COMPANY LTD.
166 Caobao Road              Tel: (86)021-61234567
Shanghai 200233              Fax: (86)021-61234666
P. R. China                  E-mail: abcsale@163.com
```

✧ Date（日期）

Date is a vital part in business letters, which has special relevance: it might be a decisive factor as to whether an order is executed, a bill is paid, or a guarantee claim is met. Therefore, never omit the date in business letters. The placements of the date in English business letters are much different from those in Chinese letters. It can be aligned with the left or right margin below the letterhead. Usually there are two styles in which business letters are dated:

(1) The American style is:
◆ month, spelled out in full;
◆ day of the month, in digit, without th., nd, etc., followed a comma;
◆ year in digit.

For example: September 10, 2012   October 4, 2012

(2) The British style is:
◆ day of the month, in digit;
◆ month, spelled out in full;
◆ year, in digit.

There is no comma between the name of the month and the year.

For example: 10 September 2011   4 October 2012

<Sample 1>

```
              SHANGHAI FOXBORO COMPANY LTD.
        166 Caobao Road, Shanghai 200233, P. R. China
   Tel: 021-61234567  Fax: 021-61234666  E-mail: abcsale@163.com
September 10, 2012
```

<Sample 2>

```
              SHANGHAI FOXBORO COMPANY LTD.
166 Caobao Road              Tel: (86)021-61234567
Shanghai 200233              Fax: (86)021-61234666
P. R. China                  E-mail: abcsale@163.com
4 October 2012
```

❖ Inside Address（信内地址）

We include the address in the letter although it already appears on the envelope, because the envelope is usually thrown away. The inside address is often put two lines under the date line, aligned with the left margin. Generally, the inside address should include any or all of the following: the person's name and title, company name, street address, city, state or province, ZIP code and country.

<Sample>

> Mr. Roland Smith, Sales Manager
> ABC Company
> 123 Berry Drive
> Minneapolis, MN55667
> USA

❖ Salutation（称呼）

A salutation is the complimentary greeting with which the writer opens his letter. It is typed flush with the left margin below the inside address. In a very formal letter, you always need to address the reader with his/her surname, such as "Dear Mr. Smith", "Dear Ms. Green". If you have a close relationship with the receiver, you can use his/her first name such as "Dear Eager" or "Dear Jennifer". Be sure to salute to the correct addressee appeared in your inside address. Salutations in business letters can be followed by a comma or no punctuation at all.

❖ Body of a Letter（信的正文）

This is the most important part of a letter. And the following parts of this book will offer detailed advice for making this part as effective as possible. Attention here should be paid to the physical precision of the body. It usually begins one or two lines below the salutation.

❖ Complimentary Close（信尾敬语）

The complimentary close, like the salutation, is purely a matter of convention and a polite way of ending a letter. Therefore we should carefully select the most appropriate complimentary close to match the character of our communication and salutation. The correct punctuation for the complimentary close is a comma. Notice also that only the first word in a complimentary close is capitalized.

The following are the usual matches used in modern business letters:

	Salutation	Complimentary Closing
Formal	Dear Sir or Madam,	Very truly yours,
		Yours very truly,
		Very sincerely yours,
		Very cordially yours,
Semi-formal	Dear Mr./Mrs./Ms.,	Sincerely yours,
		Cordially yours,
		Yours sincerely,
Informal	Dear Lisa,	Sincerely,
		Cordially,
		Yours truly,
		Yours,

✧ Signature（签名）

The signature is the signed name or mark of the person writing the letter or that of the company he/she represents. In both cases, there should be a typed version of the name underneath the signature. The signature is put at the margin, leaving three-line spaces for the signature before typing the writer's name, title and department.

Never sign your letter with a rubber stamp.

<Sample>

> Yours sincerely,
> *Michel Chen* (signature)
> **Michel Chen**
> Sales Manager

In addition, business letters still have some special elements apart from the above seven essential elements:

✧ Reference Number（案号）

In some business letters, reference number is written for reference, quoting or filing. Its specific position is right below the writer's address and above the date.

<Sample>

> SHANGHAI FOXBORO COMPANY LTD.
> 166 Caobao Road
> Shanghai 200233
> P. R. China
> **Our Ref. No. FPB/SB-95**
> **Your Ref. No.**
> 4 October 2012

✧ Attention Line（注意项）

Usually, when the inside address doesn't contain the individual's name, attention line is used to name the specific person the letter is addressed to. Attention line is put between the inside address and the salutation, or within the inside address.

<Sample>

```
ABC Company
123 Berry Drive
Minneapolis, MN55667
USA
Attention: Mr. Roland Smith
Dear Sir,
```

✧ Subject Line（事由）

Subject line is right below the salutation, at the centre or the left place. It is usually underlined so as to arrest the reader's attention. Since it is briefly written, denoting the name of goods, the number of contract or letter of credit, it is convenient for reference and filing.

<Sample>

```
ABC Company
123 Berry Drive
USA
Dear Sir,
          Re. /Subj.: L/C No. 228 for 3500 Dozen Shirts
```

✧ IEC Block (initials, enclosures and carbon copies)（缩写名、附件及分送标志）

The IEC block appears on the left-hand margin two or three lines below the signature block (including complimentary close, signature, and typewritten identification).

(III) *Format of Business Letters*

✧ Full-Block Format（全齐头式）

<Sample>

```
                    Letterhead
Date
Inside address
_____
Salutation
```

```
┌─────────────────────────────────────────────────────────┐
│  Body of letter                                         │
│  _____  │
│  _____  │
│  _____  │
│                                                         │
│  Complimentary close                                    │
│  Signature                                              │
└─────────────────────────────────────────────────────────┘
```

In the full-block format, all lines begin at the left margin. There is no indention in the letter at all. This format is simple, easy to type, and is often used in business letters.

❖ Semi-Block Format（半齐头式）

<Sample>

```
┌─────────────────────────────────────────────────────────┐
│                        Letterhead                       │
│   Date                                                  │
│   Inside address                                        │
│   _____                                      │
│   Salutation                                            │
│                       Body of letter                    │
│   _____ │
│   _____ │
│   _____ │
│                                                         │
│                                   Complimentary close   │
│                                          Signature      │
└─────────────────────────────────────────────────────────┘
```

This format is a more conservative one of layout. In this format, the date, complimentary close and signature begin to the right of the centre of the paper. All the other elements are blocked against the left margin.

❖ Conventional Format（传统式）

<Sample>

```
┌─────────────────────────────────────────────────────────┐
│                        Letterhead                       │
│                                                  Date   │
│   Inside address                                        │
│   _____                                      │
│   Salutation                                            │
│                       Body of letter                    │
│   _____ │
│   _____ │
└─────────────────────────────────────────────────────────┘
```

```
_____
_____

                                    Complimentary close
                                         Signature
```

The difference between this format and the semi-block format is that it takes four or five spaces in the first line of each paragraph of the letter. The positions of other elements are quite similar to those in the semi-block.

(IV) *Addressing an Envelope*

The envelope helps to convey the image of a company. Basically, the addressing of the envelope for a business letter is the same as that for a personal letter. Here are two samples:

✧ Block Form（齐头式）

<Sample >

```
Jennifer Green
78 Cowpepper Road, Jericho            [Stamp]
Oxford X2 6DP England
                    Purchase Manager
                    Huapu Chemicals
                    Import and Export Corporation
                    29 Baishiqiao Road
                    Haidian District
                    Beijing 100034
                    P. R. China
By Air
```

✧ Indented Form（缩进式）

<Sample >

```
Overseas Trading Co.
  88 Market Street                     [Stamp]
    London, E. C. 3.
                Huapu Chemicals
                  Imp. & Exp. Corporation
                    Li Qing
                      Chaoyang District
    [Registered]        Beijing 100022
                          P. R. China
```

Writing Tips

❖ Writing Procedures（写信步骤）

Generally, there are five steps in letter writing to help you achieve your final aims. While writing, ask yourself the relevant questions following each step:

(1) Determine your writing purpose.（确定写作目的）

You should ask yourself why you write this letter.

(2) Analyze your reader.（分析阅信人）

You should think what you know about the receiver and what kind of relationship between you and receiver.

(3) Organize your thoughts.（构思信函内容）

What and how will you write?

(4) Write your drafts.（拟草稿）

Write and think if it is the best way to say what you want to say in this letter.

(5) Polish your writing.（修改信件）

Please go over the letter and check if this is a really effective business letter.

Be sure that in writing a business letter, there is no need to spend much time in finding colourful words and using complicated and beautiful modifiers in sentences. Simple English with brief but clear and accurate words is generally required. More often, some special terms and expressions in business are used.

❖ Outline（框架）

A typical business letter usually has three paragraphs in the body of letter, they are:

(1) Opening Paragraph

The opening paragraph of a business letter is like a headline in the newspaper. It should obtain the reader's attention at the first sight, and help to gain a positive response from the reader. In order to accomplish this aim, the following points should be considered:

◆ Be brief.（言简意赅）

As a general rule, keep the paragraph short—two or three sentences.

◆ Indicate what the letter is about.（点明信的主旨）

Get to the point immediately in the first paragraph and let the reader find the key information quickly.

◆ Refer to previous correspondence, if appropriate.（如果合适，提及以前的通信）

When there has been previous communications concerning the subject, reference to them is necessary. This may help the reader to get the point promptly.

◆ Set a positive and friendly tone.（设定积极友好的语气）

Setting a positive and friendly tone in the opening paragraph may help to evoke the positive reaction the writer desires.

(2) Middle Paragraph(s)（中间段落）

Middle paragraph support the first paragraph and provide more information. After finishing the opening paragraph, think about what the reader still needs to know so that he/she may react as you desire. Here necessary background and supporting information should be provided. Usually, information concerning these aspects should be considered: Who, What, Why, When, Where and How.

(3) Last Paragraph（结尾）

The last paragraph usually serves as a summation, suggestion or further request. It should:
- ◆ Conclude or restate the key point.（总结或重申重点）
- ◆ Request necessary action, if appropriate.（如果合适，请对方采取行动）
- ◆ Further confirm a positive image.（进一步加强积极的形象）

Exercises

I. *Look at the following letter, which breaks some of the rules we have just mentioned above. Identify each of the mistakes, and then rewrite the letter.*

```
                    Business International Co., Ltd.
                           68 Xingfu Street
              Dongcheng District Beijing 100032, P. R. China
                 Tel: 86-10-67554422   Fax: 86-10-67554424
9.8.2012
Purchase Manager
ABC Company
New York 66783
USA
                                                    Subject:

Dear Sir or Madam,
```

II. *Design an envelope and fill it with the address in the above letter.*

Supplementary Reading

How to Write Business Letters?

A business letter is a formal means of communication between two people, a person and a corporation, or two corporations. Business letters differ from personal letters because they follow very strictly set rules for composition. Many people are intimidated by the prospect of writing to strict guidelines, however business letters are nothing to be afraid of. Before you begin writing, answer the following questions:

- What is my purpose in writing this letter/memo/report?
- What does my reader want or need to know to understand my message?
- Have I answered important questions and provided the necessary information for the reader?
- Did I accomplish my purpose?
- Have I included boring, confusing, or distracting information?
- What do I want the reader to do when he or she is done reading this?
- Is that clear to the reader?
- Have I included all the information necessary for the reader to take this action?

The 7 C's of Business Letter Writing

Most problems with business letters are they are either hard to understand or very long and drawn out. One solution that many writers use to correct this problem is to double check the writing to make sure it follows the seven C's of business writing. The seven C's are: Clarity（清楚）; Conciseness（简洁）; Correctness（正确）; Courteousness（礼貌）; Completeness（完整）; Concreteness（具体）; Consideration（体谅）.

If you as a writer are able to effectively do all or part of these seven guidelines, then your paper will be on its way to being a good business letter.

Keeping Your Letter to the Point

The first thing you need to make sure of when writing a business plan is to make sure that you are not wasting the reader's time. There are two questions to make sure that you are not wasting their time and they are, "why am I writing" and "what do I want to achieve." If you are able to answer theses two questions, then you writing will be a third of what it would have been if you as a writer just sat down and started to write. It is a good thing that your letter is short because that way you are getting straight to the point of what you want you readers to know.

Business Writing Checklist

Once you have completed your business letter, there is a checklist that you can go through in order to make sure you letter is up to par. The basic idea of the checklist is to make sure the letter is: short, simple, strong, and sincere. If you go back and find that your letter has all of these qualities, then there is a good chance you have written an effective business letter.

Unit 2　Establishment of Business Relations

Learning Aims

After you finish learning this unit, you are requested to:

(1) Acquire how to obtain the information about your potential trade partners in foreign trade;

(2) Study some useful expressions and sentence patterns concerning the establishment of business relations;

(3) Master how to write a good and effective letter for entering into business relations.

Unit 2 Establishment of Business Relations

Background Knowledge

(I) *Significance of Establishing Business Relations*

Establishing business relations[1] is the first step of a transaction[2] in foreign trade. The development and expansion of a business depends on your customers. Needless to say[3], that no customer, no business. Seeking prospective[4] clients and establish business relations is one of the most important undertakings for a newly established firm or an old one that wishes to expand its market and enlarge its business scope and turnover[5].

(II) *Access to Your New Potential Customers*

Before entering into business relations with your new clients in foreign trade, you should have a thorough understanding of the following channels from which you may obtain the necessary information about your potential trade partners:

(1) Chamber of Commerce;
(2) Commercial Counselor's Office[6];
(3) Your branch offices[7] abroad;
(4) Trade Directories[8];
(5) Advertisements;
(6) Exhibitions and trade fairs[9];
(7) Banks;
(8) Internet;
(9) Market survey[10];
(10) Trade press.

Writing Tips

When writing letters to establish business relations in foreign trade, you should pay attention to the following points:

(1) To state the source of information and the intention of the letter;
(2) To introduce briefly one's own company, such as nature of company, business scope[11], financial standing, etc;
(3) To express the purpose of writing the letter;
(4) To express to the wish of setting up business relations and early reply.

If you reply to a letter of this kind, you should try to answer all the questions with necessary information the other party required. Please remember to reply promptly and politely even if you are unable to meet some specific requirements.

13

Sentence Patterns & Examples

【Pattern 1】learn/obtain/have… from…　　从……(渠道)获悉……

We learn that you are one of the leading exporters of electronic toys in China from Italian Greenland Trading Co., Ltd.
我们从意大利 Greenland 贸易有限公司处获悉贵公司是中国电子玩具的主要出口商之一。
We obtained your name and address from the commercial counselor of our embassy in Beijing.
我们从驻北京商务参赞处得知贵公司的名称和地址。
类似的表达还有:"owe…to…",表示从……渠道或途径获取相关信息。

【Pattern 2】be in the market for　　欲购,求购

You are in the market for black tea.
贵公司欲购红茶。
We learned from China Council for the Promotion of International Trade that you are in the market for Longquan celadon.
从中国国际贸易促进会获悉,你们有意采购一批龙泉青瓷。

【Pattern 3】establish/enter into/set up business relations with…　　与……建立业务关系

We have seen your advertisement in China Daily and are writing this letter to you with a view to establishing trade relations with you.
我们看到你方在《中国日报》上登的广告,现写信来希望与你们建立业务关系。
We are willing to enter into business relations with your company on the basis of equality and mutual benefit.
我们愿意在平等互利的基础上与你公司建立业务关系。

【Pattern 4】under separate cover/post　　另封邮寄

We are sending you under separate cover by airmail a copy of the latest catalogue.
现另封航邮寄去最新产品目录一份。
We are sending by separate post a statement of account, from which you will observe that there is a balance in our favor of USD 6,900.
我们现另封邮寄去账目明细表一份,从中你们可以看到你方尚欠我方 6,900 美元未付。

【Pattern 5】rest assured　　放心

You may rest assured that the superior quality of the material will give you every satisfaction.
请放心,料子的质量上乘,定会令你方满意。
You may rest assured that our quotation will prove to your satisfaction.
请放心,所报价格包您满意。

Unit 2 Establishment of Business Relations

【Pattern 6】appeal to   对……有吸引力；引起兴趣；投其所好

We are confident that the design and color of products will appeal to your market.
我们坚信我们产品的款式与颜色将会受到你方当地市场的欢迎。

We think the superb workmanship as well as the novel design will surely appeal to your customers.
我们认为其高超的工艺和新颖的设计必将吸引你方客户。

【Pattern 7】enjoy good reputation, enjoy great popularity   享有……声誉；受……欢迎

Our products enjoy good reputation all over the world.
我们的产品享誉世界。

Our products enjoy a great popularity at home and abroad due to their high quality and reasonable prices.
我们的产品品质优良、价格合理，深受国内外用户欢迎。

【Pattern 8】be of interest to …   对……是有意义的；对……有趣的

If any of our products are of interest to you, please send us your inquiry sheet.
若对我们的任何产品感兴趣，请给我们寄询价单。

If this offer be of interest to you, please advise us promptly.
如贵方对该报价感兴趣，请立即告知。

【Pattern 9】fall/come/lie within the scope of…   属于……的（经营）范围

We note with pleasure the items of your demand just fall within the scope of our business line.
我们很高兴地了解到您需要的产品正好属于我们的业务范围。

Items of this kind fall within the scope of our business activities.
此类商品在我方经营范围之内。

【Pattern 10】take the opportunity to…   借此机会……，利用此次机会……

May I take the opportunity to express my thanks?
我可不可以利用这个机会来表达我的感谢？

We take this opportunity to introduce ourselves as large exporter of leather goods in our country.
我们借此机会做自我介绍，我们是本国大的皮革制品出口商。

Specimen Letters

<Letter 1> Establishment of Business Relations

Dear Sirs,

　　We have learned from the Commercial Counselor's office of our Embassy that you are in the market for 100% cotton women's jackets, which just fall into our business scope. We are writing to enter into business relations with you on the basis of equality and mutual benefits.

Our corporation is specialized in[12] manufacturing women's garment, and we have got a lot of experience. Our own brand "Happiness" has won a high reputation at home and the abroad. They sell well in Russia, Occident, the Middle East and Southeast Asia area.

Our products are made of environmental-friendly[13] material, 100% cotton, good in airiness, moisture absorption, fashion in design, and comfortable in wear.

Enclosed is our latest catalogue of women's jacket, which may meet your demands. It will be a great pleasure to receive your inquiries for any of the items against which we will send you our best quotations.

We are looking forward to your early reply.

Yours sincerely,

<Letter 2> Reply to Letter One

Dear Sirs,

We acknowledge with thanks for the receipt of your letter of September 9, 2011 and take the pleasure of establishing business relations with you.

Your products are attractive and we plan to place large orders with you if your prices are competitive. We shall be obliged if you could send us sample books and best quotations on CIF New York basis.

We look forward to your favorable reply.

Yours faithfully,

<Letter 3> Self-introduction by Exporter

Dear Sirs,

We obtain your name and address from the website of alibaba.com and note with pleasure the items of your demand just fall within the scope of our business line. First of all, we avail ourselves of[14] this opportunity to introduce our company in order to be acquainted with[15] you.

Our firm is a Chinese exporter of various canned foodstuffs. We highly hope to enter into business relations with your esteemed company on the basis of mutual benefit in an earlier date. We are sending a catalogue and a pricelist under separate cover for your reference. We will submit our best quotation to you upon receipt of your concrete inquiry.

We are looking forward to receiving your earlier reply.

Yours faithfully,

<Letter 4> Importer's Request for Setting Up Business Relations

Dear Sirs,

We have seen your cotton garments displayed at Shanghai International Clothing

& Textile Expo and have a pleasure to ask you to send us details of your goods with the lowest CIF New York price.

We are one of the largest dealers of garments in America and our annual requirements for cotton garments are considerable[16]. We will place large orders with you if your price are competitive and your deliveries prompt. Meanwhile, we'd like to set up direct business relations with you after this transaction.

We are looking forward to hearing from you soon.

Sincerely yours,

<Letter 5> Exporter's Reply to Importer

Dear Sirs,

Thank you for your letter dated October 8. We are glad to learn that you are interested in entering into business relations with our corporation in the line of garments.

As requested, we are now sending you separately our catalogue and latest price list. If any of the items listed meets your requirement, please let us have your specific enquiry and we shall deliver the goods one month after receipt of your L/C.

We look forward to receiving your reply soon.

Yours faithfully,

Notes

1. establish business relations with   与……建立业务联系
2. transaction   交易
   transaction cost   交易费用，交易成本
   cash transaction   现金交易
3. needless to say   毋庸置疑
4. prospective clients   潜在客户
   prospective buyer   有意购买者，潜在的购买者
   They want to sell their house and already have a prospective buyer.
   他们想卖房，并且已经有了一位有意向的买主。
5. turnover   n.   营业额
   With our rich experience in marketing your products in our city, we have the ability to increase the turnover to $50, 000.
   我们在本地市场拓展贵司产品方面具有丰富经验，并且有能力将销售额提高 50,000 美元。
6. chamber of commerce   商会
   Your firm has been recommended to us by the Chamber of Commerce in Vancouver, Canada.

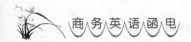

加拿大温哥华商会已向我公司推荐贵公司。
commercial counselor's office   商务参赞处
We learn from the commercial counselor of our embassy in Ottawa that you deal in table cloth.
我们从我国驻渥太华大使馆商赞处得知贵公司经营桌布生意。

7. branch office   分公司
8. trade directories   贸易行名录
9. exhibitions and trade fairs   展销会
10. market survey   市场调查

We conducted a market survey in July.
我们在七月做了一项市场调查。

11. business scope   经营范围

After the pioneering efforts, the company has a business scope to cover Beijing, Shanghai, Zhejiang, Guangdong and other places.
在前期努力下，公司已将经营范围覆盖至北京、上海、浙江、广州及其他地区。

12. be specialized in = specialize in   专营
13. environmental-friendly *adj.*   有利于环境的，环保的
14. avail oneself of   利用
15. be acquainted with   与……相识；与……熟悉
16. considerable   相当大的；重要的，值得考虑的

Exercises

I. *Translate the following terms into English:*

1. 商务参赞处
2. 报价
3. 订单
4. 商会
5. 经营
6. 另封邮寄
7. 习惯做法
8. 商品目录
9. 潜在客户
10. 价格表

II. *Translate the following terms into Chinese:*

1. establish business relations
2. business scope
3. importer
4. exporter
5. be in the market for
6. trade directory
7. specialize in
8. head office
9. reference sample
10. original sample

III. *Choose the best answer to complete the following sentences:*

1. We will _____ you as soon as the crop comes to the market.
   A. contact with   B. contact   C. get in touch   D. get contact

Unit 2 Establishment of Business Relations

2. We deal in decorative fabrics _____ different varieties.
   A. on   B. of   C. in   D. for
3. We shall do everything possible to assist you in _____ a mutually beneficial trade.
   A. developing   B. to develop   C. develop   D. development
4. The design of the goods is very nice but the color does not _____ to us.
   A. attract   B. appeal   C. appreciate   D. suit
5. Your firm has been referred to us by the ABC Co. of Canada, _____ we have done business for many years.
   A. which   B. with that   C. whom   D. with whom
6. I'm sure that the quality of our new products will _____ you in every respect.
   A. satisfy   B. satisfactory   C. satisfied   D. satisfaction
7. Should your products prove _____ in quality and reasonable in price, I trust substantial order will follow.
   A. satisfy   B. satisfactory   C. satisfied   D. satisfaction
8. The goods you offered are _____ line with the business scope of our clients.
   A. out of   B. without   C. outside   D. not
9. It will be _____ if you can give us your favorable reply.
   A. appreciate   B. appreciating   C. appreciated   D. appreciate it
10. We shall _____ if you will quote us the best price.
    A. appreciate   B. appreciating   C. appreciated   D. appreciate it

IV. Read the following sentences and try to find out the mistakes and make corrections. There is one mistake in each sentence.

1. We have obtained your name and address to Singapore Chamber of Commerce.
2. We are in the market on Groundnuts.
3. We are a state-operated corporation dealing with both the import and export of textiles.
4. We wish to enter business relations with your corporation for the supply of light industrial products.
5. We are sending you catalog in separate cover.
6. Would you please let us have a copy of your sample book so that we may acquaint ourselves in your business line?
7. Should any of the items be of interest to you, please let us know.
8. Our mutual understanding and cooperation will certainly result from important business in the future.
9. We have the pleasure of writing to contact with you in the hope of doing business with you.
10. In order to acquaint you with the chemical products we handle, we take pleasure in sending you on air our latest catalogue for your reference.

V. Translate the following sentences into Chinese:

1. We have been handling light industrial products for 20 years.

2. We have learned from the Chamber of Commerce that you are in the market for a large quantity of black tea.

3. If you find our price reasonable, please contact us.

4. We shall be pleased to receive your latest catalogue.

5. We have learned your name and address from the Internet.

VI. Translate the following sentences into English:

1. 我方愿在平等互利、互通有无的基础上与贵公司建立业务关系。

2. 我方专门出口中国工艺品，愿与贵方开展这方面业务。

3. 为促进双方业务往来，另封航邮寄上样品，供你方参考。

4. 如果贵方对我公司的经营范围感兴趣的话，我方将非常高兴地给贵方寄去我们的产品目录。

5. 我方预料到你方产品在我方市场会有着广阔的前景，我方保证随时给予你方密切合作，盼速复。

VII. Simulated writing:

Now you are required to write a letter to Bright Trading Co., Ltd. of USA, to inform them the following details:

敬启者：

　　承蒙金太阳贸易责任有限公司推荐，获悉贵公司的名称。我公司已与该公司有多年的贸易来往。

　　我公司专营中国龙泉青瓷产品的出口，该产品在世界上享有盛誉。现随函附寄目录一份供你参考，若贵方对某一产品感兴趣的话，希望与我方取得联系。

　　期盼早日回复。

谨启

Dear Sirs,

Yours faithfully,

Supplementary Reading

The Canton Fair

The Canton Fair is a trade fair held in the spring and autumn seasons each year since the spring of 1957 in Guangzhou, China.

The Fair is co-hosted by the Ministry of Commerce of China and People's Government of Guangdong Province, and organized by China Foreign Trade Centre.

Its full name since 2007 has been China Import and Export Fair（中国进出口商品交易会）, renamed from Chinese Export Commodities Fair（中国出口商品交易会）[1][2], also known as Canton Fair（广州交易会）, which abbreviation is "广交会" in Chinese.

The Fair is the largest trade fair in China. Among China's largest trade fairs, it has the largest assortment of products, the largest attendance, and the largest number of business deals made at the fair. Like many trade fairs it has several traditions and functions as a comprehensive event of international importance.

Contents

Fifty trading delegations, being composed of thousands of China's best foreign trade corporations (enterprises), take part in the Fair. These include private enterprises, factories, scientific research institutions, wholly foreign-owned enterprises, and foreign trade companies. The 101st fair saw 314 different companies from 36 countries.

Functions

The fair leans to export trade, though import business is also done here. Apart from the above-mentioned, various types of business activities such as economic and technical cooperations and exchanges, commodity inspection, insurance, transportation, advertising, consultation, etc. are also carried out in flexible ways.

Basic facts

First held: April 1957.

Interval: Three phases per session; two sessions per year.

Spring session: April 15-19 (Phase 1); April 24-28 (Phase 2); May 3-7 (Phase 3).

Autumn session: October 15-19 (Phase 1); October 23-27 (Phase 2); October 31- November 4 (Phase 3).

Venues:

China Import and Export Fair (Pazhou) Complex, 380 Yuejiangzhong Road, Haizhu District, Guangzhou 510335

Liuhua Complex: The Complex was first put into use in 1974. It was discontinued as a venue for the Canton Fair, starting from the 104th Session (Autumn 2008).[3]

Gross exhibition space: 1,125,000 m².

Number of booths: Over 55,800 standard stands (105th Session).

Varieties: Over 150,000.

Business turnover: 262.3 Million USD (105th Session).

Number of trading countries and regions: 203 (103rd Session).

Number of visitors: 165,436 (105th Session).

Exhibitors: Over 22,000 (with 21,709 Chinese exhibitors, 395 international exhibitors, 105th Session).

After-Class Study

世界主要会展

一、家具家居类

1. 科隆国际家具展　　　imm cologne　　德国
2. 拉斯维加斯家具展　　Las Vegas Market　　美国
3. 意大利米兰国际家具展　　Salone Internationale del Mobile di Milano　　意大利
4. 美国高点家具展　　Highpoint Market　　美国
5. 科隆国际办公家具及管理设备展　　Orgatec　　德国
6. 阿联酋迪拜国际家具展　　INDEX　　阿联酋

二、汽车配件类

1. 印度新德里汽车配件展览会　　AUTO EXPO　　印度
2. 中东（迪拜）国际汽车零部件展览会　　Automechanika Middle East　　阿联酋迪拜
3. 德国埃森轮胎展　　REIFEN　　德国
4. 俄罗斯莫斯科国际汽车配件展　　Automechanika　　俄罗斯
5. 美国拉斯维加斯汽车改装车展　　SEMA　　美国
6. 德国埃森改装车展　　ESSEN MOTOR SHOW　　德国

三、珠宝钟表类

1. 日本东京国际珠宝展　　IJT　　日本
2. 瑞士巴塞尔国际钟表与珠宝展览会　　BASEL WORLD　　瑞士
3. 阿联酋阿布扎比国际珠宝与钟表展　　JWS ABU DHABI　　阿联酋
4. 美国拉斯维加斯珠宝展　　LUXURY & PREMIERE　　美国
5. 拉斯维加斯钟表制造与珠宝展　　THE JCK SHOW　　美国
6. 阿联酋迪拜国际珠宝展览会　　Dubai Jewellery Show　　阿联酋

四、服装皮革鞋帽包类

1. 美国拉斯维加斯国际鞋类展览会　　WSA　　美国
2. 意大利米兰皮包展览会　　MIPEL　　意大利

3. 意大利米兰鞋类展览会　　　MICAM　意大利
4. 意大利米兰皮革皮毛展　　　MIFUR　意大利
5. 德国杜塞尔多夫国际鞋类展览会　　GDS　德国
6. 法国国际服装展览会　　FATEX　法国

五、能源光伏类

1. 阿联酋迪拜国际电力、照明及新能源展览会　　MEE　阿联酋
2. 英国阿伯丁国际能源展　　All-Energy Aberdeen　英国
3. 德国慕尼黑国际太阳能技术博览会　　INTER SOLAR　德国
4. 印度新德里国际可再生能源展　　Renewable Energy India Expo　印度

Chinese Version of Specimen Letters

<例信 1> 建立业务关系

敬启者：

　　我方从中国驻贵国大使馆商务参赞处获悉贵方欲购一批全棉女士夹克衫。由于该产品恰好属于我方的经营范围，因此我方致函以期在平等互利的基础上与贵方建立业务关系。

　　我公司专门生产女士服装并具有丰富的经验。我们的自创品牌"幸福"牌在国内外享有盛誉，产品畅销俄罗斯、欧美、中东、东南亚地区。我们的产品采用全棉的环保材料制作，透气性好、吸湿性强、设计时尚、穿着舒适。

　　随函附上最新的女士夹克衫的目录，相信能满足你方要求。期盼收到贵方的询盘，我方将发送最低报价于贵方。

　　希望贵方早日回复。

谨启

<例信 2> 回复例信一

敬启者：

　　收到你方 2011 年 9 月 9 日来信，谢谢。我们愿与你方建立业务关系。

　　你们的产品非常吸引人，如果价格也具有竞争力的话，我们一定会大批量订购。如你方能寄来样品薄和报纽约到岸价的最低价，我们将不胜感激。

　　期盼你方佳音。

谨启

<例信 3> 出口商作自我介绍

敬启者：

　　我们从阿里巴巴网站上看到您公司的名称和地址，并且很高兴地了解到您需要的产品正好符合我们的业务范围。我们很荣幸有这个机会向您介绍我们的公司。

　　我公司是一家中国的出口企业，主营各类罐头食品。我们非常希望能在双赢

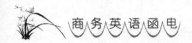

的基础上尽早同贵公司建立业务关系。我们给您发出了产品目录和价格表以供参考。如果能够收到您具体的询盘,我们将为您提供最优惠的价格。

期待您的尽早回复。

谨启

<例信 4> 进口商要求建立业务关系

敬启者:

我们在上海国际服装纺织品贸易博览会上见过贵方参展的棉质服装,请来函告知商品详情并报纽约到岸价的最低价。

我公司是美国最大的服装经销商之一,对棉质服装的年需求量相当大。如果贵方价格具有竞争力、交货及时,我方将大量订购。同时,我方愿意以此笔交易后与贵公司建立直接的业务关系。

盼早日复函。

谨启

<例信 5> 出口商回复进口商

敬启者:

贵方 10 月 8 日来函收悉,谢谢!我方很高兴获悉贵公司有兴趣在服装行业与我公司建立业务关系。

应贵方要求,兹另邮寄目录和最新的价目单。如果所列的任何商品符合贵方要求,请具体询价,我方会在收到贵方信用证后一个月之内交货。

盼早日复函。

谨启

Unit 3 Enquiries and Replies

Learning Aims

After you finish learning this unit, you are requested to:

(1) understand some basic knowledge about enquiry[1] and reply in foreign trade;
(2) acquire some writing skills and principles about enquiries and replies.

Background Knowledge

(I) *The Definition and Classification of Enquiry*

An enquiry is a request for information[2] on goods, it is regarded the first real step in business negotiation. When business people intend to import a product, they usually send an enquiry to an exporter. It may ask for a quotation[3] or an offer[4] for the goods they wish to buy, which can be made by writing correspondence, such as a letter, telex, fax, E-mail or by chatting through "MSN" "SKYPE" "Trade Manager" etc., or talk in person.

Enquiry can be of two types: general enquiry[5] and specific enquiry[6].

General Enquiry: The buyer asks for general information he needs, such as catalogue, price list, quotation sheet, sample[7], illustration[8] or a brochure, etc., which the exporter is in a position to supply.

Specific Enquiry: It may include great details such as the name of the commodity, quality, specification, quantity, price, discount, terms of payment[9], time of shipment, packing, etc., required by the buyer so as to enable the seller to make proper offers.

(II) Reply to Enquiry

Reply to enquiry is actually a response to the received enquiry. The relevant answer to every detailed question put forward by the buyer will be given by the seller. More important, the seller should try to push the sale of his commodities by giving the realistic description of commodities and other attractive terms and conditions.

Writing Tips

1. Enquiry

Enquiry is usually made by the importer to seek detailed information about specific goods. When you write an enquiry letter, the following guidelines should be followed:

(1) Mention how you get the relevant information (name, address etc.) about the exporter.

(2) Tell the exporter the items you are interested in and express your initial intention for purchasing.

(3) Invite a quotation or an offer asking for details (price list, catalogue, samples etc.) of your desired commodities.

(4) State the possibility of placing an order and hope to receive an early reply.

2. Reply

As we all know, enquiry means potential business. Therefore, reply to enquiry must be prompt, accurate, courteous and clear. It includes the following parts:

(1) An expression of thanks for the enquiry.

(2) Cover all the details that your clients asked for, such as name of commodities, quality, quantity, and specifications, unit price, terms of payment, packing method, shipment, illustrated catalogues, samples, etc.

(3) Express your hopes of doing business with your clients.

Sentence Patterns & Examples

【Pattern 1】enquire for / make enquiry for　　询购

A lot of customers have approached us to enquire for mohair sweaters.
许多客户向我们询购马海毛毛衣。

We will make enquiry for the articles we are interested in upon receipt of your catalogue.
一俟收到你方的产品目录，我们将立即对感兴趣的商品进行询购。

【Pattern 2】quote sb. for sth. / make quotation for…　　对……进行报价

Do you quote FOB or CIF for the goods?
就这批货，贵方是报 FOB 价还是 CIF 价？

Thank you for your quotation for the refrigerators.
感谢你方寄来的电冰箱报价函。

Please make your quotation for the lot on a CFR basis.
请你方按 CFR 方式报这批货的价格。

【Pattern 3】be in the market for　　欲购

We are in the market for a used car.
我们想买一辆二手车。

ABC company has spent much money on advertisement for potential customers who are in the market for their products.
为吸引潜在客户欲购其产品，ABC 公司在广告宣传上已投入不少。

【Pattern 4】place an order with sb. for sth.　　向某人订购某物

If your prices are competitive, we shall be pleased to place an order with you for gloves.
如你方价格具有竞争力，则我方将向你方订购手套。

We are ready to place an order with you for the garments, but only one condition is that the goods are confined to Australia.
我们准备向你们订购服装，但是唯一的条件是，货物只限卖给澳大利亚的公司。

【Pattern 5】at your request　　应你方要求

We send the counter sample at your request.
应你方要求，寄上对等样品。

At your request, we have amended the contract.
应你方要求，我们已经修改了合同。

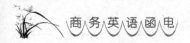

【Pattern 6】particulars   详细情况

We shall appreciate it if you will send us particulars of bed sheets and pillow cases.
若贵公司向我们寄送有关床单和枕套的详细情况,我方将不胜感激。

Particulars of our products are illustrated in this brochure.
我们产品的详细情况在这本小册子中有说明。

【Pattern 7】We regret to inform/ note you that …   我们很遗憾地告知你方……

We regret to note you that we cannot accept your price.
很遗憾这个价格我们不能接受。

We regret to inform you that we are unable to reduce the price.
很抱歉,我们不能减价。

We very much regret being unable to offer you this article at present.
很抱歉我们现在不能向你方提供这种商品。

【Pattern 8】We shall appreciate it if you…   若贵方……,我们将不胜感激

We shall appreciate it very much if you will give us your most favorable price.
若贵方能向我方报最优惠的价格,不胜感激。

We shall appreciate it if you will send us your latest catalogue for our reference.
若贵公司能寄给我方你们最新的产品目录作参考,我方将甚为感谢。

【Pattern 9】look forward to…   盼望,期待,希望

We are looking forward to your visit.
我们期待您的来访。

We are looking forward to receiving your early reply.
我们希望尽早收到你的回复

【Pattern 10】in reply to   回复,答复

In reply to your inquiry, we have sent you our latest price list.
为答复你方的询价,我们寄去了最新的价格单。

In reply to your telex dated April 2, we are enclosed this order sheet No. T135.
兹回复贵方4月2日电传,随函附上我方第T135号订单。

Specimen Letters

<Letter 1> A General Enquiry for Synthetic Fiber Goods and Reply

Dear Sirs,

　　Seeing your advertisement in the China Trade Directory, we ask you to kindly send us your latest price list of synthetic fiber goods with the lowest quotations as soon as possible, together with an illustrated catalogue.

We shall appreciate it if you could provide your best terms and conditions.

We are looking forward to receiving your immediate reply.

Yours faithfully,

(*Reply Letter*)

Dear Sirs,

In reply to your letter of May 10, we are now enclosing[10] you our latest price list for synthetic fiber goods, together with our illustrated catalogue. As you will see in the above list, we have quoted you the lowest prices, offering you our best quality goods which we believe will induce you to favor us with valued orders.

As for the samples, we shall be pleased to send you if you require.

We await with deep interest to receive your immediate reply.

Yours faithfully,

<Letter 2> A Specific Enquiry for Silk Blouses and Reply

Dear Sirs,

We have received many reports from our sales agents in Hong Kong[11], indicating there are brisk demands[12] for the captioned garments.

We are pleased to learn that your mill is the most well-known producer of this item in China. We, therefore, are writing to you for quotations for silk blouses of all three sizes: large, medium, and small. We hope you can quote us your best prices since we will place large orders with you.

When quoting, please state your prices on CIFC 2% Los Angeles[13] and be sure that your prices are competitive.

Your prompt reply to this enquiry will be much appreciated[14].

Yours sincerely,

(*Reply Letter*)

Dear Sirs,

We are please to learn from[15] your enquiry dated Nov.5, from which we find you are interested in our silk blouses.

We are now in a position to supply you with a wide range of silk blouses[16] we make for all age groups. Enclosed please find our Quotation Sheet No.257 covering different sizes and colors, all of them can be shipped from stock[17]. In addition, all the prices quoted are net, to which please add your commission[18]. If your orders exceed USD 50,000, we will offer you a quantity discount[19] of 4%.

We are confident that you will find a ready sale for our products in your market.

Any order you may place with us will have our prompt attention.

Yours truly,

<Letter 3> A Specific Enquiry for Fancy Buttons and Reply

Dir Sirs,

We thank you for your letter of May 3 and shall be glad to enter into business relations with you.

We have seen your brochures and are interested in your fancy buttons of all sizes. Please give us your best firm offer[20] for spring coats No.12 and No.18. We shall be pleased if you will kindly send us samples and all the necessary information regarding these products. Besides, please let us know the packing, weight, payment, shipment and other essential details.

We are looking forward to your early reply.

Yours faithfully,

(Reply Letter)

Dear Sirs,

Thank you very much for your enquiry of May 8. We are please to send you samples of our fancy buttons for spring coats No.12 and No.18.

Pattern No.12: $26 per box CIF Bombay, each box containing 5 dozen.

Pattern No.18: $35 per box CIF Bombay, each box containing 5 dozen.

The above prices are subject to market fluctuations. For quantities of more than 150 dozen, we will reduce[21] the price by three percent.

These buttons are of exceptional beauty and are packed in wooden cases, each containing 20 boxes. Shipment will be made within 3 weeks from acceptance of our order. Our terms of payment are draft at sight under an irrevocable letter of credit.

Thank you again for your interest in our products. We are looking forward to your order and you may be assured that it will receive our prompt and careful attention.

Yours faithfully,

<Letter 4> The Enquiry for Textiles and Reply

Dear Sirs,

Recently, we saw your advertisement in *International Trade* and would like you to send us details of your bed-sheets and pillowcases in wide ranges, including sizes, colors, prices as well as the samples of different types.

We are large dealers in this line and believe there is a promising market in our area for moderately priced bedding products.

When replying, please state your terms of payment and discount you would allow on purchases of quantities for not less than 100 dozen of individual items.

Yours faithfully,

(Reply Letter)

Dear Sirs,

We are very pleased to receive your enquiry of 15 June, and enclose our illustrated catalogue and price list giving the details you ask for. In addition, we are sending you some samples by separate post. We feel confident that when you have examined them you will agree that our commodities are both superior in quality[22] and reasonable in price[23].

On regular purchases in quantities of not less than[24] 100 dozen of individual items we would allow you a discount of 2%. Payment is to be made by irrevocable L/C at sight.

Because of their softness[25] and durability[26], our all cotton bed-sheets and pillowcases are rapidly becoming popular. After studying our prices, you will not be surprised to learn that we are finding it difficult to meet the huge demands. However, if you place your order not later than the end of this month, we would ensure prompt shipment.

We invite your attention to our other products such as table cloth and table napkins, details of which you will find in the catalogue.

We look forward to receiving your first order.

Yours faithfully,

Notes

1. enquiry (inquiry)　　 n.　　 询盘，询价，询购（指明具体商品时，通常接介词 for）
   We thank you for enquiry for carpets.
   谢谢贵公司对地毯的询盘。
   enquiry (inquiry)　　 v.　　 询价，询购，询问
   Thanks for your e-mail of June 16 enquiring for foodstuffs.
   感谢贵公司在 6 月 16 日电子邮件中对食品的询价。

2. information　　 n.　　 消息，情报
   We wish to get from you more information on (about) the item.
   我们希望从贵公司得到这一商品的更多资料。

3. quotation　　 n.　　 报价
   Would you please fax us a FOB quotation for 500 units.
   请传真五百台的 FOB 报价。
   quote　　 v.　　 报价
   Would you please quote us your best price CIF Sydney?
   可否请报最优惠的悉尼 CIF 价？
   区别：quota　　 n.　　 配额
   import quota　　 进口配额　　　　　export quota　　 出口配额

4. offer　　 v.　　 报盘（包括交易的各种条件，如：货名、规格、数量、价格、船期及答复期等）
   We can offer you various kinds of socks.
   我们可以就各类袜子向你方报盘。
   We can offer you large quantities of this year's groundnuts at attractive price.
   我们能以极具吸引力的价格就大量今年产的花生向你方报盘。
   offer　　 n.　　 发盘
   Please make us an offer for shoes.
   请报鞋子的价格。

5. general enquiry　　 一般询盘

6. specific enquiry   具体询盘
7. sample   n.   样品
   Quality must be up to sample.
   质量必须与样品完全相同。
8. illustration   n.   插图（图解）
   illustrated catalogue   带有插图的产品目录
9. terms of payment   付款条件
10. enclose   vt.   随函附寄
    We are enclosing a price list for your reference.
    我们随函附寄一份价格单以供参考。
    enclosure   n.   附件
11. Many reports have been received from our sales agents in Hong Kong,
    已收到许多来自香港销售商的报告。
    have received = be in receipt of   收悉
    以下几种表达方式，意义相同，常用在函件的开头。
    We are in receipt of your letter…
    We have received your letter…
    We acknowledge your letter…
    We have the pleasure of acknowledging receipt of your letter…（多用于正式场合）
12. brisk demand   旺盛的需求
13. CIFC2% Los Angeles   洛杉矶 CIF 价加 2%佣金
    C = Commission   佣金，提成
    CIF = Cost Insurance Freight   成本+运费+保险费（到岸价）
14. appreciate   v.   感激，感谢
    We shall appreciate your quoting us the best price at the earliest date.
    如果你方能够尽快报给我方最低价，我们将不胜感激。
15. learn from   从……得知（了解到）
    We learn from the Internet that your corporation handles foodstuffs for export.
    我们从网上了解到贵公司经营食品出口。
16. wide range of silk blouses   各式各样的丝绸女衬衫
    a wide range of   各式各样的，范围很广的
    We can supply wool carpets in a wide range of designs.
    我们可以供应花样繁多的羊毛地毯。
17. stock   n.   现货，存货
    in stock   有库存，有现货
    Please make us your lowest quotation CIF London for what you have in stock now.
    请报现货 CIF 伦敦最低价。
    out of stock   无现货，缺货
    We regret to inform you that the goods are out of stock for the time being.
    很遗憾告知你方目前无现货。
    supply from stock   现货供应，从库存中供应

18. commission   *n.*   佣金

   Please quote us your lowest prices, CIF Liverpool, including our 5% commission.
   请报 CIF 利物浦最低价，包括我方 5%的佣金。

19. discount   *n.*   折扣

   If you order for 6,000 sets, we would grant you 8% discount.
   如果你方能订购 6,000 台，我们将给予 8%的折扣。

20. firm offer   实盘   non-firm offer   虚盘

21. reduce   *vt.*   减少

   to reduce the price to USD30   降价至 30 美元
   to reduce the piece by 10%   降价 10%

22. superior in quality   品质优良（质量上乘）

   You'll find the socks are superior in quality.
   你会发现，这些袜子质量上乘。

23. reasonable in price   价格合理

   I can assure you that our commodities are reasonable in price and good in quality.
   我可以向您保证，我方所供货品价格公道、品质优良。
   表示"价格合适、适中"还可以说：moderate in price。

24. not less than   不小于，不少于，至少

25. softness   *n.*   柔软性

26. durability   *n.*   耐用

Exercises

I. Translate the following terms into English:

1. 佣金
2. 价格合理
3. 另邮
4. 供你方参考
5. 缺货
6. 最新的商品目录
7. 报价
8. 付款条件
9. 具体询盘
10. 欲购

II. Translate the following terms into Chinese:

1. sample
2. enter into business relations
3. discount
4. high quality
5. general enquiry
6. prompt reply
7. appeal to
8. business line
9. superior in quality
10. illustrated catalogue

III. Choose the best answer to complete the following sentences:

1. We thank you for your letter of March 12 and the _____ catalogue.
   A. sent   B. enclosed   C. given   D. present

2. We _____ if you could give us whatever information you can in this respect.
   A. should appreciate   B. appreciate
   C. appreciate it   D. shall appreciate it
3. We _____ the fact that the market is declining.
   A. are aware of   B. aware
   C. aware of   D. are aware
4. If you are interested, we will send you a sample lot _____ charge.
   A. within   B. for   C. with   D. free of
5. While _____ an enquiry, you ought to enquiry into quality, specifications and piece etc.
   A. making   B. offering   C. bidding   D. sending
6. We enquire _____ glassware available _____ export.
   A. for, to   B. for, for   C. to, for   D. of, about
7. We regret _____ entertain your order for our Green Beans as we are in short supply at present.
   A. not able to   B. are unable to   C. can not   D. our inability to
8. We are pleased to inform you that the item you requested can be supplied _____.
   A. from stock   B. in stock   C. out of stock   D. of stock
9. Please reply as soon as possible, _____ the earliest shipment date and terms of payment.
   A. stated   B. as stated   C. stating   D. state
10. We are pleased _____ your enquiry of July 15 for our toys.
    A. to receiving   B. as received   C. receiving   D. to have

IV. Fill in the following blanks with the words and expressions in the box, change the form when necessary:

| quote | decline | interest | to | available |
| on | acceptance | commission | for | appreciate |

1. We find the price you _____ rather _____ the high side.
2. As the market is _____, we recommend your immediate _____.
3. We regret that the items you enquire about are not _____.
4. We would prefer CIF Lagos, including our _____ of 5%.
5. One of our clients has made us an enquiry _____ 300 dozen blouses.
6. Your prompt attention _____ this enquiry is much appreciated.
7. Many Korean customers have expressed their _____ in our baby's toys and inquired about the quality and prices.
8. We would very much _____ if you can give us a special discount.

V. Translate the following sentences into Chinese:

1. Please quote us your best price CIF Hamburg for the chairs.
2. We shall be very glad to place our order with you if your quotation is competitive and delivery date is acceptable.
3. We look forward to placing further orders with you and trust that you will make every

effort to satisfy our particular requirements.

4. Please send us your best offer by fax indicating packing, specification, quantity available and earliest time of delivery.

5. If your prices are competitive, we are confident in selling the goods in great quantities in our local market.

VI. *Translate the following sentences into English*:

1. 是否能向我方报最低的利物浦离岸价？
2. 一旦收到你方具体询价单，我们马上寄送样品并报最优惠的价格。
3. 你方必须降价5%，否则没有成交的可能。
4. 我方对进口你方产品感兴趣，如有可能可否请向我方寄送产品目录、价格单和样品？
5. 若你方能立即航空邮寄给我们剪样（sample cutting），我们将不胜感激。

VII. *Simulated writing*:

Now you are required to write an enquiry letter based on the following main points:

（1）我们从芝加哥Sparking有限公司获悉贵公司是中国五金配件（hardware accessories）的主要出口商。

（2）我们非常感兴趣进口你们的商品，若贵方能向我们寄送最新的带插图的产品目录和价格单的话，我们将不胜感激。

（3）请给我们详细的出口信息，如CIF纽约价、折扣、包装方式以及支付条件等。

（4）我们真诚希望这将是我们双方建立长久贸易关系的良好开端。

（5）盼早日回复。

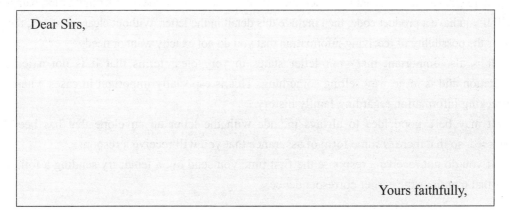

Supplementary Reading

How to Write an Inquiry?

What is a letter of inquiry? More often than not, a letter of inquiry is written to garner information about certain products or services, but occasionally it can also be used to conduct inquiries about job vacancies or even to conduct investigations into the history of a family and to trace their genealogy. While a letter of inquiry can take on a personal tone, if written as a part of your professional commitments, then you will need to ensure that the letter is written formally. In this article, we tell you how to write an inquiry letter and give you an example of the same so that you can understand the format of such a letter.

Writing a Letter of Inquiry

In order to write a letter of inquiry, there are a few basic things that need to keep in mind. In this section, we list out those pointers that will help you draft a good letter that will ensure that you receive all the information that you need without unnecessary delay.

First and foremost, before drafting the letter, it is important to ascertain the purpose for which the letter is being written. If the information that you are seeking is personal, then it may be a good idea to keep the tone less formal. While with professional letters, the tone will be determined by the information you are seeking.

- If you are writing the letter on behalf of the organization that you are working for, then it is important that you use the letterhead of the company. Also include important information that is not mentioned on the letterhead, like your e-mail id or your phone number at work.
- If the letter is being written on a personal basis, then you will need to include information like your name, address, and your contact details.
- If you are unsure of whom you need to address the letter to, then use salutations like Dear Sir/Ma'am, or To Whomsoever It May Concern.

Ensure that you mention in clear terms what is the information that you are seeking for. If you want more details about a certain product, then mention the name of the product in the first paragraph itself. If you have a product code, then include this detail in the letter. Without clear questions, there is always the possibility of receiving information that you do not exactly want or need.

It is also important that your letter states in very clear terms that it is not a letter of solicitation and is in no way selling something. This is especially important in cases where you are seeking information regarding family history.

It may be a good idea to always include with the letter an envelope that has been self addressed, so that there is some form of assurance that you will receive a response.

If you do not receive a response the first time you send out a letter, try sending a follow-up letter that mentions the earlier correspondence.

Example of Inquiry Letter

Now that you know how to write an inquiry letter, let us take a look at the format of such a letter with the help of a sample inquiry letter. Using the proper format and following an inquiry letter template is very important when writing such a letter.

Cole Austin
896, Elm Avenue
Olympia, WA – 95766

Date: 15 April 2011

Harold's
865, Wall Street
New York, NY – 79677

Subject: With reference to advertisement in New York Times

Dear Sirs,

    This is with reference to the advertisement regarding your Spring/Summer collection in the New York Times dated 14 April 2011. With reference to the same, I would like to place an order for your latest catalog. I would also like to receive information on whether or not it is possible to make online purchases at your website, as there is no information regarding the same.
    Awaiting your response.

Yours sincerely,
(*Signature*)
Cole Austin

Hopefully, the example of an inquiry letter given in this article and the tips given will help you write such a letter as and when the need arises. Remember that as with any other letter, it is important that you check it for any spelling, grammatical, or factual errors.

After-Class Study

(I) *The Types of Sample*

original sample	原样	duplicate sample	复样/留样
counter/return sample	对等样/回样	test sample	测试样
pre-production sample	产前样	approved sample	确认样
production sample	生产样	modified sample	修改样
shipping sample	出货样/船样	sealed sample	封样
pattern sample	款式样	size/ color set sample	齐色齐码样
salesman sample	广告样	washed sample	水洗样
lab dip	色样		

(II) The Incoterm 2010 Rules

Group	Abbreviation	Full Name	Chinese Mean	Insert named place	Mode or modes of transport
E 组	EXW	Ex Works	工厂交货	…指定地点	任何运输方式
F 组	FAS	Free Alongside Ship	装运港船边交货	…指定装运港	海运及内河水运
	FCA	Free Carrier	货交承运人	…指定目的港	任何运输方式
	FOB	Free On Board	装运港船上交货	…指定装运港	海运及内河水运
C 组	CFR	Cost and Freight	成本加运费	…指定目的港	海运及内河水运
	CIF	Cost, Insurance and Freight	成本、保险费加运费	…指定目的港	海运及内河水运
	CIP	Carriage and Insurance Paid	运费及保险费付至目的地	…指定目的地	任何运输方式
	CPT	Carriage Paid To	运费付至目的地	…指定目的地	任何运输方式
D 组	DAT	Delivered At Terminal	目的港集散站交货	…指定目的港	任何运输方式
	DAP	Delivered At Place	目的地交货	…指定目的地	任何运输方式
	DDP	Delivered Duty Paid	完税后交货	…指定目的地	任何运输方式

Chinese Version of Specimen Letters

<例信1> 对合成纤维的一般询盘及回复

敬启者：

我们在《中国贸易目录》上看到贵公司的广告，真诚地希望贵方能尽快将合成纤维制品最新价格单寄给我们并报最低价格，同时附上产品的图解目录。

贵方如能提供最优条款和条件，我方将不胜感激。

盼复。

谨启

（回复信函）

敬启者：

兹回复你方5月10日的来信，我方已随信附寄合成纤维制品最新的价目表及产品图解目录。正如您在所附报价单上看到的，我们已经报了最低价格，我们相信为您提供优质优价的商品将使您为我们带来有价值的订单。

至于样品，如果贵方需要的话，我们将非常乐意地寄送于你。

我们期盼您的回复。

谨启

<例信2> 对丝绸女衬衫的具体询盘及回复

敬启者：

我们已经收到许多来自香港销售商的报告，标题项下的服装有旺盛的市场需求。

很高兴获悉贵公司是中国生产该产品的最知名厂家,因此我们去函请你方对大号、中号和小号三种尺寸的丝绸女衬衫进行报价。我方将大量订购,因此希望贵方能报最优惠的价格。

报价时,请在洛杉矶 CIF 价基础上加 2%的佣金并确保所报价格具有竞争性。速复为感。

谨启

(回复信函)

敬启者:

我们很高兴从 11 月 5 日的询盘中获悉贵方对我们的丝绸女衬衫感兴趣。

目前我们能提供各种年龄段的各式丝绸女衬衫,现随函寄去 257 号报价单,内含不同尺寸和颜色,所有产品均可现货发送。此外,所报价格都是净价,请加上你们的佣金。如果贵方订单金额超过 5 万美元,我们将给予 4%的数量折扣。

相信这些产品在你方市场上会很畅销。

来单即复。

谨启

<例信 3> 对花式纽扣的具体询盘及回复

敬启者:

非常感谢您 5 月 3 日的来信,同时很高兴与您建立业务关系。

我们看过您发来的小册子,并对各种型号的花式纽扣非常感兴趣。请向我们报款式号为 12 和 18 春装上纽扣最优惠的实盘。如能寄送样品以及所有涉及这些产品相关的信息,我们将不胜感激。此外,请告诉我们有关包装、重量、付款方式、装运以及其他一些必要的细节。

期盼早日回复。

谨启

(回复信函)

敬启者:

谢谢您 5 月 8 日的询盘。我们非常乐意寄上款式号为 12 和 18 的春装上花式纽扣的样品。

款式号 12:孟买到岸价每箱 26 美元,每箱 5 打。

款式号 18:孟买到岸价每箱 35 美元,每箱 5 打。

上述价格根据市价浮动。如订单数量超过 150 打,我们将降价 3%。

这些纽扣极其美观,采用木箱包装,每只木箱装 20 盒。

在接受你方订单后的三周内安排装运。我们采用不可撤销的即期信用证支付。

再次感谢您对我们产品的兴趣。期待您早日下单,我们确保您的订单将得到我们及时细致的关注。

谨启

<例信 4> 纺织品的询盘及回复

敬启者：

  最近我们在《国际贸易》杂志上看到贵公司刊登的广告。我们希望你能将各种系列床单枕套产品的详细信息，包括尺寸、颜色、价格以及不同型号的样品寄送给我们。

  我们是该行业的大经销商，相信价格适中的床上用品会在我们当地市场有广阔的前景。

  回复时，请说明你们的付款条件，以及采购数量在每个型号不低于 100 打情况下你们能够给予的折扣。

谨启

（回复信函）

敬启者：

  我们很高兴收到您 6 月 15 日的询盘，并且按您的要求附上我们详细的产品图解目录以及价格单。此外我们另行邮寄了一些样品给您，相信当您对它们进行检查后，您会同意这些商品品质优良、价格合理。

  按常规，采购数量在每个型号不低于 100 打的情况下我们将给予您 2%的折扣。采用不可撤销即期信用证支付。

  由于它们的柔软度和耐久性，我们的床单和枕套非常受欢迎。当研究过我们的价格后，您将对我们的供货很难满足巨大需求这一现状不会感到惊讶。但是如果您能在这个月底之前下订单的话，我们会确保及时装运。

  请您关注我们的其他商品，如桌布和餐巾，详细的情况可在产品目录中查询。

  我们期待收到您的首次订单。

谨启

Unit 4 Offers, Counter-offers and Acceptance

Learning Aims

After you finish learning this unit, you are requested to:
(1) understand some basic knowledge about offers, counter-offers and acceptance.
(2) master some business negotiation strategies.
(3) acquire how to write a good and effective letter of offer, counter-offer and acceptance.

Background Knowledge

In international business, the export procedures on the side of seller can be illustrated by the following chart.

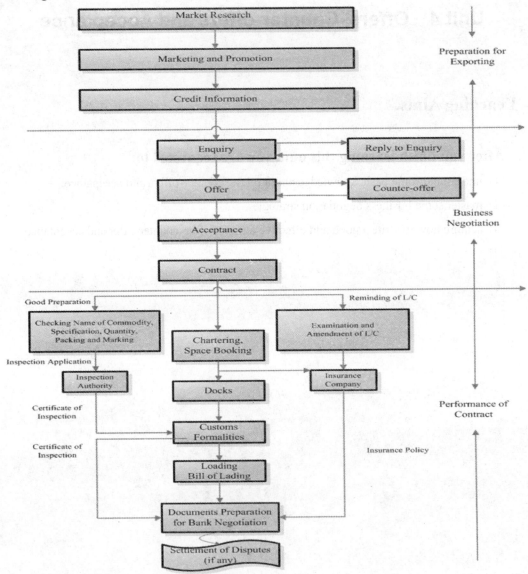

Among all of these procedures, offer, counter-offer and acceptance are decisive for a successful business transaction.

(I) What is Offer?

Offer usually refers that the seller gives some sales terms and conditions to the buyer for confirmation and expresses to sign a legal and effective contract based on these terms and conditions. An offer from an individual or a firm to another is a declaration or a formal presentation that he or it is willing to sell a certain amount of specified goods, at specified price under specified terms and therein for the buyer's acceptance. In the international business, offers can be divided into two kinds:

◆ **Firm offer:** A firm offer is a promise indicating main transaction conditions such as: exact description of goods, quantity, packing, unit price, shipment, insurance, payment term and validity. If the buyer accepts within its validity, then it is a contractual obligation. A firm offer must not contain vague words such as "about", "roughly", "approximately", "for reference" or "for information"; and it must also be final, without reserve. Therefore, it should not have words such as "subject to our confirmation", "subject to prior sale" or "without engagement".

Attention: (1) A firm offer is a contractual obligation. Once it has been accepted unconditionally within the term of validity, it can not be withdrawn. (2) The validity period is indispensable to a firm offer. Specifically, the beginning and the ending date of the validity must be given.

◆ **Non-firm offer:** A non-firm offer is an offer without engagement. It is not binding upon the sellers and the details of the offers may change in certain situation. In most cases, the contents of a non-firm offer are not clear and definite. The main terms and conditions are not complete.

(II) What is Counter-offer?

A counter-offer is virtually a partial rejection of the original offer or a bid, but suggests a change or changes. It also means a counter proposal put forward by the buyer or the offeree. There are several kinds of counter-offer:

◆ Counter-offer on price
◆ Asks for reduction of minimum quantity
◆ Counter-offer on payment terms
◆ Asks for earlier delivery
◆ Asks for changing the package
◆ Counter-offer on the discount of the goods
◆ Asks for more commissions

In the counter offer, the buyer can show his disagreement to the certain term or terms, and state his own idea instead. Additional or different terms, put forward by the offeree, relating to the price, payment, quality and quantity of the goods, place and time of delivery, extent of one's party's liability to the other or the settlement of disputes are considered to alter the terms of offer materially. The appearance of the counter-offer indicates or signifies that business has to be negotiated on the renewed basis, the original offerer or the seller now becomes the offeree and he has the full right to accept or refuse the counter-offer sent by the buyer. In the latter case, the seller may make another counter-offer of his own. This process can go on for several rounds till business is finalized or called off.

Offer and Counter-offer

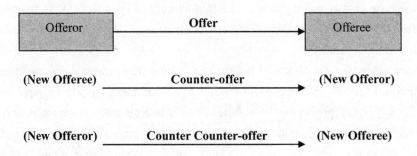

(III) *What is Acceptance*?

An acceptance is a total assent to the terms and conditions of an offer or counter-offer, which means that the buyer and the seller have come to an agreement on the sale. It is binding on both parties

An acceptance must meet the following requirements:

✧ The acceptance must be made by the offeree.

✧ The acceptance must be presented in oral or written form.

✧ The acceptance must reach the offeror within the time of validity the offer.

✧ The acceptance must be unconditional, that is an acceptance can contain no additions, modifications, or limitations to the offer.

As soon as an offer is accepted, a written sales contract or sales confirmation is usually required to be signed between the buyer and the seller to confirm the sales and stipulate their rights and obligations respectively. A sales contract or sales confirmation contains some general terms and conditions as well as the specific terms that vary with the commodity. But such terms as the name of the seller, the description of the goods, quality and specification, quantity, packing, unit price, amount, payment, date of delivery, shipment, insurance, inspection, claim and arbitration are indispensable. The sales contract is normally made out in two originals, one for the buyer himself and the other for his seller.

Writing Tips

(I) *Firm Offer Letter*

1. Letters of a firm offer can be written in the following structure：

(1) Express thanks for the enquiry & briefly state the content of the enquiry, if any;

(2) Explain detailed business terms: supply all the information requested including name of commodities, quality, quantity, and specifications;

(3) Give details of prices, terms of payment, commissions, or discounts, if any;

(4) Indicate packing and date of delivery; state clearly the validity of the offer;

(5) End the letter by asking for an early reply or expressing willingness to further business.

2. Some typical expressions about time of validity can be used in a firm offer.

(1) Be valid until (till, before) …　　有效期至……；在……前有效

(2) Be valid for … days　　有效期……天；

(3) Subject to your reply reaching us by (before) …　　以我方在……前收到你方答复为条件/以……前复到为条件

(4) Subject to your reply reaching us not later than …　　以我方在不晚于……收到你方答复为条件；以不晚于……复到为条件

(5) Subject to your reply within … days　　以我方在……日内收到你方答复为条件；以……日内复到为条件

3. Some typical sentences can be used in a firm offer.

(1) We make you a firm offer for 1,000 tons of iron & steel subject to your reply reaching us by July 2;

(2) We offer you 1,500 Forever Bicycles at USD32 per piece CIF London for delivery in May;

(3) Thank you for your inquiry of April 5, in reply to which we have faxed our firm offer;

(4) The firm offer is subject to your reply reaching us within 10 days;

(5) The offer will be kept open until 12 March.

(II) *Non-firm Offer Letter*

1. Letters of a non-firm offer can be written in the following structure：

(1) Open the letter by expressing thanks for the inquiry & briefly state the content of the inquiry, if any;

(2) Provide details of quantity, quality, price, discount, payment, packing and so on;

(3) Express the hope for a favorable reply.

2. Some typical expressions can be used in a non-firm offer.

(1) Subject to our/seller's final confirmation　　以我方/卖方最后确认为准

(2) Subject to goods being unsold　　以货物尚未售出为有效

(3) Subject to prior sale　　以先售为准/以（商品）未售出为准

(4) Subject to change without notice　　不经通知可以改变

(5) An offer without engagement (obligation)　　无约束性报盘

3. Some typical sentences can be used in a non-firm offer.

(1) We are now making you an offer subject to our final confirmation.

(2) We are now making you the following offer without engagement.

(3) We are now making you a special offer subject to the goods being unsold.

(4) We are now making an offer for cell phone as follows, subject to prior sale.

(III) *Count-offer Letter*

1. A counter-offer letter can be written in the following structure：

(1) Open the letter by thanking the recipient for the offer;

(2) Express regret at inability to accept;

(3) Decline the original offer by providing the recipient with detailed and appropriate

reasons;

(4) Make counter-offer, put forward the desired business conditions and try to persuade the recipient to accept them;

(5) Close the letter by expressing expectations for a favorable reply.

2. Some typical expressions can be used in a counter-offer letter:

How to express your regret

(1) We regret that we are not in a position to accept your offer.

很遗憾,站在我方的立场,将无法接受贵方的发盘。

(2) We regret being unable to accept your offer.

很抱歉,我方无法接受贵方的发盘。

(3) We are regretful that we are unable to entertain your offer.

非常遗憾,恕我方无法接受贵方的发盘。

What are the reasons

(1) The market is declining.

行市下降。

(2) Your price is out of line with the prevailing/ruling price in the market.

你方价格与现行世界市场行情不一致。

(3) Your price is on the high side.

你方价格偏高。

(4) Your price is too high.

你方价格太高。

(5) Your price is a bit high.

你方价格有点高。

(6) Your price is excessive.

你方价格过高。

(7) Your price is rather stiff.

你方价格相当高。

(8) Your price is prohibitive.

你方价格令人望而却步。

(IV) Acceptance Letter

1. A counter-offer letter can be written in the following structure:

(1) Open the letter by thanking the recipient for the counter-offer;

(2) Express the willingness to accept the counter-offer;

(3) Make a new offer according to the buyer's requirements;

(4) Close the letter by expressing expectations for an order and future cooperation;

2. Some typical sentences can be used in an acceptance letter.

(1) I'll respond to your counter-offer by reducing our price by three dollars.

(2) We are able to offer you the goods at a discount of 3 percent off our recent price, but we

can only hold open this advantages offer for two weeks.

(3) We look forward to receiving a trial order from you soon.

(4) We trust you will find our quotation satisfactory and look forward to receiving your order.

Sentence Patterns & Examples

【Pattern 1】offer sb. sth.　　向某人报盘

We offer you 1,500 Forever Bicycles at USD32 per piece CIF London for delivery in May.
我方向贵方报盘 1,500 辆永久自行车，CIF 伦敦价，每辆 32 美元，5 月份交货。
Please offer us firm 20 tons of wool FOB Sydney.
请报 20 吨羊毛实盘，FOB 悉尼价。

【Pattern 2】make/give/send sb. an offer for/on sth.　　向某人就某产品报盘

Please make us an offer CIF New York for 10 tons of frozen fish.
请报 10 吨冻鱼 CIF 纽约价。
We take pleasure in sending you an offer for 50 sets of machine tools Model 70 as follows.
我方高兴地向贵方寄送 50 台 70 型机床的报盘，（详情）如下。

【Pattern 3】advise sb. to accept an offer　　建议某人接受报盘

As the prices quoted are exceptionally low and likely to rise, we would advise you to accept the offer without delay.
由于所报价格特低，并可能上涨，我方劝贵方立即接受此报盘。

【Pattern 4】make a counter-offer　　给予还盘

If you cannot accept it, please make best possible counter-offer.
如不能接受，请尽力给一个最好的还盘。
Your offer is unworkable, however, in view of our long-standing business relationship we make you such a counter-offer.
你方报盘无法接受，但鉴于我们之间的长期贸易关系，特向你方作此还盘。

【Pattern 5】counter-offer　　作出还盘

Your price is on the high side and we have to counter-offer as follows, subject to your reply received by us on or before 8 April.
你方价格偏高，我们不得不作如下还盘，以我方在 4 月 8 日或以前收到你方答复为有效。

【Pattern 6】out of line with the market　　与市场不一致

in the line with the market　　与市场一致

The price you counter-offered is out of line with the market, so it is beyond what is acceptable to us.
你方还价与市场不一致，故我方无法接受。
Our quotation always comes in line with the world market.
我们的报价总是与世界市场价格保持一致。

【Pattern 7】 to entertain business at…price   考虑按……价格成交

We can't entertain business at your price, since it is out of line with the prevailing market, being 20% higher than the average.
我们不能考虑按你方价格成交，因为你方价格与现时市场不一致，要比一般价格高20%。

It's impossible for us to entertain business at such price, since it is far below our cost price.
我方无法以此价格与你方交易，因为它远远低于我们成本价。

【Pattern 8】 enjoy fast sales = selling fast / sell fast / popular with customers / command a good market   （商品）畅销

The goods enjoy fast sales are selling fast.
这些商品非常畅销。

类似的表达还有 "The goods are most popular with customers." 或 "The goods have commanded / found a good / ready market."

【Pattern 9】 invite one's attention to other products   请某人注意其他产品

We invite your attention to our other products, details of which you will find in the catalogue
敬请垂询我方其他产品，详情见目录。

【Pattern 10】 be in a position to do sth.   能够做……事

We are not in a position to entertain your claim.
我们不能接受你们提出的索赔要求。

We do our best to gear our production to your requirements and shall soon be in a position to accept your substantial order.
我们尽力使我方的生产与你方的要求相适应，不久将能够接受你方的大宗订单。

Specimen Letters

<Letter 1> Firm Offer

Dear Sirs,

Thank you for your enquiry of May 24. At your request[1], we are making you the following offer subject to your reply arriving here before June 23[2].

Article: Brocade Handbags

Price: USD 12.00/pc CIF Vancouver

Quantity: 5,000 pcs

Shipment: August, 2003

Packing: 20 pieces to one carton

Terms of Payment: By irrevocable documentary Letter of Credit[3] in the seller's favor[4]

We hope that the above will be acceptable to you, and await with keen interest your formal orders[5].

Yours faithfully,

<Letter 2> Non-firm Offer

Dear Sirs,

With reference to your enquiry of May 24, we take pleasure in making the following offer[6]:

"5,000 pieces of brocade handbags, at USD 12.00/pc CIF Vancouver for shipment in August, 2003, for payment by irrevocable documentary L/C in seller's favor, which we hope you will find in order. Please note that[7] this offer is subject to goods being unsold.

As we have received large number of orders from our other clients, it is quite probable that our present stock may soon run out[9]. We would therefore suggest that you take advantage of[10] this attractive offer.

We look forward to receiving your order.

Yours faithfully,

<Letter 3> Counter-offer

Dear Sirs,

We are in receipt of your letter of June 1 offering us 5,000 pieces of brocade handbags at USD 12.00/pc CIF Vancouver.

In reply[11], we regret to inform you that[12] our end-users here find your price too high and out of line with the prevailing market level[13]. You may be aware[14] that some Indonesian dealers are lowering their prices. No doubt there is keen competition in the market.

We do not deny that the quality of your brocade handbags is slightly better[15], but the difference in price should, in no case, be as big as 5%[16]. To step up the trade[17], we, on behalf of[18] our end-users, make counter-offer as follows[19]:

"5,000 pieces of brocade handbags, at USD 11.40/pc CIF Vancouver, other terms as per[20] your letter of June 1."

As the market is declining[21], we recommend your acceptance.

We are anticipating your early reply.

Yours faithfully,

<Letter 4> Acceptance

Dear Sirs,

We are appreciative of[22] your letter of June 14 which requested a 5% discount.

It is our company's policy not to give a discount on our standard prices. However, we are glad to make an exception[23] in this case as an introduction to our brocade handbags. Thus, we accept your counter-offer for a 5% discount based on a purchase of

5,000 pieces by July 15, as follows:

"Brocade handbags at USD 11.40/pc CIF Vancouver for shipment in August."

We look forward to receiving your order, and to developing our continuing, profitable relationship in the future.

Yours faithfully,

Notes

1. At your request... 应你方要求
   这是商业信函中的常用语，用作状语。
   At your request, we have amended the L/C.
   应你方要求，我们已经修改了信用证。
   也可用：as requested/at the request of sb.　　应某人的要求
   As requested, we are giving you an estimate of approximate requirements for next year.
   应你方要求，寄上一份明年所需货物的预估表。
   We are sending the counter sample at the request of your agent.
   应你方代理商要求，寄上对等货样。

2. subject to your reply arriving here before June 23　　以你方答复于6月23日前到达为有效
   subject to　　以……为条件，以……为有效（这里subject是形容词，subject to 引起的短语作表语）
   在报盘信中常用以说明报盘的性质，即报的是实盘还是虚盘。
   subject to our final confirmation　　以我方最终确认为准（虚盘）
   subject to your acceptance within two weeks　　以你方在两周之内接受为条件（实盘）
   subject to your immediate acceptance　　以你方立即接受为条件（实盘）

3. by irrevocable documentary Letter of Credit　　凭不可撤销的跟单信用证
   Letter of Credit 是可数的普通名词，在商业书信中常用大写，单数为(a) Letter of Credit，复数为 Letters of Credit，且常用大写缩写形式，即 L/C 和 Ls/C。当 credit 表示信用证时，复数为 credits。

4. in seller's favour=in the favor of the seller　　以买方为受益人
   这是外贸业务术语，尤指信用把信用证开给某人名下。表示"以某人为受益人"，"对……有利"可以说：in one's favor, in the favor of sb.
   We have made arrangements with the Bank of China, to open a credit in your favor.
   我们以安排由中国银行开立以你方为受益人的信用证。

5. ...and await with keen interest your formal orders, ...　　并殷切地等待着你方正式下单
   with keen interest　　殷切地
   await　　v.　　(formal) wait for　　等待，期待
   We await your final confirmation.
   盼你方最终确认。

6. take pleasure in doing sth.　　很高兴地做某事

在较正式场合使用的客套用语，也可用以下的句型，意义相同。

(1) We have (take) the pleasure of doing sth.

(2) We have (take) the pleasure to do sth.

(3) It's a (great) pleasure for us to do sth.

(4) We are pleased to do sth.

7. Please note that…　　请注意……

这是商业信函中的常用句型，用以提醒收信人对信中的某一内容给予特别关注。

Please note that the market for the goods is rising and our price cannot remain unchanged for long.

请注意，目前这种产品的市场行情看涨，我们的价格不会保持很长时间。

类似的表达有：

Please pay attention to the fact that…

Please be aware that…

8. run out　　用完，耗尽

9. take advantages of　　利用

10. be in receipt of =have received　　……已经收悉

11. in reply　　作为答复

这个短语可以放在句首。倘若放在一封信的句首，则应写为：In reply to your letter of…，意为"作为答复你方×月×日的来信"。

In reply to your letter of September 23, we take great pleasure to inform you that the goods under Contract No.8776 are now ready for shipment.

兹复你方9月23日来信，我们很高兴告知8776号合同项下之货物即将装运。

其他类似的表达法：in response to, in reply (to), replying to/ as a reply

In response to your enquiry of May 1, we now offer you men's shoes as follows.

就你方5月1日对男鞋询盘一事，我方现报盘如下。

12. We regret to inform you that…　　我们很遗憾地告知你方……

regret　v.　抱歉，惋惜，引为遗憾（后面可接名词，动名词，不定式，that引导的从句）。

（1）接名词

We very much regret our inability to comply with your wishes.

我们很抱歉未能依照你方的要求办理。

（2）接动名词

We regret being unable to offer you this article at present.

很抱歉我们现在不能向你方报这种商品。

（3）接不定式

We regret to note that you cannot make any headway with our offer.

获悉你们对我方报盘未能取得任何进展，甚为遗憾。

（4）接从句

We regret that the business has fallen through.

我们很遗憾交易未能达成。

regret 也可作名词，意思是"抱歉，遗憾"。

Much to our regret, we are unable to even shade (=change slightly) the price.
非常抱歉，我们甚至一点也不能减价。

13. …find your price too high and out of line with the prevailing market level.
……发现你方价格太高，与现行的行市水平不一致。

out of line with the prevailing market level　　与市场价不符

in line with　　　与……相一致

Your price is quite in line with the market.
你方价格非常符合市价。

14. (be) aware of / that　　知道

We are aware of the fact that the market is declining.
我们知道市价下跌的事实。

We are aware that the market is declining.
我们知道市价下跌。

15. slightly better　　稍微好些

16. But the difference in price should, in no case, be as big as 5%.　　但价差决不应高达 5%。

in no case　　决不

The goods should in no case be packed in wooden.
货物无论如何不能用木箱包装。

in no case 放在句首，则应用倒装句。

In no case should the shipping marks be misprinted.
运输标志决不能印错。

17. to step up the trade　　为了促进贸易

18. on behalf of　　代表

19. we counter-offer as follows　　我们作如下还盘

as follows= as what follows　　如下

注意：

"as"是关系代词，不论句子的主语是单数或复数，只可用"as follows"而不可用"as follow"、"as following"、"as followed"三类错误表达。

Our prices are as follows:　　我方的价格如下：

Our price is as follows:　　我方的价格如下：

We quote the prices as follows:　　我方报价如下：

20. as per　　根据，依照

常用于询价单、报价单、价目单、装运须知和规格表，也用于来电、来函等。

We handle a wide range of textiles as per list enclosed.
我们经营多种纺织品，见附表。

As per your request, we enclose a copy of our latest catalogue.

我们已按你方要求随函寄去一本最新目录。

21. As the market is declining...　　由于行市下降（行市转疲）……
    这里的 market 作行市或市场需求或销路解。

注意：

下列一些形容词经常和 market 搭配使用：

declining（行市）下跌；advancing 上涨；strong 十分坚挺（迅速持续上涨）；firm 坚挺（有上涨表现）；weak 疲软（有下跌趋势）；brisk（active）活跃等。

22. be appreciative of　　对……表示感谢，感激
23. make an exception　　破例

Exercises

I. Translate the following terms into English:

1. 发盘人　　　　　　　　　2. 受盘人
3. 规格　　　　　　　　　　4. 付款条件
5. 佣金　　　　　　　　　　6. 优先报盘
7. 报盘的有效期限　　　　　8. 确认报盘
9. 可撤销报盘　　　　　　　10. 有权先售的报盘

II. Translate the following terms into Chinese:

1. CFR Singapore　　　　　　2. descriptive leaflet
3. substantial order　　　　　4. out of stock
5. favorable price　　　　　　6. original offer
7. non-firm offer　　　　　　8. quotation
9. withdraw offer　　　　　　10. as per

III. Choose the best answer to complete the following sentences:

1. If you could make a reduction _____ 5% in quotation, please let us know.
   A. to　　　　B. for　　　　C. of　　　　D. at
2. Much to our regret, we are unable to _____ the price to your level.
   A. change　　B. reduce　　C. decline　　D. lower
3. It is _____ that the matter should still be hanging unsettled.
   A. regretful　　B. with regret　　C. regretted　　D. regrettable
4. We think it advisable for you to make a _____ if you wish to remain competitive.
   A. reducing in price　　　　B. price reduction
   C. cutting price　　　　　　D. price cutting
5. We will place an order without delay if you would reduce your price _____ 5% _____ your cotton shoes.
   A. of/to　　B. of/to　　C. by/in　　D. by/at

6. You may be aware that some Indian dealers are lowering their prices. No doubt there is _____ competition in the market.
   A. high   B. sharp   C. keen   D. large
7. What we can do best is to _____ you half way.
   A. reduce   B. come   C. meet   D. bring
8. Information indicates that some parcels of similar quality from other sources are being sold _____ a level about 8% lower than yours.
   A. at   B. of   C. by   D. with
9. If you could see any chance to reduce the price to our _____, there is a possibility to conclude the business.
   A. approval   B. level   C. request   D market
10. Information _____ that the market is declining, so we recommend your acceptance.
    A. indicates   B. demands   C. makes   D. brings

IV. Fill in the following blanks with the words and expressions in the box, change the form when necessary:

| recommend | quote | opportunity | various | purchase |
| major | regular | subject | freight | substantial |

1. We would like to take the _____ to establish business relations with you.
2. Your company is kindly _____ by Mr. Lee.
3. We are considering to _____ 100,000 dozen of cotton from your company.
4. When_____, place state your terms of payment and the possible discount.
5. Please send us_____ catalogue and pricelist at your earliest convenience.
6. If the price is reasonable, we will place _____ orders with you for mobile phones.
7. This offer is firm, _____ to your reply reaching us before March 31.
8. We have learned that you are _____ dealers of porcelain in U.S.A.
9. Leather bags exactly come within the _____ of our business activities.
10. CIF price should include cost, insurance and _____.

V. Translate the following sentences into Chinese:

1. The above offer is made without engagement and is subject to our final confirmation.
2. While thanking you for your offer of yesterday, we regret being unable to work on it as the time of delivery is too distant. In our letter of enquiry, we have stated that time of delivery is of utmost importance.
3. We sincerely hope to conclude the business at a price 10% lower than those of similar products in America.
4. We make you the following offer, subject to your reply reaching us before September 24.
5. The price you counter-offered is not in line with the prevailing market.

Unit 4 Offers, Counter-offers and Acceptance

VI. *Translate the following sentences into English*:

1. 很抱歉,我方不能接受你方还盘,因为我方报的价格是很实际的。
2. 虽然你方能在报价上减少 2%,我们仍然不能接受。
3. 从目前迹象来看,市场将继续下降。
4. 我们不妨在这里补充说明一下,由于需求量大,该盘有效期到 1 月 10 日截止,过期后我们无法再把货物保留着不出售。
5. 你方必须降价 3%,否则没有成交的可能。

VII. *Simulated writing*:

Now you are required to write a counter-offer letter to inform them the following details:

敬启者:
　　你方 6 月 18 日来信收到,谢谢。
　　我们棉制台布(cotton table-cloth)的价格定得很合理,歉难给你们任何折扣。
　　关于付款条件,我们希望指出在同贵国所有客户的交易中惯用信用证,因此,我们不能对你方有所例外。
　　因我们与其他客户按我们现行价格和条款达成大笔交易,希望你方重新考虑并早日通知接受。
　　静候回复。

谨上

Dear Sirs,

                                                    Yours faithfully,

Supplementary Reading

Sellers Counter Offer Strategies

　　The art of the deal is negotiating. The goal, when you're countering a buyer's offer, is to get the highest price and best terms possible. Once you reject the initial offer, you must decide how much to counter. The answer is easy when the market is hot. You will counter at full price or more.

　　If the market is normal, you may receive less than full price for your property. In this case,

55

one strategy would be to set your asking price higher than normal. How much lower than your asking price will you counter-offer?

Beware of Setting a Minimum Counter Price

Setting a firm minimum counter price is a big mistake that some sellers make. Depending on the deal and the buyer your counter offer should be flexible. For example, after investigating the market, you set your asking price at USD 350,000. Your minimum price may be USD 320,000. If you are offered your minimum, you sell. If you are offered lower, you don't sell. It sounds simple.

Unfortunately, in this mindset, you box yourself into a limited deal. You want to be flexible when negotiating. Let us review our last example. The buyer offers USD 300,000. The seller rejects and counters with the minimum of USD 320,000.

The buyer counters with USD 305,000 again. Where do you go from here? You have already offered your lowest minimum counteroffer. The only recourse would be to repeat your same offer.

One strategy would be to counter lower at USD 315,000. Or what if the buyer is willing to pay more than your minimum?

The buyer might be willing to pay USD 330,000. You will actually have lost money again by countering too low.

There are housing situations where you are just lucky to be paying off the mortgage, commission, and closing costs. You might be offered a little less but you accept to some cash to save your credit. In this case, setting a minimum price would be reasonable.

If you do feel the need to set a minimum counter price, don't set it in stone.

Try to Get a Sense of the Buyer

Your counteroffer is not the final transaction. It is one step in the negotiating process. You counter. The buyer will counter your offer. You will then counter back. This process will repeat until the deal is made.

Therefore, your counteroffer should not be your best and lowest. The buyer's first offer is usually a low-ball offer. A seller's first counter is a high-ball offer. Both parties are testing to see how the other will respond.

Let the buyer know you are willing to negotiate. You ask USD 340,000, the buyer offers USD 300,000. You counter USD 335,000. You must also send the message that you are not willing to drop your price too much.

Some buyers will cave and accept the counteroffer and others will not. Anytime you reject and counter, you are opening negotiations but you are also taking the risk of losing the deal.

There are some buyers who are just looking for a desperate seller. They make a lot of low-ball offers until they find the property. You are not going to find a good price with that type of buyer.

Others will counter with close to what they originally offered, in this case say USD 305,000 (now you're still USD 30,000 apart).

What If You're Close Together in Price?

After a few counters, you are only a few thousand dollars apart. You countered at USD

335,000 and the buyer countered back at USD 330,000. Now you're only USD 5000 apart. Should you accept the buyer's counter?

You can simply accept the deal. Another strategy would be to tell the buyer or the agent that you want to split the difference. They accept. You will then have sold your property at USD 332,500.

Splitting the difference can be an effective way of closing out negotiations to bring about a win-win situation.

What If You're Far Apart?

You counter at USD 335,000 and the buyer counters at USD 305,000. You're USD 30,000 apart. That's serious money.

There are only two ways of handling this situation. You could hold your original counter. The buyer would understand that this is your final offer. This could be a deal breaker. If you were highly motivated to sell, a steep decline of your price would get the ball rolling again. You counter at USD 320,000 saying this is your best but last offer.

This action could spark the buyer's interest. He/She could accept or at least make a higher counteroffer.

Is There a Time to Walk Away?

There are only two reasons to walk away from negotiations. You are truly angry and will not lower your price.

The second is for effect. You are willing to take less, but you want the buyer to think you've made your last, best offer. You say, "Take my last offer or leave it. I'll give you an hour to decide."

As a tactic, walking away can start negotiations. You could get your price or lose the deal.

There are no guarantees when negotiating real estate. The final outcome is often determined by the following percentages:

10%—how good you are at negotiating
45%—how motivated you are to sell
45%—how motivated the buyer is to purchase
100%—luck

After-Class Study

(I) *List of Commonly-used Offer Terms and Phrases*

offeror 发价（盘）人
offeree 被发价（盘）人
offering 出售物
offer letter 报价书
offer sheet 出售货物单
offer list/book 报价单

offer price　　售价
offering date　　报价日
preferential offer / the preference of one's offer　　优先报盘
cost of production　　生产费用
inland / domestic / local invoice　　国内发票
consular legalized invoice　　领事发票/领事签证书
pro forma invoice / skeleton invoice　　形式发票
to extend an offer　　延长报盘
to renew an offer / to reinstate an offer　　恢复报盘
to withdraw an offer　　撤回报盘
concentration of offers　　集中报盘
to decline an offer/ to turn down an offer　　谢绝报盘
combined offer　　联盘，搭配报盘
lump offer　　综合报盘（针对两种以上商品）
to extend an offer　　延长报盘
official offer　　正式报价（报盘）
offer subject to our written acceptance　　以我方书面接受为准的报盘
offer subject to sample approval　　以样品确定后生效为准的报盘
offer subject to our final confirmation　　以我方最后确认为准的报盘
offer subject to export / import license　　以获得出口（进口）许可证为准的报价
offer subject to prior sale　　以提前售出为准的报盘
offer subject to goods being unsold　　以商品未售出为准的报盘
offer subject to your reply reaching here　　以你方答复到达我地为准的报盘
offer subject to first available steamer　　以装第一艘轮船为准的报盘

(II) *List of Commonly-used Counter-offer Words and Phrases*

wild speculation　　漫天要价
enjoy great popularity　　享有盛誉
ready seller / quick seller / quick-selling product　　畅销品
favorable price　　优惠价格
favorable terms　　优惠条件
unacceptable　　不可接受的
workable　　可行的
reasonable　　合理的
competitive　　有竞争性的
at wide intervals　　间隔时间太长
make headway　　有进展
trade terms　　贸易条件
trade agreement　　贸易协定
trade fair　　交易会
trade mark　　商标
foreign trade　　对外贸易

trade in sth　　经营某物
trade with sb.　　与某人交易
quotation　　行情
discount quotation　　贴现行情
exchange rate quotation　　外汇行情
commission　　佣金
general practice　　惯例
meet sb. half way　　各让一半，折中处理
on the high side　　偏高
leave…with only a small profit　　无利可图，获利很低

(III) *List of Commonly-used Acceptance Words and Phrases*

sales conditions　　销售条件
to make delivery　　交货
to make prompt-delivery　　即期交货
payment terms　　付款方式
special orders　　特殊订货
to be equivalent to　　相当于
to employ　　用……计价，采用……
exchange rate　　汇率
price terms　　价格条款
conclude business with sb.　　与某人达成交交易
close business / close a deal / close a transaction / close a bargain　　达成交易
gross price　　毛价
price effect　　价格效应
price contract　　价格合约
price calculation　　价格计算
price limit　　价格限制
price control　　价格控制
price theory　　价格理论
price regulation　　价格调整
price structure　　价格构成
price support　　价格支持

(IV) *List of Commonly-used Abbreviations in Offer, Counter-offer and Acceptance*

Ackmt　　acknowledgement　承认，收条
adv.　　advice　通知（书）
A.N.　　arrival notice　到货通知
Cert.　　Certificate　证明书
I/P　　Insurance Policy　保险单
C.I.　　Certificate of Insurance　保险单
CK　　Check　支票

Disc.	Discount	贴现；折扣
F.A.Q	Fair Average Quality	良好平均品质
G.M.B.	Good Merchantable Brand	品质良好适合买卖之货品
G.M.Q.	Good Merchantable Quality	良好可售品质
G/N	Guarantee of Notes	承诺保证
G.S.W.	Gross Shipping Weight	运输总重量
G.W.	Gross Weight	毛重
IOU	I owe you	借据
L/A	Letter of Authorization	授权书
L/I	Letter of Indemnity	赔偿保证书
L/G	Letter of Guarantee	保证函
L/U	Letter of Undertaking	承诺书
M.T.,	metric ton	公吨
M/T	Mail Transfer	信汇

(V) List of Commonly-used Price Terms

1. FOB

FREE ON BOARD (…named port of shipment)　　装运港船上交货（……指定装运港）

此术语是指卖方在指定装运港于货物越过船舷时即完成交货义务。而买方承担自货物在装运港越过船舷后的风险和责任。由于在 FOB 风险、责任划分上以越过船舷为界，卖方要负责支付货物装上船之前的一切费用，但历史上对"装船"的概念没有统一的解释，因而在装船费用方面就出现了许多的争议。为了解决这个问题，双方往往在 FOB 属于后面加列附加条件，这就形成了 FOB 的变形。常见的 FOB 变形主要有：

(1) FOB 班轮条件，即指装货费用和卸货费用由买方承担。

(2) FOB 吊钩下交货，即从货物起吊开始装货费用由买方承担。

(3) FOB 包括理舱，即卖方负担将货物装入船舱并支付包括理舱费在内的装货费用

(4) FOB 包括平舱费，即卖方负担将货物装入船舱并支付包括平舱费在内的装货费用。

此术语只能适应于海运和内河运输。

2. CIF

COST, INSURANCE AND FREIGHT (…named port of destination)　　成本加保险费、运费（……指定目的港）

此术语是指当货物在指定装运港越过船舷时，卖方即完成交货义务。卖方必须支付将货物运至目的港所必需的费用和运费，但卖方在装运港越过船舷完成交货义务后所发生的一切风险由买方承担，并且买方还承担自此以后由于各种事件造成的任何额外费用。卖方还需负责办理租船或订舱、支付运费、办理货物运输保险和支付保险费。CIF 合同下，在目的港卸货费用由谁负担，可采用 CIF 变形来表示：

(1) CIF 班轮条件，即卸货费用由支付运费的一方卖方负担。

(2) CIF 舱底交货，即买方负责从舱底起吊卸到码头的费用。

(3) CIF 吊钩下交货，即卖方负担将货物从舱底吊至船边卸离吊钩为止的费用。

(4) CIF 卸到岸上，即卖方负担将货物卸到目的港岸上的费用。

3. CFR

COST AND FREIGHT (…named port of destination)　　成本加运费（……指定目的港）

此术语是指装运港货物越过船舷，卖方就完成了交货义务，卖方必须支付将货物运至指定目的港所需的费用和运费。但在装运港越过船舷之后，货物发生灭失或损害的风险，以及由于各种事件造成的任何额外费用由买方负担。

4. FCA

FREE CARRIER (…named place of)　　货交承运人

此术语是指卖方在指定地将经过出口海关的货物交给买方指定的承运人，卖方就完成了交货义务。承运人是指在运输合同中承担履行铁路、公路、海洋、航空、内河运输或多式运输，或承担取得上述运输履行的人。如果买方指定一个非承运人的人收取货物，当货物被交给该人时，应认为卖方已履行了交货义务。

由于本术语适用于任何运输方式，包括多式运输，所以在交货点和风险划分上《2010年国际贸易术语解释通则》作了明确的规定：如在卖方所在处交货，卖方负责将货物装上由买方指定承运人的收获运输工具上。如在其他指定地交货，卖方不负责将货物从其送货工具上卸下。

5. CPT

CARRIAGE PAID TO (…named place of destination)　　运费付至（……指定目的地）

此术语是指当货物已被交给由卖方指定的承运人时，卖方即完成交货义务。货交承运人后，货物发生灭失或损坏的风险，以及由于发生事件而引起的额外费用，由买方负担。但卖方必须支付货物运至目的地的运费。

6. CIP

CARRIAGE AND INSURANCE PAID TO (…named place of destination)　　运费，保险费付至（……指定目的地）

此术语是指当货物已被交给卖方指定的承运人时，卖方即完成交货义务，但卖方必须自负费用订立运输合同，支付将货物运至指定目的地的运费，同时卖方还需自负费用，取得按合同规定的货物保险，并向买方提供保单。买方负担在货物被交货后发生的一切风险和任何其他费用。

在使用 FCA、CPT、CIP 三种贸易术语时，如果讲货物运至目的地需要经过多个承运人方可完成，那么卖方完成交货义务的分界线是货交第一承运人后，卖方即完成了交货义务。

六种主要报价方式的异同：

报价方式	办理出口清关手续	交货地点	风险转移划分点	承担运输义务	承担保险义务	办理进口清关手续	货物所有权转移方式	适用运输方式
FOB (…named port of shipment)	卖方	装运港	装运港越过船舷为界	买方	买方	买方	随交单而转移	适合海运和内河运输
CFR (…named port of destination)	卖方	装运港	装运港越过船舷为界	卖方	买方	买方	随交单而转移	适合海运和内河运输

续表

报价方式	办理出口清关手续	交货地点	风险转移划分点	承担运输义务	承担保险义务	办理进口清关手续	货物所有权转移方式	适用运输方式
CIF (…named port of destination)	卖方	装运港	装运港越过船舷为界	卖方	买方	买方	随交单而转移	适合海运和内河运输
FCA (…named place)	卖方	出口国指定地点	货交第一承运人	买方	买方	买方	随交单而转移	适合一切运输方式
CPT (…named place of destination)	卖方	出口国指定地点	货交第一承运人	卖方	买方	买方	随交单而转移	适合一切运输方式
CIP (…named place of destination)	卖方	出口国指定地点	货交第一承运人	卖方	卖方	买方	随交单而转移	适合一切运输方式

Chinese Version of Specimen Letters

<例信 1> 实盘

敬启者：

感谢贵公司 5 月 24 日的询盘。应你方要求，报盘如下，以贵公司的答复于 6 月 23 日前到达有效。

商品：锦缎手袋

价格：每个 12 美元，温哥华到岸价

数量：5,000 个

装运期：2003 年 8 月

包装方式：纸箱，每箱 20 个

付款条件：凭以卖方为受益人的不可撤销跟单信用证支付

希望以上条件能为贵公司接受，并殷切期盼您的正式订单。

大卫·陈

<例信 2> 虚盘

敬启者：

就贵公司 5 月 24 日来函询价，现报盘如下：

"5,000 个锦缎手袋，每个 12 美元温哥华到岸价，2003 年 8 月装运，以卖方为受益人的不可撤销跟单信用证支付。望妥善查收。请注意此报盘以货物未售为准。"

因为我们已从其他客户处接到大量订单，我们现有的库存很可能告罄。因此建议贵公司利用这次具有吸引力的报价。

盼望收到贵公司订单。

大卫·陈

<例信 3> 还盘

敬启者:

贵公司 6 月 1 日函悉,报盘 5,000 个锦缎手袋,单价每个 12 美元,温哥华到岸价。

兹复,很遗憾,我处客户认为你方价格过高,且与现行市场水平不一致。贵公司可能了解,一些印度尼西亚商人正在削价销售。毋庸置疑,市场竞争激烈。

我们不否认贵公司锦缎手袋质量稍好,但差价决不至于高达 5%。为促进贸易,谨代表客户还价如下:

"5,000 个锦缎手袋,每个 11.4 美元温哥华到岸价,其他条件按你方 6 月 1 日函办理。"

由于行情下跌,建议你方早日接受。

盼望早日得到答复。

马丁·克朗

<例信 4> 受盘

敬启者:

感谢贵公司 6 月 14 日要求减价 5%的来信。

我公司的政策是对标准价格不打任何折扣。不过,我们可为你方破一次例,以推广我公司之锦缎手袋。因而,若你方在 7 月 15 日前购买 5,000 个锦缎手袋,我们便接受你方要求减价 5%的还盘。

"锦缎手袋,每个 11.40 美元温哥华到岸价,8 月份装运。"

期盼收到你方订单,并持续发展双方互惠互利的业务关系。

大卫·陈

Unit 5 Sales Promotion

Learning Aims

After you finish learning this unit, you are requested to:

(1) understand some basic knowledge and strategies concerning sales promotion[1] in foreign trade;

(2) acquire how to write good and effective sales letters for your products;

(3) understand the function of reviver letter and its application;

(4) understand the function of follow-up letter and its application.

Background Knowledge

(I) About Sales Letter

Sales letter, as a particular kind of commercial letter, its purpose is to persuade your customers (namely the buyer or importer) to purchase your products or services supplied by your company or your suppliers. It has been defined as "A form of direct mail in which an advertiser sends a letter to a potential customer."

Since the development of the internet, sales letter has become an integral part of internet marketing, and typically takes the form of an email or webpage. A good sales letter will help you to make profits, expand your business scope and raise the commercial image and reputation of your company while a poor sales letter will probably make you suffer from a heavy loss of orders and opportunities.

(II) The "AIDA" Principle[2]

In order to achieve your final aims successfully, we might as well adopt the so-called *AIDA* principle which is widely-used in foreign trade, that is:

(1) Catch the potential buyers' *Attention* by introducing your product;
(2) Arouse their *Interest* by comparing the similar products;
(3) Stimulate their *Desire* by offering fashionable terms;
(4) Induce them to take *Action* of purchase your product.

(III) Two Other Related Commercial Letters

✧ **Reviver Letter[3]**: It is a close relative of sales letter, the main function of reviver letter is to retain or regain old customers instead of developing new ones. Statistics show that almost 80% of the company profit is usually created by the old customers compared to 20% profit created by new customers in foreign trade. Therefore the old customers are often regarded as the backbones of sales potential. Reviver letter together with sales letter are often written in the form of circular since they are often supposed as junk mails without being read.

✧ **Follow-up Letter[4]**: Follow-up letter is usually written by the seller to express regret or surprise that no response or reply has been received for the inquiry or offer previously made and discreetly inquire into the reason. An effective follow-up letter should be short and concise. In the first paragraph, it is necessary to state the intention of your letter since it will help the reader in clear understanding. The letter has to use formal language with soft and polite tone as well as positive attitude. In addition, a well drafted follow-up letter often creates a good impression on the reader and he or she is more likely to take up the issue that you mentioned in the letter.

Writing Tips

When writing a sales letter, it is important to have a good attitude ("You Attitude[5]") in order to sell your product or service, because the reader will want to know why they should spend their valuable time reading the letter. Therefore, you need to provide clear, specific information that will explain to the reader why they should be interested in buying your product or service.

A good sales letters usually have the following essential writing strategies:

(1) Catch the reader's eye: it is very crucial in a sales letter to attract the reader's attention, or you will probably fail to see your product or service.

(2) Describe the product or service you are trying to sell.

(3) Convince your reader that your claims are accurate: support your comments with research and facts.

(4) Give the reader opportunities to learn more about your product or service: you can provide the reader some necessary information, such as a phone number, a Web site address, an E-mail, or some other way for them to seek out information on their own.

Sentence Patterns & Examples

【Pattern 1】take the opportunity to introduce…　　借此机会介绍

We take the opportunity to introduce our company as the leading exporters dealing with animals by-products[6] in our area.

我们借此机会介绍我公司是当地规模最大的经营畜产品出口的公司。

I'd like to take the opportunity to introduce our new-developed energy-saving lighting products.

借此机会介绍我们新研发的节能照明产品

【Pattern 2】take the liberty of doing …; take the liberty to do…　　冒昧做某事

We have taken the liberty of sending some samples of our products to you and hope you will be interested in them.

我们冒昧地向你们寄送了一些我们公司产品的样品，希望你方能对此感兴趣。

We take the liberty to enclose the sample and price list of our new season silk fabric.

我们冒昧随信附寄新款丝绸的样品与价目表。

【Pattern 3】superior in quality; moderate / reasonable in price; skilful / excellent in workmanship / craftsmanship; elegant in style; matching in colour; novel in design 质量上乘，价格合理，工艺精湛，样式美观，颜色匹配，设计新颖

We assure you that our T-shirts are superior in quality, elegant in style and reasonable in price.

我们向你方保证我们公司的T恤衫质量上乘，样式美观，价格合理。

Being moderate in price, stable in performance, novel in design, our new coffee makers enjoy fast sale in European markets.
我们的新款咖啡机由于价格适中，性能稳定，款式新颖，在欧洲市场上非常热销。

【Pattern 4】sell fast / well; have a good / ready market; enjoy fast sales   产品销路好

Our "DELL" computers sell fast in domestic market.
"戴尔"牌电脑在国内市场销路很好。
The "VK" Brand deep-sea fish oil exported from USA enjoys fast sales in China.
从美国进口的"维之冠"牌深海鱼油在中国销路很好。

【Pattern 5】meet with warm reception   很受欢迎

"Citizen" watches meet with warm reception for its high-quality.
西铁城牌手表由于质优，因而很受欢迎。
We are confident that our toys will meet with warm reception in your local market.
我们自信我们的玩具产品会在贵方当地市场上深受欢迎。

【Pattern 6】entitle sb. to a discount; give / allow / offer sb. a discount   给某人打折

This coupon will entitle you to a 20% discount on any purchase of our products.
使用此券购买任何我公司的产品，将享受八折的优惠。
We will give you 10% discount in view of the previous substantial orders.
鉴于过去的大量订购，我公司将给予贵方10%的折扣。

【Pattern 7】to one's advantage to do...   做……是有利的

We think it to you advantage to enter into long-term business relation with us.
我们认为与我公司建立长期的业务关系对你方有利。
It will be to our mutual advantage to cooperate closely.
密切合作将使我们双方都受益。

【Pattern 8】recommend / advise sb. to do...   建议某人做……

Since you are interested in our products, we recommend you to place an order with us without hesitation.
既然你方对我们产品感兴趣，我们建议你方马上订货。
We advise you to accept our counter-offer since it is based on our latest market survey.
我方建议贵公司能接受我们的还盘，因为这是基于我们最新的市场调研做出的。

【Pattern 9】work fast   迅速做出决定

In view of the huge demand of "HP" printers, we advise you to work fast in case they are sold out.
由于惠普牌打印机的需求量很大，我方建议你方迅速做出决定以免产品售空。

Please work fast and place an order with us a month before the Christmas rush so that we can supply the goods from stock.

为确保我们能现货供应此类商品，请在圣诞销售旺季前一个月迅速做出决定并向我们订购。

【Pattern 10】in stock / out of stock　　有现货 / 缺货

They have plenty of stonewashed jeans in stock.
他们有大量的库存磨砂牛仔裤。

We are sorry to inform that the articles you ordered last week are out of stock at present, therefore we recommend some similar ones for your reference.

我们非常遗憾地告知你方上周所定购的货品现在缺货，故特意向你方推荐一些其他类似的产品供你方参考。

Specimen Letters

<Letter 1> A Sales Letter for Bamboo Floorboard

Dear Sirs,

　　We are specialized in[7] bamboo products and the "Green Paradise" brand bamboo floorboard is our knock-out product. This kind of bamboo floorboard is made of high quality bamboo through a series of strict craftsmanship. Level, smooth, bristletail-resistant[8] and distorting-resistant[9] are the main characteristics of our products. Besides it has the elegant color and luster[10], clear veins[11] which any other similar bamboo floorboard can't match it. This kind of product is suitable for top grade apartment, office, bedroom, hotel, sports places and outdoor recreation ground. The perfect combination of nature and modern technology will make you fell the nature in the home.

　　For above reasons, "Green Paradise" bamboo floorboard meets with warm reception[12] and enjoys fast sales both in domestic and overseas markets.

　　We deem it to your advantage to choose our products; therefore we write this letter herewith[13] some illustrated catalogues[14] of the products for your reference and look forward to your early reply.

Yours faithfully,

<Letter 2> A Sales Letter for Cosmetic Products

Dear Sirs,

　　Our company is a cosmetics enterprises specializing in the production of various middle and high class color cosmetics series such as make-up pencils, lipsticks, nail enamels, foundation, and so on.

　　Through decades of years of effort, our company has enjoyed good reputation with "SMART" and "ELFS" world-wide famed brand. With the adherence of "Perfect

Service to Customers" as production idea and "Quality First" as principle of business, we will endeavor to provide better products and after-sale services[15] for global customers based on ISO 9001:2000[16].

We enclose the coupons which entitle[17] you to receive a free sample (while in stock) and enjoy a buy-one, get-one-free full moisture lipcolor at selected cosmetics shops.

We hope you will be keen on our products by this way of sales promotion. Don't hesitate to place an order with us if you'd like.

Yours truly,

<Letter 3> A Sales Letter for Huzhou Writing Brush

Dear Sirs,

Huzhou, Zhejiang is the birthplace of writing brush. Huzhou writing brush has a long history and a strong cultural connotation. They together with Hui ink sticks, Xuan paper and Duan ink slabs are called the four treasures of the study[18] in China, which are the important symbols of Chinese long and splendid civilization.

Our Huzhou Wang Yipin Writing Brush Company, which has a history of more than 260 years, is the oldest professional enterprise that produces and deals in Huzhou writing brushes. Enjoying the reputation of "First of writing brush making skill is all over the world." we achieve the success by refining the traditional craftsmanship. "Sharp, neat, round and strong" are the four virtues of our products. In 1995, we obtained the Best Image AAA Grade Brand and certificate of Chinese enterprises and won the Gold Medal of Asian-Pacific International Trade Fair.

Chinese leaders and celebrities such as Mao Zedong, Deng Xiaoping, Guo Moruo ever showed their calligraphy by using our writing brushes.

Since it's the first time that you will place an order with us, we offer you a special discount[19] as follows,

Items	Quantities	Discount
YH-20 Series	50-100	5% off
YH-20 Series	100-200	10% off
YH-20 Series	above 200	20% off
LH-18 Series	20-50	5% off
LH-18 Series	50-100	10% off
LH-18 Series	above 100	15% off

Yours sincerely,

<Letter 4> A Reviver Letter

Dear Sirs,

Looking back through our sales records, we find that from 2008 to 2010 you bought from us a large quantity of computerized flat knitting machines in Models SJ-120 and SJ-150, but unfortunately we haven't received your any new order during 2011.

Last year, we innovated the core processing technology and upgraded our products. The Model SJ-200 computerized flat knitting machine is now our latest series product and has a good market in overseas markets. Being stable in performance, easy to install and maintain, safe in operation, our products compare favorably with[20] those of other suppliers in quality. In view of your previous substantial orders with us, we are willing to allow you a special discount on the current market price for our Model SJ-200 products, i.e. 3% for an order for below 100 sets, 6% for an order for 100 sets to 300 sets, 10% for an order for 300 and above. This offer is subject to your reply reaching us not later than Oct. 20.

Enclosed, please find a set of literature[21] for Model SJ-200. We are looking forward your favorable reply.

Yours faithfully,

<Letter 5> A Follow-up Letter

Dear Sirs,

We take the liberty of sending this letter to you to acquire some new information about your interest towards our ball bearing[22] products.

We think you have received the sample and illustrated catalogues that we sent you tow months ago. However, to our surprise, up to now we still haven't got your response whether you were satisfied with them or not.

Have you had an opportunity of checking the sample and relevant report? Didn't our ball bearing meet your requirements? Or you have found other better supplier?

Whatever the reason, we are keen on receiving your reply at your earliest convenience so that we can make timely arrangement to improve the quality and related service of our products.

Yours truly,

Notes

1. sales promotion   促销，推销某种（产品或服务）的活动
   sales letter   推销信函
2. "AIDA" principle
   "AIDA"原则是广告促销中对顾客产生作用的四个阶段，即：
   （1）引起顾客的注意（Attention）；
   （2）让顾客对商品产生兴趣（Interest）；
   （3）刺激其购买的欲望（Desire）；
   （4）使顾客采取实际行动（Action）满足其购物欲。

3. reviver letter　　振兴信
   振兴信以重新联系老客户并获得其订单为目的，此类信函与促销信函在外贸中通常以"通函"形式出现。

4. follow-up letter　　随访信
   这是在产品推销过程中经常出现的一种信函；撰写此类信函主要因为你的客户在一段比较长的时间内没有向你方下订单或给予必要的回复。在随访信中，可先提及客户过去产品的询价及公司过去提出的报盘，然后对一直没有收到订单而表示惊讶或遗憾，并谨慎地询问其中的原因。在信末也可提出一些对推销有利的新观点、优惠条件或改进措施。

5. You Attitude　　对方本位
   即站在对方的立场上，说明能够给予对方的利益及效用。

6. by-product　　副产品
   Silver is often obtained as a by-product during the separation of lead from rock.
   从矿石中提取铅时，往往可获得银这种副产品。
   animal by-product　　畜产品
   agricultural product　　农产品
   forest product　　林产品
   aquatic product　　渔产品

7. specialize in = be specialized in　　专营

8. bristletail-resistant　　防蛀

9. distorting-resistant　　不变形

10. color and luster　　颜色和色泽
    在外贸进出口业务中，商品的外在特性主要反映在 modeling（样式）、structure（结构）、color（颜色）、luster（色泽）、taste（味觉）上，而内在特性则主要反映在 chemical composition（内在组成）、mechanical performance（机械性能）、biological features（生物特性）上。

11. vein　　*n.*　　（植物的）叶脉，纹理

12. meet with warm reception　　受欢迎
    meet　　*v.*　　相遇；与某人相识；满足（欲望或要求）
    meet someone's requirements　　符合某人的需要（求）
    We can't find the product that meets our requirement.
    我们找不到一种能够符合我们要求的产品。
    meet with sb. / sth.　　偶然发现（人或某物）遭到
    They met with an accident on their way back.
    他们在归来途中发生了车祸。

13. herewith　　随函附上
    I send you herewith two copies of the contract.
    我随函附寄上合同副本两份。

14. illustrated catalogues　　带有插图的(产品)目录

15. after-sale service　　售后服务
    "4S"：4S 是英文单词（Sale）销售、（Service）维修、（Spare Parts）配件和（Survey）

信息反馈的 4 个开头字母。

"4S 店"是个近几年才时兴起来的名词，指的是"四位一体"的汽车销售专卖店，即集整车销售、零配件供应、售后服务、信息反馈于一体的销售服务店。

16. ISO 9001：2000　　质量管理体系——要求
    ISO (International Organization for Standardization)　　国际标准化组织
    ISO 9000：2000　　基本原理和术语
    ISO 9004：2000　　质量管理体系——业绩改进指南

17. entitle sb. to (do) sth.　　授予某人获得某事物（做某事）的权利或资格 [常用于被动语态]
    This ticket entitles you to a first class seat.
    凭此票，你可以坐头等舱。
    You are not entitled to the discount if you are not our VIP membership.
    假如你不是我们的贵宾会员就没有资格享受打折优惠。

18. the four treasures of the study　　文房四宝（即：湖笔、徽墨、宣纸、端砚）

19. discount　　v./n.　　打折扣；折扣

注意：

discount 原意为"不算在内"，因此指某物减价出售时所减去的那个百分比，例如：
他以八折的价钱买了那件衬衫。
He bought the shirt at an 80% discount.（误）
He bought the shirt at a 20% discount.（正）
言下之意，也就是中文说打八折，英文应是 20%；九折就是英文应是 10%，以此类推。

20. compare favorably with　　比……要好，比……有优势
    The price we offer compare favorably with other quotations you can get elsewhere.
    我们的报价要比你其他地方得到的报价优惠。

21. literature　　n.　　（产品）宣传资料

22. bearing　　n.　　轴承
    ball bearing　　滚珠轴承
    roller bearing　　滚柱轴承
    air bearing　　空气轴承
    plain bearing　　滑动轴承

Exercises

I. Translate the following terms into English:

1. 专营
2. 价格适中
3. 畅销
4. 现货供应
5. 缺货
6. 深受青睐

Unit 5 Sales Promotion

7. 拳头产品   8. 质量上乘
9. 通函   10. 打九折

II. Translate the following terms into Chinese:

1. novel in design   2. stable performance
3. by-product   4. illustrated catalogue
5. special allowance   6. excellent in craftsmanship
7. work fast   8. compare favorable with
9. be subject to   10. after-sale service

III. Choose the best answer to complete the following sentences:

1. No discount will be granted_____ you could place an order of more than 10,000 dozens.
   A. until   B. unless   C. otherwise   D. except

2. If you can make us a firm offer at a _____ price, we will place an order with your company.
   A. competitive   B. comparative   C. subjective   D. objective

3. As it involves only a small _____, we hope you will have no difficulty on promotion.
   A. quality   B. figure   C. quantity   D. number

4. We can _____ you a special discount of 15% on orders exceeding $50,000. The word "allow" can be replaced by the following words except_____.
   A. give   B. grant   C. offer   D. permit

5. We assure you _____ the goods can be supplied from stock _____ you order early.
   A. that…if   B. that…whether C. if…not   D. whether…if

6. We can _____ men's shirts _____ stock.
   A. provide…if   B. supply…in   C. provide…with   D. supply…from

7. In view of the large demand of the goods, we suggest you to _____ fast and place an order with us as soon as possible.
   A. decide   B. take action   C. work   D. run

8. We are sending you with pleasure_____ fax the latest _____ catalogue of our "Canon" Brand printers.
   A. through…illustrated   B. through…illustrating
   C. by…illustrated   D. in… illustrating

9. A set of _____ about our new products has been sent to you _____ separate cover and we think it to your advantage to purchase them.
   A. description…in   B. literature…by
   C. prescription…with   D. instruction…for

10. _____ in quality, _____ in price, _____ in design, our portable computers sell fast all over the country.
    A. superior…cheap…stable   B. excellent…reasonable…advanced
    C. excellent…reasonable…skilful D. superior…moderate…novel

IV. Fill in the following blanks of each sentence, pay attention to first letter of each word has been given:

1. We are glad to enclose the latest catalogue of our products that are superior in q_____ and moderate in p_____ and are sure to have a r_____ market.

2. Novel d_____ and reasonable price make our YF-5000 series vacuum cleaner meet with warm r_____.

3. In order to encourage to p_____ orders with us, we would a_____ you a 10% special d_____ for our items.

4. Recently we have received large numbers of orders, therefore we r_____ you to w_____ fast and place an order with us early in case the products are out of s_____.

5. Don't hesitate to p_____ our "Nikon" Brand digital cameras because we have been s_____ in this field for many years, which make us provide you the best commodities and a_____ service.

V. Translate the following sentences into Chinese:

1. This coupon entitles you to enjoy a 10% discount off regular-priced items and receive a free gift with any purchase of HKD 300 at Wise-Kids Toys.

2. Owing to its superior quality, skilful workmanship and moderate price, our 18K jewelry items are very popular with customers in Southeast Asia.

3. In order to enable you to have better understanding of products, we enclose the illustrated catalogues and a set of relevant literature by separate post for your reference.

4. Although the price of our MP3 is 10% higher than that similar product of Korean origin, we compare favorably in quality and performance.

5. We are going to clear our stock by offering you a special discount of 30% if you purchase at least 500 sets.

VI. Translate the following sentences into English:

1. 我们借此机会介绍我们的体育运动器材并随信附上产品目录及价格单。

2. 我们公司已有 15 年的出口经验，我们下属工厂月生产 60 万套男式衬衫，全供出口。

3. 鉴于我们长期的业务关系，我们愿意给你方提供八折的优惠。

4. 在过去的 10 年中，我们公司已经在商业和金融圈里享有诚信的名誉，产品备受用户的青睐。

5. 我们公司是中国茶叶最大的供应商，可提供各类茶叶，产品在市场上非常走俏，故我们建议你方向我们订购。

VII. Simulated writing:

Now you are required to write a sales letter of GPS navigator to Evergreen Trading Co., Ltd. of Canada based on the following information:

敬启者：

我们很高兴从中国驻加拿大大使馆参赞处获悉贵公司的名称和地址，现冒昧去函介绍我方公司和主营出口产品——GPS 导航仪。

我们公司目前是中国最大专业生产 GPS 导航仪的厂商，已有 12 年的历史，在国内外市场享有盛誉。我们的产品质量上乘，价格合理，操作简单，款式新颖，深受世界各国和地区用户的青睐。

现随函附寄我方产品的价格单和带有插图的目录供你方参考。我们认为贵公司在你方当地市场推销我们的产品是有利的。如果你方首次订购超过 1,000 台，我们愿给予 10%的折扣。

鉴于我公司产品需求量较大，建议贵公司从速决定并向我们下单，盼早日回复。

Dear Sirs,

Yours faithfully,

Supplementary Reading

How to Write an Effective Sales Letter

Sales letters are the most common marketing strategies of companies who look forward to sell their products or services. This is a very effective marketing strategy that however ends up in the recycling bin. Why is it that most sales letters meet the same fate? The answer is incorrect sales letter format. Sales letters are either too long or full of information that the reader does not comprehend. So what should a sales letter format be like? The following paragraphs will discuss some pointers on letter writing that will help you draft an effective sales letter.

An effective sales letter should contain the message that the reader is looking for. You should first understand the needs of the client and whether your products and services match their requirements. The letter should be addressed to the targeted audience. Do not write a letter to the company CEO, when it is the purchase manager who will decide upon buying your products or services.

The first few lines are very crucial, as it will give the reader a gist of what you intend to offer. Do not write in a general or hazy manner, as the reader will lose interest and won't read till the end. The most important message to send through your sales letter is mentioning the benefits the client will get after using your products or service. Many businessmen make a mistake of just mentioning the product features, but forget talking about end-user benefits.

The tone of the letter should not be similar to a business letter type. A sales letter should sound more personal and warm. Speak to the reader in a sincere and genuine language. You should not mix a sales letter with the actual sales process. A sales letter helps open the doors for queries, faxes, quotes, etc. Making the actual sales is the next step after getting a positive response from a sales letter.

The language should be easy to understand and simple. Do not use too difficult words and technical terms. If you need to use technical language, be sure you explain it in a simple manner. Do not use too big paragraphs as it puts off the reader. Explain your products and services in short and simple sentences. Never exceed more than one page. The people who are going to make a decision are very busy and do not have the time to read two or three page long sales letters.

Provide a product sample, free tutorial or free demo of the product or service offered. Always give a deadline for the offer. Even if you won't use the product deadline in reality, mentioning a deadline helps limiting the time for making a decision by the reader. Write the lines like, "Call to order..." or "Call our toll free line xxx-xxx." Also makes sure you send a business reply card along. It should have a pre-paid postage, as you do not want to lose a customer for the price of a stamp.

Finally, provide guarantee for your customer service, delivery, pricing, etc. This helps in building trust and integrity of the customer with your company. You can even include testimonials from satisfied users. Make sure you have taken a signed authorization form them, as you do not want to breach someone's right to privacy. The following sales letter templates will help you draft a proper sales letter example for your company.

After-Class Study

The Classification of Common Export Commodities in Foreign Trade

Picture	Category	Sample Goods
	Agriculture & Food	Food Additive, Garlic, Tea & Tea Leaf, Rice
	农业食品	食品添加剂、蒜、茶和茶叶、大米
	Apparel & Accessories	Athletic & Sports Shoes, Slippers & Sandals, Belt & Accessories, T-shirts
	服装饰件	运动鞋、拖鞋和凉鞋、腰带及饰物、T恤衫
	Arts & Crafts	Promotion Gifts, Christmas Gifts & Crafts, Painting & Calligraphy
	工艺品	广告礼品、圣诞礼物与手工艺品、油画与书画
	Auto Parts & Accessories	Car Audio & Video, Tyre, Car Light & Auto Mirror
	汽摩及配件	车载影音、轮胎、车灯和反光镜
	Bags, Cases & Boxes	Backpack, Trolley & Luggage, Specialized Case & Box
	箱包和礼盒	背包、拉杆箱和行李箱、专用盒子和箱子

Unit 5 Sales Promotion

续表

Picture	Category	Sample Goods
	Chemicals	Plastic Products, Pigment & Dye, Rubber Products
	化工	塑料制品、颜料和染料、橡胶垫
	Computer Products	USB Flash Disk, Memory Card & Card Reader, Mouse
	计算机产品	U 盘、储存卡与读卡器、鼠标
	Construction & Decoration	Laminate Flooring, Mosaic Tile, Countertop & Vanity Top
	建筑和装饰材料	复合地板、马赛克、工作台面
	Consumer Electronics	MP4 Player, MP3 Player, TV & Parts
	电子消费品	MP4 播放器、MP3 播放器、电视机及配件
	Electrical & Electronics	Battery, Storage Battery & Charger, Electric Motor, Plug
	电工电气	电池、蓄电池和充电器、电动机、插头
	Furniture & Furnishing	Sofa, Furniture Parts & Accessories, Bedroom Furniture
	家具摆设	文件柜、家具部件、卧室家具
	Health & Medicine	Pharmaceutical Chemicals, Health Care Appliance, Disposable Medical Supplies
	医药卫生	医药化学品、保健器材、一次性医用耗材
	Industrial Equipment & Components	Water Pump, Sealing & Gaskets, Motor & Engine
	工业设备及组件	水泵、垫片、发动机内燃机
	Instruments & Meters	Physical Measuring Meter, Geographic Surveying Instrument, Electronic Instrument
	仪器仪表	量具、地理测量勘测仪器、示波器
	Light Industry & Daily Use	Kitchen Implements, Exhibition and Advertising Equipment, Cup & Mug
	轻工日用品	厨房用具、易拉宝、杯具
	Lights & Lighting	LED Display, Table Lamp & Reading Light, Stage Lighting
	照明用具	LED 显示屏、台灯、激光灯
	Manufacturing & Processing Machinery	Plastic Machinery, Packaging Machinery, Casting & Forging
	制造加工机械	注塑机、封口机、铸造和锻压
	Metallurgy, Mineral & Energy	Alloy, Magnetic Material, Fireproof Material
	冶金矿产和能源	合金、磁性材料、耐火和耐高温材料
	Office Supplies	Pen, Pencil & Brush, Printer, Cartridge & Paper, Notebook
	办公文教	笔类、打印机及耗材、笔记本

续表

Picture	Category	Sample Goods
	Security & Protection	Surveillance, Control & Protection, Alarm & Security Systems, Safety Products & Supplies
	安全与防护	监视器、报警器、安全和防护产品
	Service	Commercial Service, Exhibition, Design & Photography
	服务	商业服务、展览、设计与摄影
	Sporting Goods & Recreation	Barbecue, Tent, Fishing Tackle
	运动健身与休闲娱乐	烧烤用具、帐篷、垂钓用具
	Textile	Cotton, Towel & Handkerchief, Carpet
	纺织品	原棉和棉织物、毛巾、浴巾和手帕、地毯
	Tools & Hardware	Pneumatic Tools, Hardware Accessories, Knife
	五金工具	气动工具、五金配件和刀
	Toys	Wooden Toys, Inflatable Toys, Intellectual & Educational Toys
	玩具	木制品玩具、充气玩具、益智和娱教玩具
	Transportation	Barrow, Trolley & Cart, Gas Scooter, Truck & Bus
	交通运输	手推车、汽动车、货车和客车

Chinese Version of Specimen Letters

<例信 1> 竹制地板促销信函

敬启者：

我们是专营竹制产品的公司，"绿色天堂"牌竹制地板是我们公司的拳头产品。这类竹制地板采用优质毛竹，经一系列严格工艺流程加工而成，产品具有平整、光滑、防蛀及不变形等特点；除此之外，该产品色泽高雅、纹理清晰，是其他同类竹制地板所无法比拟的，适用于高档公寓、住宅、办公室、卧室、宾馆饭店、体育场所以及户外娱乐场所。自然与现代科技的完美结合，使您足不出户便能感受到大自然的气息。

由于以上诸原因，"绿色天堂"牌竹制地板备受客户青睐，在国内外市场上十分走俏。

我们认为你们公司选择我们的产品是相当有利的，故我方特地写信并随信附寄此类产品的最新插图目录供你方参考并希望尽早收到你们的回复。

谨启

<例信 2> 化妆品促销信函

敬启者：

　　本公司是专业生产各类中高档化妆笔、口红、指甲油、粉饼等彩妆系列化妆品的企业。

　　经过几十年的努力，我们拥有了"SMART"、"ELFS"（"斯马特"、"艾尔芙斯"）等世界知名品牌。

　　公司遵循"完美顾客服务"的生产理念，坚持质量为先的商业原则。我们将在 ISO 9001：2000 国际质量认证体系基础上始终如一地为全球客户提供更加优质的产品及售后服务。

　　为此我公司特随信附上这些优惠券，该券将使你在我公司化妆品店里免费获赠样品试用装一件（数量有限）并享有丰盈水分唇膏"买一送一"的优惠。

　　我们希望通过此促销方式你方对我公司的产品感兴趣，假如你方中意的话请尽快向我公司订货。

谨启

<例信 3> 湖笔促销信函

敬启者：

　　浙江湖州是毛笔的发源地，湖笔文化源远流长，内蕴丰盈，与徽墨、宣纸、端砚并称为"中国四大文房四宝"，是中华文明悠久灿烂的重要特征。

　　我们湖州王一品湖笔公司是湖州当地最老的一家生产和经营湖笔的专业毛笔企业，具有 260 多年的历史。公司通过对传统手工工序的精炼和改进获得成功，所生产的毛笔素有"湖颖之技甲天下"之美誉；"尖、齐、圆、健"是其四大美德。我们的产品在 1995 年获中国企业最佳形象 AAA 级标牌和证书，并获"亚太国际贸易博览会金奖"。

　　近现代中国家领导人和文化名人，如毛泽东、邓小平、郭沫若，曾使用我们生产的毛笔题字。

　　考虑到你公司第一次向我们订货，我方特给予以下特别优惠：

商品名称	数量（支）	折扣
羊毫-20 系列	50～100	9.5 折
羊毫-20 系列	100～200	9 折
羊毫-20 系列	200 以上	8 折
狼毫-18 系列	20～50	9.5 折
狼毫-18 系列	50～100	9 折
狼毫-18 系列	100 以上	8.5 折

谨启

<例信 4> 振兴信

敬启者：

　　经查阅销售记录，我们发现贵公司在 2008 年至 2010 年期间向我们购买了大量

SJ-120 和 SJ-150 型号的电脑横编织机,但令人遗憾的是在 2011 年我们却再未收到贵公司的新订单。

去年,我们革新了纺织机的核心生产技术并更新了自身的产品,SJ-200 型号的电脑编织机是目前我公司最新系列的产品并在海外市场上非常热销。由于该产品性能稳定、安装保养简单、操作安全性高,我们的编织机产品在质量上较其他供应商同类产品都更胜一筹。鉴于贵公司过去的大量订购,我方此次愿意给贵公司在现行市场价的基础上给予特别的优惠,即购买 100 台以下优惠 3%,100 台至 300 台优惠 6%,300 台以上优惠 10%。此报盘以贵方的回复信函在 10 月 20 日前到达我方为有效。

随信附寄 SJ-200 型号编织机的宣传资料一套。静候佳音。

谨启

<例信 5> 随访信

敬启者:

我们冒昧再次写信以图获取你公司对我们生产的滚珠轴承产品的最新消息。

两个月前寄送的样品和产品插图目录想必一定收到,但是使我们纳闷的是直至现在我们仍然没有收到你公司对我们产品是否满意的回复。

我们不知道贵公司有没有抽空看过我方的样品及相关的产品报告?是不是我们的滚珠轴承产品尚未达到你方的要求或者你方已经找到了其他更理想的供应商?

无论哪种原因,我们都热切期望收到贵公司早日的回复以便我们可以做出及时安排,改进产品的质量与相关服务。

谨启

Unit 6　Orders and Acknowledgements

Learning Aims

After you finish learning this unit, you are requested to:
(1) know about how to place and confirm an order;
(2) master how to write letters concerning orders and their acknowledgements[1];
(3) understand some basic knowledge about sales contract in foreign trade.

Background Knowledge

(I) *About Orders*

An order is a request to supply a specified quantity of goods. It can be an acceptance of an offer or sent voluntarily by a buyer. Under any circumstances, an order should be clearly and accurately written out and state all the terms of transaction. Once the order is confirmed or accepted, it may be regarded as part of the contract between the exporter and importer, therefore both parties should ensure that no important information will be neglected in their orders before sending in order to avoid any possible mistakes which may lead to subsequent loss or trouble.

Generally speaking, an order usually contains the following information:

(1) The name and address of exporter and importer;

(2) Catalogue number;

(3) Quantities ordered;

(4) A full and accurate description of the commodities (such as name, type, size, color, specification etc.);

(5) Price of the commodities, including unit price and total value;

(6) Packing and marking;

(7) Shipping company, shipping method, time of shipment, port of loading, port of destination;

(8) Terms of payment;

(9) Other necessary information, including order number, order types, validity of the order etc.

(II) *About Acknowledgements*

An acknowledgement is a reply to an order, either to accept or to reject. When a seller receives his customer's order, he should acknowledge receipt of the order immediately.

A deal is concluded when the seller's offer is accepted by the buyer, or confirmed by the seller. In cases the buyer has made a counter-offer, or placed a firm order, or confirmed a purchase with the seller, it should contain all necessary terms and conditions. After acceptance and confirmation, a Sales Contract/Confirmation made out by the seller is to be signed by both parties.

Writing Tips

A letter of placing an order written by the buyer is usually composed of the following three parts:

(1) Refer to the previous contact, acknowledging receipt of the offer and tell the seller of the buyer's intention to place an order.

(2) Give the detailed description of your order and state the terms of payment and the anticipated date of delivery and the mode of transportation.

(3) Close the letter by expressing willingness to cooperate or suggesting future business dealings with the seller.

Unit 6 Orders and Acknowledgements

When the seller received the buyer's letter, the seller also adopts three steps to complete the letter:

(1) Confirm that you have received the letter and express your pleasure.

(2) Give your reply of agreeing or refusing and your reasons.

(3) State your good will to do business with the buyer, or hope for further orders.

Sentence Patterns & Examples

【Pattern 1】place an order with sb. for sth.   向某人下某货的订单/向某人订购某货

We thank you for your quotation of September 20 and now place an order with you for the following items.

谢谢你方9月20日的报价，现向你方订购下列商品。

In reply to your quotation of May 10, we are pleased to place an order with you for the products mentioned in the enclosed sheet.

兹回复贵方5月10日报价函，现向你方订购如所附订单所示商品。

This is only a small trial order[3], but, if satisfactory, we shall be able to place large and regular orders with you.

此次仅为小量试销订单，但是，如果商品令人满意，我们将与你方定期大量订购该商品。

【Pattern 2】confirm one's order   确认订单

Thank you very much for your order of May 5 for 5,000 cases canned beef. We are pleased to confirm our acceptance as shown in the enclosed Sales Contract.

贵方5月5日订购5,000箱罐头牛肉的订单已收到，谢谢。对此订单我方乐意确认予以接受，如附寄的销售合同所示。

We shall be grateful if you could confirm your order on the revised conditions.

如果你方能按照修改的条件确认你方订单，我们将不胜感激。

【Pattern 3】to accept (decline or cancel) one's order   接受（拒绝/取消）某人订单

Owing to heavy commitments, many orders haven't been completed. Therefore, we can only accept your orders for October shipment.

由于大量承约，许多客户的订货都未发出，因此我们目前只能接受你方10月船期的订单。

To our regret, we are unable to accept your order at the price requested, since our profit margin does not allow us any concession by way of price discount.

很抱歉，我们不能按你方所要求的价格接受订单，因为我方利润已不允许我们再打任何折扣。

【Pattern 4】to execute / fulfill / work on an order   执行订单

We have received your order No. 667 which will be executed to your satisfaction.

我们已收到你方667号订单，该订单的执行将使你方满意。

We are executing your Order No. 668 at present and please rest assured that we will effect[4] the shipment within the time you specified.

目前我们正在执行你方668号订单，请放心我们定将在你方所规定的期限内安排装运。

Your repeat order No. 782 has been accepted and we are now working on it.
我方已接受你方编号为782的续购订单，现在该订单正在执行中。

【Pattern 5】order sth. at ... price   按……价格订购

We have ordered 500 sets of milling machines at 1,400 Euros per unit FOB Lisbon.
我们已订购了500台铣床，每台1,400欧元，里斯本离岸价。

We plan to order the following goods at the prices named after we received your catalogue and price list.
在收到你方寄来的产品目录及价格单后，我们打算按所示价格订购下列商品。

【Pattern 6】to sign and return a copy of ... for one's file   签退一份……以供某人存档

We have pleasure in informing you that we have booked your order No. 123. We are sending you our Sales Confirmation No. 632 in duplicate, one copy of which please sign and return for our file.
我们高兴地告知已接受你方第123号订单。现寄上第632号销售确认书一式两份，请签退一份供我方存档。

Specimen Letters

\<Letter 1\> Place an Order for Men's Shirts

Dear Sirs,

  Many thanks for your quotation of October 10 and the samples of men's shirts. We are satisfied with the quality of the items and pleased to enclose our Order No. 682 for sizes listed in your quotation.

  We learn that you are able to supply the above mentioned goods from stock and hope you will deliver the goods within the next six weeks.

  We wish to effect payment by D/P 60 days. Please let us have your confirmation at your earliest convenience.

Yours faithfully,

Encl.

ORDER No. 682			
Buyer:		**Seller:**	
Qingdao Garments Imp/Exp Corp.		Alice Trading Co. Ltd.	
Qingdao, P. R. China			
Quantity(doz)	Item	Size	Unit Price(Per doz) CFR Singapore
20	Men's shirts	S	USD 160.00
30	Ditto	M	USD 240.00
25	Ditto	L	USD 200.00

Unit 6 Orders and Acknowledgements

<Letter 2> A Letter for Declining an Order

Dear Sirs,

<u>Re: Order No. CS213—Chinese Silk Goods</u>

We thank you very much for your fax of May 15, in which you informed us that you will place a repeat order[5] with us.

Much as we sincerely appreciate your interest, we regret that we cannot at present entertain[6] any fresh orders for the above-mentioned goods, owing to heavy commitments[7]. However, we will contact you as soon as our new stocks come in.

Regarding stock Chinese silk goods, we are also enclosing a list for your reference in case you are interested in any other items. If possible, please feel free to send us your specific enquiries which can be assured of our best attention at all times.

Yours faithfully,

<Letter 3> Acknowledgment for 6,000 Sets of Full Automatic Washing Machine

BEIJING JINGHUA ELECTRIC APPLIANCE CORPORATION

86 Guangqumen Street, Dongcheng District, Beijing

Tel: (010) 65200693   Fax: (010) 65200698

Dear Sirs,

Thank you for your order No. _____.

We accept your order for 6,000 sets of full automatic washing machine and will arrange shipment accordingly.

Our letter of acceptance will reach you in a few days.

Yours sincerely,

<Letter 4> A Letter for Sending a Sales Confirmation/Contract

Dear Sir or Madam,

<u>Subject: Your Order No. 223-CS002</u>

Thank you for your order No.223-CS002 for 1,000 TCL Brand TV sets which you faxed us yesterday. We are glad to tell you that all the items can be delivered by the end of October. Enclosed you will find our Sales Contract No. 122 in triplicate[8]. Please sign and return one copy to us for our file.

We trust you will open the relative L/C in our favor at an early date. Meanwhile, you may rest assured[9] that we shall effect shipment without delay upon receipt of the L/C.

We appreciate your co-operation and look forward to your further orders.

Yours truly,

<Letter 5> A Letter for Counter-Signature

Dear Sirs,

We have duly received your Sales Conformation No. 32CS003HL. As requested, we return herewith one copy completed with our counter-signature.

We have established the relative L/C in your favor[10] with the Bank of China, London. It will reach you soon. Upon receipt, please arrange shipment and advise us of the name of steamer and date of sailing by fax.

Yours faithfully,

Notes

1. acknowledgement   *n.*   （对收到来信等的）确认；回音
2. proforma invoice   形式发票
   这是一种非正式发票，是卖方对潜在的买方报价的一种形式。一般小额贸易国外客户是很少签正式出口合同的，形式发票往往就起着约定合同基本内容以实现交易的作用。如果形式发票被用来做信用证，那么信用证上的条款便应与形式发票上的一致。
3. trial order   试购订单
   在国际贸易中常见的订单类型还有：
   initial order / first order   首次订单
   regular order   定期订单
   repeat order   续购订单
   substantial order   大宗订单（大量订购）
   additional order   补充订单
4. effect   *v.*   实现，完成；使生效
   At present, supply can be effected only in small quantities.
   目前，仅能供应少量货物。
5. repeat order   续订订单；续订的货物
   repeat order 与原订单除装运期不同外，价格、数量及详细规格也可能不同。若只是装运期不同，其他一些条件都相同，则称之为 duplicate order。
6. entertain=ready to consider   *v.*   准备考虑（引申为接受）
   We cannot entertain any price higher than USD320 per long ton.
   我方不能接受（考虑）高于每长吨 320 美元的价格。
7. commitment   *n.*   所承诺的事；所承担的责任
   Heavy commitments prevent us from accepting new orders.
   由于订单太多无法接受新的订单。
8. in triplicate   一式三份
   in duplicate   一式两份
   in quadruplicate   一式四份

一式四份及以上也常说 in four copies，in five copies，……或 in fourfold，in fivefold……

9. rest assured   放心

   Please rest assured that repayment is ensured.
   请您放心，还款是有保障的。

10. in one's favor / in favor of sb.   以……为受益人

    The letter of credit has been opened in your favor.
    以你方为受益人的信用证已经开立。

    favor   v.   有利于

    The opportunity does not favor our making a binding arrangement.
    机会不利于我们做出具有约束力的安排。

Exercises

I. Translate the following terms into English:

1. 试订购
2. 样品
3. 销售确认书
4. 销售合同
5. 形式发票
6. 会签
7. 折扣
8. 单价
9. 库存
10. 支付条款

II. Translate the following terms into Chinese:

1. acknowledgement
2. regular order
3. repeat order
4. fulfill an order
5. in your favor
6. arrange shipment
7. payment by D/P 30 days
8. for one's file
9. in triplicate
10. rest assured

III. Choose the best answer to complete the following sentences:

1. We are confident that such an arrangement will prove_____.
   A. satisfactory   B. satisfaction   C. satisfied   D. satisfying
2. We hope you will give your best attention_____this order.
   A. to the execution of   B. for carrying out
   C. in the performance of   D. by filling out
3. _____heavy commitments, we cannot accept any fresh orders.
   A. Since   B. Because   C. Owing to   D. In addition
4. The_____order is given strictly on the condition that shipment must be made not later than the first day of march.
   A. enclosing   B. enclosed   C. enclose   D. enclosure

5. According to the terms_____payment in the contract, we have established an L/C in your favor.

  A. on   B. for   C. of   D. at

6. We hope to book _____ you a repeat order _____ the following lines _____USD210 per set CIF London.

  A. from, for, at   B. for, of, on   C. with, for, at   D. \, with, on

7. We must apologize_____you_____being unable to fill your present order.

  A. to, on   B. to, as   C. for, about   D. to, about

8. We would like to suggest that you_____orders for Christmas gifts earlier

  A. will place   B. place   C. have to place   D. shall place

9. _____in your fax, we have sent you the latest catalogue

  A. At request   B. As requested   C. On requested   D. are interested in

10. If you _____earlier, we would have reserved the goods for you

  A. will inform us   B. inform us

  C. had informed us   D. have informed

IV. Fill in the following blanks of each sentence, pay attention to first letter of each word has been given:

1. We will try our b_____to find a ready market for your products.

2. Please s_____and return one signed copy of the Contract for our f_____.

3. Our contract stipulates that payment should be m_____by irrevocable letter of credit payable by sight d_____, so you must act accordingly.

4. Since your o_____covers such a big quantity, we are unable to meet your r_____for the moment, but we will do our utmost to secure supply for you.

5. We will request our bankers to o_____an L/C in your f_____upon receipt of your confirmation of this order.

V. Translate the following sentences into Chinese:

1. We have accepted your order No. 13E for 60 tons of grapefruit. Please open the covering L/C in our favor according to the terms contracted.

2. We find both the quality and price of your products satisfactory and are pleased to give you an order for the following items on the understanding that they will be supplied from current stock at the prices named.

3. Since both of us two parties have affixed the signatures to the contract, it is effective and binding on both parties.

4. We regret that we haven't had any stock of the article required by you.

5. We regret to inform you that, as some items under your Order No. FL34 are beyond our business scope, we can only accept your order partially.

VI. Translate the following sentences into English:

1. 如果你方认为一切无误，请签退合同一份以供我方存档。

2. 我们很高兴与你方订购 1,500 台 DVD 机，随信附寄订单一份，订单号是 WL120。
3. 兹通知你方，有关信用证已由中国银行开出。
4. 我方已向贵公司随信附寄了编号为 DM-56 号一式两份的销售确认书。
5. 非常高兴与贵公司达成这笔交易。

VII. *Simulated writing*:

Write a letter for Universal Trading Co., Ltd. (55 Maple Street, London) to their Chinese supplier, ABC Imp. & Exp. Corp., confirming an order for 20 dozens each size of Blouses. The letter should be written according to the instructions below:

1. 谢谢对方 6 月 6 日报价和寄来的样品。
2. 对对方的女士外套样品质量和价格感到满意。
3. 随信附寄大中小三类尺寸各 20 打女士外套的订单一份，订单号为 LB120。
4. 要求最好现货供应，7 月底交货。
5. 由于客户急需该批货，希望尽快交货。

Dear Sirs,

Yours faithfully,

Supplementary Reading

An order or an order letter should be clearly and accurately written out and state all the terms of transaction. It should include the following points:

(1) description of the goods, such as specifications, size, quantity, quality and article number (if any);

(2) prices (unit prices as well as total prices);

(3) terms of payment;

(4) mode of packing;

(5) time of transportation, port of destination and time of shipment etc.

Many buyers use printed order forms which ensure that no important information will be neglected.

When acknowledging an order received, the following structure may be used:

(1) Express appreciation for the order received.

(2) Assure the buyers that the goods they have ordered will be delivered in compliance with their request. It is also advisable for the sellers to take the opportunity to introduce other products to the buyers.

(3) Close the letter by expressing willingness to cooperate or suggesting future business dealings.

When a seller or a buyer agrees completely with the terms and conditions of an offer, order or a counter-offer, he will send a Sales Contract (or Sales Confirmation) or a Purchase Contract (or Purchase Confirmation) to the other side to ask for counter-signature.

A contract is an agreement between two or more competent parties in which an offer is made and accepted, and each party benefits. It is an agreement which sets forth binding obligations of the relevant parties.

The agreement can be formal, informal, written oral or just plain understood. Some contracts are required to be in written in order to be enforced.

A contract proper includes: (1) the full name and address of the buyer and seller; (2) the commodities involved; (3) all the terms and conditions agreed upon; (4) indication of the number of original copies of the contract, the languages used, the term of validity and possible extension of the contract.

A contract or confirmation can be drawn up either by the seller or the buyer. Respectively, they are called a sales contract/confirmation or a purchase contract/confirmation.

Following is a specimen of a Sales Contract:

货物销售合同
(Sales Contract)

正本
ORIGINAL

编号(No.)：_____

签约地点(Signed at)：_____

日期(Date)：_____

卖方(Seller)：_____   **买方**(Buyer)：_____

地址(Address)：_____   地址(Address)：_____

电话(Tel)：_____   电话(Tel)：_____

传真(Fax)：_____   传真(Fax)：_____

电子邮箱(E-mail)：_____   电子邮箱(E-mail)：_____

买卖双方经协商同意按下列条款成交：

The undersigned Seller and Buyer have agreed to close the following transactions according to the terms and conditions set forth as below:

1. 货物名称、规格和质量(Name, Specifications and Quality of Commodity);

2. 数量(Quantity);

3. 单价及价格条款(Unit Price and Terms of Delivery);

除非另有规定，FOB、CFR 和 CIF 均应依照国际商会制定的《2010 年国际贸易术语解释通则》办理。

The terms FOB, CFR or CIF shall be subject to the International Rules for the Interpretation of Trade Terms (INCOTERMS 2000) provided by International Chamber of Commerce (ICC) unless otherwise stipulated herein.

4. 总价(Total Amount):

5. 允许溢短装(More or Less): _____%

6. 装运期限(Time of Shipment):

收到可以转船及分批装运之信用证_____天内装运。

Within _____ days after receipt of L/C allowing transshipment and partial shipment.

7. 付款条件(Terms of Payment):

买方须于_____前将保兑的、不可撤销的、可转让的、可分割的即期付款信用证开到卖方，该信用证的有效期延至装运期后_____天在中国到期，并必须注明允许分批装运和转船。

By confirmed, irrevocable, transferable and divisible L/C to be available by sight draft to reach the Seller before _____ and to remain valid for negotiation in China until _____ after the Time of Shipment. The L/C must specify that transshipment and partial shipments are allowed.

买方未在规定的时间内开出信用证，卖方有权发出通知取消本合同，或接受买方对本合同未执行的全部或部分，或对因此遭受的损失提出索赔。

The Buyer shall establish a Letter of Credit before the above-stipulated time, failing which, the Seller shall have the right to rescind this Contract upon the arrival of the notice at Buyer or to accept whole or part of this Contract non fulfilled by the Buyer, or to lodge a claim for the direct losses sustained, if any.

8. 包装(Packing):

9. 保险(Insurance):

按发票金额的_____% 投保_____险，由_____负责投保。

Covering _____ Risks for_____% of Invoice Value to be effected by the _____.

10. 品质/数量异议(Quality / Quantity discrepancy):

如买方提出索赔，凡属品质异议须于货到目的口岸之日起 30 天内提出，凡属数量异议须于货到目的口岸之日起 15 天内提出，对所装货物所提任何异议于保险公司、轮船公司、其他有关运输机构或邮递机构所负责者，卖方不负任何责任。

In case of quality discrepancy, claim should be filed by the Buyer within 30 days after the arrival of the goods at port of destination, while for quantity discrepancy, claim should be filed by the Buyer within 15 days after the arrival of the goods at port of destination. It is understood that the Seller shall not be liable for any discrepancy of the goods shipped due to causes for which the Insurance Company, Shipping Company, other Transportation Organization /or Post Office are liable.

11. 由于发生人力不可抗拒的原因，致使本合约不能履行，部分或全部商品延误交货，卖方概不负责。本合同所指的不可抗力系指不可干预、不能避免且不能克服的客观情况。

The Seller shall not be held responsible for failure or delay in delivery of the entire lot or a portion of the goods under this Sales Contract in consequence of any Force Majeure incidents which might occur. Force Majeure as referred to in this contract means unforeseeable, unavoidable and insurmountable objective conditions.

12. 仲裁(Arbitration)：

因凡本合同引起的或与本合同有关的任何争议，如果协商不能解决，应提交中国国际经济贸易仲裁委员会深圳分会。按照申请仲裁时该会当时施行的仲裁规则进行仲裁。仲裁裁决是终局的，对双方均有约束力。

Any dispute arising from or in connection with the Sales Contract shall be settled through friendly negotiation. In case no settlement can be reached, the dispute shall then be submitted to China International Economic and Trade Arbitration Commission (CIETAC), Shenzhen Commission for arbitration in accordance with its rules in effect at the time of applying for arbitration. The arbitral award is final and binding upon both parties.

13. 通知(Notices)：

所有通知用_____文写成，并按照如下地址用传真/电子邮件/快件送达给各方。如果地址有变更，一方应在变更后_____日内书面通知另一方。

All notice shall be written in _____ and served to both parties by fax/e-mail/courier according to the following addresses. If any changes of the addresses occur, one party shall inform the other party of the change of address within _____ days after the change.

14. 本合同为中英文两种文本，两种文本具有同等效力。本合同一式_____份。自双方签字（盖章）之日起生效。

This Contract is executed in two counterparts each in Chinese and English, each of which shall be deemed equally authentic. This Contract is in _____ copies effective since being signed/sealed by both parties.

The Seller: The Buyer:

卖方签字：   买方签字：

After-Class Study

The Forms of Contract in Foreign Trade and Their Differences

1. Sales Contract　　销售合同　　　　Purchase Contract　　购货合同

The major deference between a sales contract and a purchase contract is that a sales contract is drawn by the seller, while a purchase contract is drawn by the buyer.

2. Sales Confirmation　　销售确认书

The major difference between a sales contract and a sales confirmation is that the contents of a contract are more formal and more detailed than that of a confirmation.

3. Agreement　　协议

The major difference between an agreement and the above-mentioned contract and confirmation is that the agreement refers to both oral and written promises, while contract and confirmation stands for written promises only.

4. Memorandum　　备忘录

The characteristics of a memorandum are equal to those of a contract, except that a memorandum does not have contractual binding force upon parties thereto.

5. Letter of Intent　　意向书

As a letter of intent merely serves as an expression of intention, it fails to be a legal document.

6. Purchase Order　　购货订单

As a purchase order only expresses the intention of the buyer, it functions as an offer or an invitation for offer. But "acceptance" of the purchase order constitutes a purchase contract and is legally binding on all parties.

Chinese Version of Specimen Letters

<例信 1> 男式衬衫订单函

敬启者：

非常感谢你方10月10日的报价及寄来的男式衬衫样品。我们对其质量感到满意并高兴地随函附上我方第682号订单，定购你方报价中所列尺寸的男式衬衫。

我方获悉你方可以现货供应上述货物，希望你方在6周内装运。

我方希望以60天付款交单方式支付。请尽快确认。

谨启

附件

<table>
<tr><td colspan="4" align="center">第 682 号订单</td></tr>
<tr><td colspan="2">买方:
青岛服装进出口公司
中国青岛</td><td colspan="2">卖方:
Alice 贸易有限公司</td></tr>
<tr><td>数量（打）</td><td>商品</td><td>尺寸</td><td>单价（每打）CFR 新加坡</td></tr>
<tr><td>20</td><td>男式衬衫</td><td>小号</td><td>USD 160.00</td></tr>
<tr><td>30</td><td>同上</td><td>中号</td><td>USD 240.00</td></tr>
<tr><td>25</td><td>同上</td><td>大号</td><td>USD 200.00</td></tr>
</table>

<例信 2> 拒绝订单函

敬启者:

非常感谢你方 5 月 15 日的传真，要与我方续订订单。

虽对你方好意不胜感激，但很遗憾，由于目前订单太多，我方不能考虑上述货物的新订单。但是，我方一有新货到库，会马上与你方联系。

考虑到目前尚有中国丝绸制品存货，我方同时随信附上一份货单供你方参考，看是否有你方感兴趣的其他货物。如有意，请告知你方详细要求，我方将随时关注。

谨启

<例信 3> 确认 6,000 台全自动洗衣机的订单函

北京京华电器公司
北京市东城区广渠门大街 86 号
电话：(010)65200693　传真：(010)65200698

敬启者:

贵方_____号订单收悉，谢谢。

我方接受贵方 6,000 台全自动洗衣机的订单，将按要求安排装运。

我方关于接受贵方的信函几天后将寄达贵方。

谨启

<例信 4> 寄送销售合同的信函

敬启者:

事由：你方第 223-CS002 号订单

感谢你方昨日传真给我方的你方第 223-CS002 号订单，订购 1,000 台 TCL 牌电视机。我方高兴地告知你方，所有货物可以在 10 月底发货。随信附上我方第 122 号销售合同一式三份。请签退一份供我方存档。

Unit 6　Orders and Acknowledgements

　　我方相信你方会尽快开出以我方为受益人的相关信用证。同时请放心，一旦收到信用证，我们将立即装运。
　　感谢你方合作，并期待你方继续订货。

谨启

<例信 5>　要求会签函

敬启者：
　　我方已按时收到你方第 32CS003HL 号销售确认书。按你方要求，特返回一份有我方连署签名的复本。
　　我方已从中国银行伦敦分行开立出以你方为受益人的相关信用证，很快会到达你方。请你方收到后立即安排装运，并通过传真通知我方货轮名称及起航日期。

谨启

Unit 7 Terms of Payment

Learning Aims

After you finish learning this unit, you are requested to:

(1) understand some basic knowledge about international payment[1] and settlement;

(2) get acquainted with various payments, especially those customarily used in import and export;

(3) know how to write letters on payments.

Unit 7 Terms of Payment

Background Knowledge

(I) *About Payments*

Payment in international trade is much more complicated than that in domestic trade. There are many ways to make payment in international trade, the basic methods are:
- remittance[2] (including payment in advance and cash with order)
- open account
- documentary credit (using letter of credit)
- documentary collection (documents against payment, D/P or documents against acceptance D/A)

The most generally used method is the letter of credit which is a reliable and safe method of payment, facilitating trade with unknown buyers and giving protection to both sellers and buyers.

(II) *Asking for D/P and D/A Payment*

Payment is sometimes made by collection through banks under the terms of Documents against Payment (D/P) or Documents against Acceptance (D/A). In this case, the banks will only do the service of collecting and remitting and will not be liable for non-payment of the importer. D/P calls for actual payment against transfer of shipping documents. There are D/P at sight and D/P after sight. The former requires immediate payment by the importer to get hold of the documents. In the latter condition, the importer is given a certain period to make payment as 30, 45, 60, 90, 120 or 180 days after presentation of the documents, but he is not allowed to get hold of the documents until he pays. D/A calls for delivery of documents against acceptance of the draft drawn[3] by the exporter/seller. D/A is always after sight.

As far as the seller's benefit is concerned, L/C is better than D/P. D/P at sight is better than D/P after sight, whereas D/P is better than D/A. In international trade, payment through collection is accepted only when the financial standing of the importer is sound or where a previous course of business has inspired the exporter with confidence that the importer will be good for payment.

(III) *Urging Establishment[4] of L/C*

When a contract is concluded, the buyer is usually under the obligation to establish an L/C with his bank within the time limit stipulated in the sales contract. Especially for bulk sale or the commodities produced according to buyer's request, it is very important for the buyer to open the L/C in time; otherwise, the seller can't arrange the production and shipment of commodities.

Normally, the buyer's L/C should reach the seller 15 days (or 30 days) before shipment. But in practice, foreign customers always delay opening the L/C when the market condition changes or the shortage of fund arises. So we should always keep an eye on it. To promote the business, we should urge the other side to open the L/C under the following conditions:

(1) The contract stipulates a relatively long shipment (e.g. 3 months), and the buyer should open the L/C several days before the shipment (e.g. 15 days). Then we should inform buyer the estimated shipment and urge him into opening the relative L/C on time.

(2) If we can advance the shipment, we may negotiate with the buyer and request advancing opening the L/C.

(3) If the buyer fails to open the relative L/C on time, the seller has the right to claim compensation for damages.

(4) Sometimes it is not the deadline, if we find that the customer's credit is not fine or the market condition is changing, we also may urge the buyer into opening the L/C.

(IV) *Asking for L/C Amendment*

As the stipulations in the L/C should be in exact accordance with[5] the terms of the contract, the sellers should examine the stipulations in the L/C carefully. If there are some discrepancies between the two documents, sellers should ask the buyers to make the corresponding amendments to the L/C.

✧ The Reasons for Amending L/C

Two reasons may result in L/C amendment. One is for the beneficiary. Generally for those who are not in accordance with our foreign trade policies or influence the performance of contract and the security of payment, we must ask customers to amend the L/C through opening bank. The other reason is for the applicant. The applicant may be forced to change some clauses of L/C because of the changing situation.

✧ The Procedures of Amendment

Amendment to L/C ought to be applied by the applicant, and takes effect after the agreement of the opening bank and the beneficiary.

(1) The applicant submit the application of amendment to the opening bank.

(2) The opening bank sends modification to the original notifying bank after examining the application, and this modification is irrevocable.

(3) After receiving the modification, the notifying bank examines its surface authenticity and transmit it to the beneficiary.

(4) The notifying procedure of modification is similar to that of the L/C. The notification should indicate: "please write back to our bank whether the modification is accepted". If the beneficiary doesn't accept the modification, he ought to return it to the notifying bank as soon as possible, so that the notifying bank can pass on the information to the opening bank.

(5) The modification comes into effect after the beneficiary accepts it. If the beneficiary rejects it and returns it to the notifying bank with documents showing his rejection, the modification is invalid. The beneficiary's acceptance or rejection of the modification will result in postponing submission of documents.

(V) *Examining the L/C*

After receiving the buyer's L/C, the seller should examine and verify it in contrast with the contract according to the UCP. The basic principle of L/C examining is that the content of L/C must be consistent with the contract.

But in practice many foreign L/C are not totally in accordance with contracts. Reasons are various. For example, some countries and areas always have special regulations in practice, some foreign customers are not familiar with our policies, some foreign customers or opening banks make mistakes, or some foreign customers deliberately add some unreasonable clauses in the L/C, and so on. So we must seriously examine and verify those foreign L/C.

❖ Main content of bank's verification

(1) Verify the L/C on politics and policy;
(2) Verify the L/C on liability;
(3) Verify the L/C on authenticity;
(4) Verify the L/C on the words that guarantee payment and restricted clauses.

❖ Main content of company's verification

(1) Verify the L/C on the variety of L/C;
(2) Verify the L/C on the applicant and beneficiary;
(3) Verify the L/C on the amount and currency;
(4) Verify the L/C on the record of commodity;
(5) Verify the L/C on the date and place of expiration;
(6) Verify the L/C on the time of shipment and validity[6];
(7) Verify the L/C on the clause of transshipment and partial shipment;
(8) Verify the L/C on the terms of payment;
(9) Verify the L/C on the required documents;
(10) Verify the L/C on the printed clauses and special clauses.

Writing Tips

Usually the buyers adopt the following three steps to write a letter to negotiate payment terms:
(1) Mention the Contract, goods etc.;
(2) Suggest the terms of payment and give out the reason;
(3) Wish the reader to accept.

When the seller received the buyer's letter, the seller also adopts three steps to complete the letter:
(1) State that you have received the letter;
(2) Give your reply of agreeing or refusing and your reason;
(3) State your good will and your wish to do business with the reader.

Sentence Patterns & Examples

【Pattern 1】for account of... / for one's account   记……的账上；由……付款

在信用证开立时，本短语有时会与 by order (of) 放在一起使用，即 by order (of) and for account of...（奉……之命并付其账户）

By order of and for account of American ABC company.

奉美国 ABC 公司之命并付其账户。

All banking charges outside China are for applicant's account.
中国境外的所有银行费用由开证申请人负担。

【Pattern 2】instruct (bank) to issue L/C for (amount) in (one's) favor　　指示（银行）签发以……为受益人的金额为……的……信用证

We are going to instruct our bank to open a letter of credit for the amount of this order.
我公司正在请银行按照本订单金额开具信用证。

We have instructed our bank, Bank of China, Shanghai branch, to issue a confirmed irrevocable L/C for USD 650,000 in your favor.
我们已指示中国银行上海分行开立金额为 650,000 美元的以你方为受益人的保兑的不可撤销的信用证。

【Pattern 3】draw on … at … for …　　开具……金额的以……为付款人的……期汇票

(1) 词性为动词，主要构成如下搭配：

draw on 或者 be drawn on somebody / something 开出、开给（以某方为付款人的）汇票（从其账上划拨款项）、出票给……

注意：

对象前面要用介词 on。

Documents to be negotiated by drafts drawn at 60 day's sight for full invoice amount on DBS Bank Ltd, Singapore accompanied with the following documents.
单证可凭按全额发票金额开给新加坡 DBS 银行的 60 天期汇票，随附下列单据议付。

You may draw on Bank of China, Tianjin branch at sight for the amount of the invoice.
你方可以开具以中国银行天津分行为付款人的发票金额的即期汇票。

(2) "draw" 表示 "开给"，在信用证里面还可以用 "value" 和 "issue" 来表示，如：

Drawn or valued or issued on us or ourselves, or Bank of China.
开给我行或我行自己，或中国银行。

(3) drawing（为 draw 的名词形式）　　出票；支取

Notwithstanding any terms and conditions in this credit, the discrepant fee of USD 70 (or equivalent) will be deducted from the amount of drawing(s) for each set of discrepant documents presented on first presentation hereunder.
尽管本信用证有其他规定，但是，如在第一次提示时所提交的单证有瑕疵，将从每套单证的出票金额中扣除 70 美元（或相当）的不符点费。

【Pattern 4】be valid / open / effective / good / firm until…　　有效期至……

The L/C will be valid for negotiation in China until November 14.
本信用证在中国议付，有效期至 11 月 14 日。

The offer is firm until next Friday.
此报盘有效期至下周五。

Unit 7　Terms of Payment

【Pattern 5】expedite / rush an L/C　　加速开立信用证

Please do your utmost to expedite the L/C to meet your requirements in time.
我们将尽快开立信用证以及时满足你方的要求。

As the goods have been ready, please rush the covering L/C so that we may execute the order without fail.
由于货已备妥，请加速开立相关信用证以便我方能顺利执行订单。

【Pattern 6】find discrepancy　　发现差错

Thank you for your L/C No. TB1306, but we regret to say that we have found some discrepancies in it after checking.
感谢贵方寄来的编号为 TB1306 的信用证，但经核查，我们遗憾地告知贵方，我们发现该信用证存在一些差错。

The original Sales Contract shall prevail when any discrepancy is found in the L/C.
信用证中若出现任何差错，均以销售合同原件为准。

【Pattern 7】amend...as / to read...　　将……改为……

Please amend the 5th clause of the L/C as "partial shipment and transshipment are allowed."
请将信用证第 5 条条款修改为"允许分装与转船"。

As to the insurance clause, "Covering W.P.A. and War Risk" should be amended to read "Covering All Risks and War Risk".
关于保险条款，"投保水渍险与战争险"应该修改为"一切险与战争险"。

【Pattern 8】extend...to...　　将（时间）延长至……

We hope you can extend the validity of the L/C to October 30 owing to the delay on the manufacturers' part.
由于厂家的延误，我方希望贵方能将信用证的有效期延长至 10 月 30 日。

Please extend the shipment date and valid date of your L/C to March 15 and March 30 respectively so that we can effect shipment smoothly.
请将你方信用证的装运日期与有效日期分别延长至 3 月 15 日和 3 月 30 日以便我方能够顺利发货。

Specimen Letters

<Letter 1> Asking for Establishing[7] L/C

Dear Sirs,

　　We are pleased to confirm your order for 600 sets of digital camera amounting to USD 18,000. As requested, we are preparing to arrange shipment by the end of October and would request you to open an irrevocable L/C in our favor valid until September 15 as soon as possible. Upon receipt[8] of your L/C, we will ship your order.

Yours faithfully,

<Letter 2> Notifying L/C

Dear Sirs,

To cover the value of goods ordered under our Purchase Confirmation No. 369, an irrevocable documentary Letter of Credit No. 567 for USD 8,768 has been established by the Bank of China in London on July 12, 2011 in your favor.

We look forward to punctual shipment of this order, according to the delivery date stipulated in the Confirmation.

Yours faithfully,

<Letter 3> Urging Establishment of L/C

Dear Sirs,

Our Sales Confirmation No. R3369

With reference to[9] the 2,000 dozen shirts under our Sales Confirmation No. R3369, we wish to draw your attention to the fact that the date of delivery is approaching, but we still have not received your covering Letter of Credit up to now. Please do your utmost to expedite the L/C so that we may execute the order smoothly.

In order to avoid subsequent amendments, please see to it that the L/C stipulations should be in exact accordance with the terms of the contract.

We hope to receive your favorable reply soon.

Yours truly,

<Letter 4> Requiring Focusing on the Date of L/C

Dear Sirs,

We appreciate the conclusion of a transaction under Sales Confirmation No. 123 and wish to remind you of the stipulation in regard to the time limit for the arrival of your L/C. It is hoped that you will abide[10] by terms and conditions agreed upon by both parties and establish the L/C to reach us before June 20, 2011.

You can expect that shipment will be arranged as soon as your L/C arrives. Meanwhile, we hope that you will continue to make an effort to place additional orders, which will certainly receive our best attention.

Yours truly,

<Letter 5> Amendment[11] to L/C (1)

Dear Sirs,

We would like to explain the matter of L/C amendment. According to the L/C we received, the payment was to be made at 90 days. But we want it to be made at sight.

Unit 7　Terms of Payment

This was agreed on by you and expressly mentioned in your order sheet. Therefore please amend it as stated in it. The goods will be shipped by the 10 of this month.

We should be obliged for your immediate amendment to the L/C as requested by us.

Yours faithfully,

<Letter 6> Amendment to L/C (2)

Dear Sirs,

Your letter of credit No. 3368 issued by the Bank of Deutschland has arrived.

On examination, we find that transshipment and partial shipment are not allowed. As direct sailings to your port are few and far between[12], we have to ship via Rotterdam more often than not. As a result, transshipment may be necessary.

With regard to partial shipment, it would speed matters up if we could ship immediately the goods we have in stock instead of waiting for the whole shipment to be completed.

With this in mind, I telexed you today, asking for the letter of credit to be amended to read[13]: "part shipment and transshipment allowed." I trust this amendment will meet with your approval and you will telex us to your final decision without delay.

Yours sincerely,

<Letter 7> Extension[14] of an L/C (1)

Dear Sirs,

Re: Your L/C No. 1211

10 m/t raw black sugar

We thank you for your L/C No. 1211 covering your order of 10 metric tons of raw black sugar[15]. We are sorry that owing to some delay on the part of our suppliers, we are unable to get the goods ready before the end of this month.

It is expected that the consignment will be ready for shipment in the early part of October and we are arranging to ship it on S.S. "Rotenberg" sailing from Shanghai on or about October 10.

We trust you will extend by fax the shipment date of your L/C to October 15 and validity to October 30, thus enabling us to effect shipment of the goods in question[16].

We thank you for your cooperation.

Yours faithfully,

<Letter 8> Extension of an L/C (2)

Dear Sirs,

Thank you for your cable of September 16 informing us that L/C No. 517 covering the order No. 18 has been extended until November 5.

Owing to the chaos[17] in Middle East, the bankers here are so cautious that they would not accept shipping documents unless against a Letter of Guarantee. We will make every effort to make shipment within the extended period of L/C validity.

However we are afraid the amended L/C also might expire[18] according to the circumstances before shipment. Therefore, please explain our position to your customers and try to get their consent to extend L/C further. The goods of No. 18 are now in store at Qingdao and please make haste to have the relative L/C No. 517 extended until August 15 so that we may ship without fail.

Yours truly,

<Letter 9> Declining Extension of an L/C

Dear Sirs,

We have received your letter of July 30 requesting us to extend the above L/C No. 1027 to September 31 and September 15 for shipment and negotiation[19] respectively.

We are quite aware of the conditions set forth in S/C No. 3369 that the goods ordered could be shipped in August if the covering L/C reached you on July 15 at the latest. However, as we had to go through the necessary formalities[20] of applying for the relevant import license, we could not open the L/C earlier. The import license was granted on July 17 and is valid only up to August 31.

We are willing to do whatever we can to cooperate with you, but as the present import regulations do not allow any extension for license, we regret having to say that it is beyond our ability to meet your request to extend the above L/C.

Please do your best to ship the goods in time and we thank you for your cooperation.

Yours truly,

<Letter 10> Documents against Payment

Dear Sirs,

The goods which you ordered on 2 October have been shipped to you today by S.S. "Red Dragon", due at Los Angles on 5 November.

We have taken special care to the items which are suited[21] to conditions in North America. We hope you will be pleased with our selection and that this, your first order, will lead to further business between us.

From the enclosed copy of invoice you will see that the price of 30,000USD is well within the maximum figure you stated. We have drawn on you for this amount at sight through the City Bank, who has been instructed to hand over documents against payment of the draft. We hope you will understand when we explain that the urgency of your order left with insufficient time to make the usual enquiries and that we therefore had no choice but to follow our standard practice with new customers of placing the transaction on a cash basis.

We look forward to your further orders, subject to satisfactory references and regular dealings, would be prepared to consider open account terms with quarterly[22] settlements.

Yours faithfully,

<Letter 11> Documents against Acceptance

Dear Sirs,

Your Order No. 678

We are pleased to inform you that arrangements have now been made to ship the wireless phone[23] you ordered on October 22. The consignment will leave Shanghai by S.S. Hongqiao, due to arrive at the port Rotterdam sometime in late November.

In conformity with our usual terms of payment, we have drawn on you at 60 days and passed the draft and shipping documents to our banker. The documents will be presented to you by the Chartered Bank against your acceptance of the draft in the usual way.

Yours truly,

<Letter 12> Declining Documents against Acceptance

Dear Sirs,

We have received your letter of November 15. As already pointed out in our previous letter, we had made arrangements with our manufacturers to make delivery as punctually as possible in future.

We shall see to it that your interest is well taken care of at all times. As to the terms of payment, we wish to stress[24] that our usual terms of payment is by confirmed and irrevocable L/C remain unchanged in all ordinary cases. For the time being, we regret our inability to accept D/A terms in all transactions with our buyers abroad.

For future shipments, however, we shall do our best to fulfill your orders within the time stipulated. If, by any chance, it is impossible for us to do so, we will effect shipment on a D/P basis, in order to avoid putting you to so much trouble in the extension of L/C.

We trust you will appreciate our cooperation.

Yours faithfully,

Notes

1. pay vt. 付（款项，费用等）；给予（主意等）；进行（访问等）
       vi. 付款；值得；合算
   pay in advance   预付
   pay by installments   分期付款
   pay on delivery   货到付款
   pay for   v.   付出代价，为了得到……而付款

payable　　*adj.*　　可付的，应付的

bills payable　　应付票据

a check payable at sight　　见票即付的支票

amount payable　　应付金额

payment　　*n.*　　（不可数）支付；（可数）支付的款

terms of payment / payment terms　　支付条款

payment on deferred terms　　迟期（延期）付款

monthly payment of RMB 3,000　　每月付人民币 3,000 元

(1) 付某种费用的款，如发票、费用、佣金等，常用 "in payment of"

We are enclosing our check No. B123 issued by the Barclays' bank, London for Stg. 2,000 in payment of your invoice No. 56.

兹寄去伦敦巴克莱银行所开的第 B123 号支票一纸，金额计 2,000 英镑，系付你方的 56 号发票之款。

(2) 付某种具体事物的款，如商品、广告、样品等，常用 "in payment for"

We airmailed you yesterday a series of "Hua Sheng" Brand Electric Fans as samples and looking forward to your USD 230 in payment for the above.

我方昨日空邮去"华生"牌电扇系列样品，并盼望收到你方金额计 230 美元的支票，以偿付上述样品。

2. remit　　*v.*　　汇寄，汇款

Kindly remit by check.

请汇支票。

remittance　　*n.*　　汇款

On receipt of your remittance, we will ship the goods immediately.

一旦收到你方汇款，我们将立即装船。

We have received your remittance for USD 1,200.

我们已收到你方 1,200 美元的汇款。

T/T (Telegraphic Transfer)　　电汇

M/T (Mail Transfer)　　信汇

D/D (Demand Draft)　　票汇

3. draw　　*vt. & vi*　　开出（汇票）

指开立票据时，及物动词 draw 作"开立"解，不及物动词 draw 作"开立票据"解，因此 draw a draft =draw。

(1) draw (a draft) on sb. for sth.　　开出向某人索取……的汇票，开具汇票向……索取

(2) draw on sb. against sth.　　开出汇票向某人索取某笔款项

As agreed, we are drawing on you at sight against your purchase of a sample lot.

按照商定，对你方所购样货我们开出即期汇票向你方索款。

As arranged, we have drawn on you against the documents for the amount of invoice through the Bank of Asia.

按照安排，我们已凭单据向你方开具汇票通过亚洲银行向你方索取发票金额。

Unit 7 Terms of Payment

We regret to note that our draft drawn on you on the terms of D/P 30 days after sight was dishonored.
我们遗憾地注意到我们开给你方的 30 天期的付款交单的汇票遭到了拒付。

(3) to draw on sb. at 60 days' sight　　向……开立 60 天期限的远期汇票
to draw at 30 days' D/A　　开立 30 天期限的承兑交单
to draw at 60 days' D/P　　开立 60 天期限的付款交单

(4) to draw D/A (or D/P) against your purchase　　对于你方这笔购货按付款交单（或承兑交单）方式收款

drawings　　n.　　用汇票支取的金额

Your letter of credit is allowed 5% more or less in drawings.
你方信用证应准许在收款时 5%的上下幅度.

Drawer　　n.　　出票人，发票人
drawee　　n.　　受票人，（汇票）付款人

4. urge　　vt.　　催促，劝说

Recently they have been urging us for execution of their order for 3,000 gross pencils.
最近他们一直在催促我们履行有关 3,000 罗铅笔的订单。（1 罗=12 打）

Your are urged to give an early reply to our enquiry for groundnuts.
请早日答复我们有关花生的询盘。

5. in accordance with (to)　　与……一致；按照，根据
in exact (full) accordance with　　与……完全一致
in strict accordance with　　与……严格一致

The quality of the goods must be in strict accordance with that of the sample.
商品质量必须严格与样品质量相符。

To avoid any possible complaint, we wish to make it clear that the goods supplied to our order No.051 must be in exact accordance with the samples in both quality and design.
为避免任何可能的异议，我们想说明供给我们的第 051 号订单的货物在品质和设计上必须与样品完全一致。

In accordance with faxes exchanged, we are glad to have purchased from you 100 dozen cotton bed-sheets.
根据往来电传，很高兴向你方购买了 100 打棉质床单。

"与……一致；符合" 还可以说：

to be in conformity with ...
to be in compliance with...
to be in line with...
to be in agreement with...

6. validity　　n.　　有效期

We have to point out that shipment must be made within the validity of our L/C.
我们强调一点，必须在我们信用证有效期内装船。

valid　　adj.　　有效的

The offer is valid for 5 days.
此报盘有效期 5 天。

Payment is to be made by an irrevocable L/C to be opened 30 days before the time of shipment and remain valid for negotiation within 15 days after the time of shipment.
以不可撤销的信用证支付，于装运期前 30 天开立，并于上述装运期后 15 天内在中国议付有效。

7. establish   *vt.*   开立；建立；确立；开设

   establish/open/issue an L/C   开立信用证

   We hope to establish mutually beneficial business relations with all prospective customers.
   我们希望与所有潜在的客户建立互利的贸易关系。

   Our brand has already established itself firmly in public favor.
   我们的品牌已在公众中确立了信誉。

   We are glad to inform you that we have established a branch office in London.
   欣然告知你方我们已在伦敦开设了一家分公司。

   establishment   *n.*   开立；建立

   We are arranging for the establishment of the relative L/C with the bank at this end.
   我们正安排此地银行开立有关信用证。

   We take this opportunity to approach you for the establishment of trade relations with you.
   我们借此机会与你们联系，希望与你们建立贸易关系。

8. upon / on receipt of   一俟……，收到……后

   Upon / On receipt of your instructions we will send the goods.
   一俟收到你方要求，我们将发货。

9. with / in reference to   关于

   With / In reference to your letter of May 5, we are pleased to inform you that we are willing to accept L/C as our terms of payment.
   关于贵方 5 月 5 日来函，我们非常高兴地通知贵方我们愿意接受信用证的付款方式。

10. abide   遵守……；依从……

    abide by the rules   遵守条律

    had to abide by the judge's decision   服从法官的判决

11. amendment   *n.*   修改，修改书

    Please send us your amendment to the above L/C as early as possible.
    请尽快将上述信用证的修改通知书寄送我方。

    We have instructed our bank to make an amendment to / of the L/C as requested.
    我们已通知银行按要求修改信用证。

    You are requested to make amendment to L/C No. 89 without delay.
    请你方立刻修改 89 号信用证。

    amend   *vt.*   修改

    Please amend your L/C No.8034 to allow transshipment at Singapore.
    请将你信用证 8034 号修改成允许在新加坡转船。

Please amend the quantity and the amount to read "5% more or less allowed."
请将信用证中的数量和金额改为"允许增减 5%"。

Please amend the port of destination as "Shanghai, China."
请将目的港改成"中国上海"。

12. few and far between   稀少

As direct steamers to your port are few and far between, we have to ship via Hong Kong more often than not.
由于到达你方港口的直达轮稀少，我们不得不经常经由香港运输。

13. read   v.   读作；内容是

We confirm your fax of the 10th, which reads as follows:
现确认你方 10 日传真，内容如下：

Please amend the price clause to read "CFR London."
请将条款更改为 CFR London。

The thermometer is reading 40℃.
温度计显示 40 度。

A sign reading "No Smoking" was stuck on the wall.
墙上贴着"请勿吸烟"的标志。

14. extension   n.   宽限期；额外延长的期限

   three months' extension on the loan   贷款的三个月宽限期

   extend   vt.   可用，提供；拖欠，宽延；奉献，增加

We extend to you this accommodation in view of our friendly relations.
鉴于我们友好关系我们给你方此次照顾。

As the L/C allows us only five days for negotiation of the document, which is far from enough, we'd appreciate it very much if you could extend the negotiation period to 15 days.
信用证只允许我们有 5 天的时间议付单据，这显然是不够的，因此请将议期延长到 15 天。

W.P.A coverage is too narrow for a shipment of this nature, please extend the coverage to include TPND.
针对这种性质的货物只保水渍险是不够的，请加保偷盗提货不成险。

15. raw sugar   原糖，粗糖

16. in question   正被讨论的，可怀疑

    out of question   毫无疑问

    out of the question   不可能，不容讨论

    beside the question   离题

    beyond (all) question   的确；毫无疑问；无可争辩

17. chaos   n.   混乱；杂乱的一堆；乱成一团

The desk was a chaos of papers and unopened letters.
桌上杂乱地堆放着一些纸张和未拆的信。

18. expire   v.   期满（指某事经过一段时间期满），到期；终止

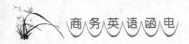

The trade agreement between the two countries will expire next year.
两国的贸易协议将在明年到期。

  expiry / expiration *n.* 终止；期满；届期
  the expiry of driving license 驾照的到期日

What is the expiry date on your library book?
你从图书馆借的那本书什么时候到期？

The President can be elected again at / on the expiration of his first four years in office.
总统第一任四年任期届满后可重新当选。

19. negotiation *n.* 谈判，磋商；议付

After our repeated negotiations, we have succeeded in closing the business.
经过我们再三磋商，最终达成交易。

The agreement was reached after a series of difficult negotiations.
该协议是经过一系列艰苦谈判之后达成的。

As the L/C allows us only five days for negotiation of the document, which is far from enough, we'd appreciate it very much if you could extend the negotiation period to 15 days.
信用证只允许我们有五天的时间议付单据，这显然是不够的，因此请将议期延长到 15 天。

  negotiate *v.* 谈判；议付

We're negotiating for a new contract at the moment.
目前我们正在谈一笔新合同。

The strike was caused by the management's refusal to negotiate with the unions.
这次罢工是由于管理层拒绝与工会谈判而引起的。

The exporters must present shipping documents when they negotiate payment with the bank.
出口商向银行议付时，必须呈递装船单据。

  negotiable *adj.* 可商量的；可以付的，可转让的

Everything is negotiable at this stage, I'm ruling nothing out.
一切都还好商量，我并没有把话说死。

A check that is not negotiable cannot be exchanged for cash and must be paid into a bank account.
一张不可议付的支票是不能兑换成现金的，只能支付到某个银行账户上。

The bill of lading is non-negotiable.
该提单是不可转让的。

20. formalities *n.* 礼节，仪式规定的程序
  trivial formality 烦琐的礼节
  go through (check in) formality 办理（飞机等）的乘坐手续
  customs formality 报关手续
  customs formality and requirements 海关手续和规定
  export formality 出口手续
  joint inspection formality 联合检查手续
  joint inspection procedure 联合检查程序
  transit formality 过境手续

21. suit to   相称
22. quarterly   *n.*   季刊   *adj.*   一年四次的，每季的   *adv.*   每季地
    a quarterly magazine   季刊杂志
    a quarterly payment   按季度付款
23. wireless phone   无线电话
    wireless operator   无线电报员
    wireless station   无线电台
    wireless device   无线电设备
24. stress   *v.*   着重强调
    stress + that clause / stess+   *n.*
    The Chinese Government stressed the point that the technology introduced from abroad should be truly advanced and appropriate to China's needs.
    中国政府强调，引进的国外技术应该是真正先进和适合中国需要的。
    stress   *n.*   重点
    It is necessary to lay stress on the packing as well as the quality.
    将重点放在包装上和在质量上是必要的。

Exercises

I. Translate the following terms into English:

1. 付款条件
2. 达成交易
3. 即期信用证
4. 见票 30 天议付的信用证
5. 保兑的、不可撤销的信用
6. 商业发票
7. 货到付款
8. 分期付款
9. 电汇
10. 信汇

II. Translate the following terms into Chinese:

1. in accordance / conformity with
2. expire
3. with reference to
4. fulfillment of contract
5. establishment of L/C
6. stipulate
7. as requested
8. in favor of
9. endorsement
10. bona fide holder

III. Choose the best answer to complete the following sentences:

1. From the enclosed copy of invoice you will see that price of USD 1,000.00 is well _____ the maximum figure you stated.
    A. in   B. within   C. between   D. at
2. We shall be glad if you agree to ship the goods to us as before _____ Cash against Documents basis.
    A. with   B. during   C. in   D. on

3. Payment should be made _____ sight draft
   A. at   B. upon   C. by   D. after
4. Mr. Wang could agree _____ D/P terms.
   A. with   B. to   C. in   D. over
5. We have opened an L/C in your favor _____ the amount of USD10, 000.00.
   A. on   B. in   C. by   D. for
6. An L/C should be opened in our favor _____ by documentary draft at 30 days' sight.
   A. paying   B. available   C. paid   D. /
7. If the amount exceeds that figure, payment _____ L/C will be required.
   A. at   B. by   C. for   D. in
8. We make purchases _____ our own account.
   A. in   B. on   C. for   D. with
9. We advised our bank to _____ L/C No. TF-512 to read transshipment to be allowed.
   A. change   B. change   C. amend   D. alter
10. Our terms of payment _____ been stipulated in the relative Sales Contract.
    A. having   B. has   C. have   D. had

IV. Fill in the following blanks with the words and expressions in the box, change the form when necessary:

| clear | exceed | amount | equivalent | to your request |
| accommodation | light | transactions | requesting | payment |

Dear Sirs,

Thank you for your letter of 3rd, April (1)____ payment against documents for contract No. 22 & 23.

We are pleased to say that we agree(2)_____. We wish, however, to make it (3) that in future (4)_____, direct payment will only be acceptable if the (5) involved for each transaction is less than $2,000 or the (6)_____ in RMB. Should the amount (7) _____ that figure, (8) _____ by letter of credit will be required.

We would like to say that we extend you this (9) _____ only in the (10)_____ of our long business relations. We sincerely hope we can enlarge the business to our mutual benefit.

Yours faithfully,

V. Translate the following sentences into Chinese:

1. In view of the amount of this transaction being very small, we are prepared to accept payment by D/P at sight for the value of the goods shipped.

2. We regret to say that the payment terms stipulated in your order are unacceptable to us.

3. As the value of this order is rather small, we trust you would agree to our making payment by mail transfer after receipt of the documents.

4. Since this is a rather substantial order and the machine is to be manufactured to your own

specifications, we can only accept your order on sight L/C basis.

5. We very much regret that we cannot agree to make payment before shipment.

6. We do not think there is any difficulty for you to establish a confirmed irrevocable L/C in our favor to cover your present order, so that we may expect to receive the money at a definite date.

7. In compliance with your request, we exceptionally accept delivery against D/P at sight, but this should not be regarded as a precedent.

8. We regret to have to decline your request for D/P terms, payment by L/C is our method of financing trade in these traditional goods.

9. We suggest payment by bill of exchange drawn on us at 60 days' sight. Please let us know whether this is agreeable to you.

10. In compliance with your request, we exceptionally accept delivery against D/P at sight, but this should not be regarded as a precedent.

VI. *Translate the following sentences into English*:

1. 为了给贵方在当地市场推销我方产品铺平道路，我方将接受即期付款交单方式付款，以示特别照顾。

2. 我们要求货款以保兑的、不可撤销的、以我方为受益人的即期信用证支付。该信用证需要在合同规定的装运期前一个月开到我方，在中国议付，有效期至装运期后15天，并允许转船和分批装运。

3. 由于开证费用颇高，故我们建议在货物装运后，你们凭装运单据向我们开立即期汇票，通过银行托收。我们保证一收到汇票，马上付款。

4. 对这次交易，我们例外同意用付款交单的方式支付，但对以后的交易，我们要求更有利的付款条件，也就是信用证方式。

5. 鉴于你我间的长期友好关系，对你方这批试购的货物，我们愿意例外地接受30天付款交单的方式付款。希望你们能接受。

6. 我们通常的做法是凭即期付款交单而不用信用证。因此，我们希望你对这笔交易和今后交易也接受付款交单方式。

7. 你方以付款交单方式付款的要求，我方已予以考虑。鉴于这笔交易金额甚微，我们准备以此方式办理装运。

8. 虽然我们对你方订购50令（ream）砂纸（glass paper）表示感谢，但歉难同意以承兑交单方式付款，因为我们一般惯例都只接受以信用证付款的方式，你方自不能例外。

9. 对你方1156号订单，我们可以接受你们所提的用远期汇票支付的建议。货物装出后，我们将向你方开出60天期的汇票。请到期即付。

10. 请注意，我们的付款方式，一般是以保兑的、不可撤销的、以我公司为受益人的、按发票金额见票即付的信用证支付。该信用证应通过我们认可的银行开出。

VII. *Simulated writing*:

Now you are required to write a letter according to the following details:

敬启者：

　　由中国银行山西分行开立的，有关 800 包女式羽绒衣，金额计 30,000 美元的第 20110908 号信用证收到。经详阅，发现该信用证不允许转船和分批装运。

　　由于开往你港的直达轮稀少，我们常常（多一半）必须经由香港转运。至于分批装运，倘若能将我们手头已有的货物立即装运，而不是等整批货齐了再装运，这对双方都会有好处的。为此，我们今日下午已去传真，要求将信用证修改为："允许转船和分批装运。"

　　由于货物包装就绪待装已有相当时日，务请立即以传真修改信用证为盼。

谨上

```
Dear Sirs,




                                                          Yours sincerely,
```

Supplementary Reading

Letters of Credit

　　The letter of credit is the most widely used instrument of international banking. It has had a long and successful history as a means of facilitating international trade, particularly during times of economic and political uncertainty.

　　The letter of credit is the bank instrument that assures the person selling merchandise of payment if he makes the agreed-upon shipment. On the other hand, it also assures the buyer that he is not required to pay until the seller ships the goods. It is thus a catalyst that provides the buyer and the seller with mutual protection in dealing with each other.

　　An international trading transaction begins when a buyer and a seller sign a contract that records all the elements of the transaction.

　　In the contract, the buyer and seller must arrange payment. The buyer will want possession before paying, and the seller will want payment before making delivery. Since each party often has an incomplete knowledge of the other, there is a certain caution to their dealings.

At this point, the letter of credit can be extremely useful. The buyer requests his bank to issue a letter of credit in favor of the seller. Assuming that the credit risk is acceptable to the bank, it issues its letter of credit. The bank has thus substituted its credit for that of the buyer, which might also be good but probably is not as well known. The letter of credit also protects the buyer, for he knows that he will not be called upon for payment by his bank until the evidence shows that the shipment has actually been effected.

The documentary requirements are designated by the buyer in his bank application for the letter of credit. The bank follows these in preparing its letter of credit.

A typical letter of credit may call for the following documents: an invoice, a hill of lading, marine insurance, a packing list, a weight list, an inspection certificate, and a certificate of origin (a consular statement of the country of origin).

Not all of these documents are required in every letter of credit transaction. Sometimes, other documents must be used. For example, food shipments coming into the United States require clearance by the Food and Drug Administration.

The customary letter of credit calls for a "full set on board ocean bills of lading to order shipper, blank endorsed." Each of these phrases will now be examined.

Full Set. Steamship companies issue more than one original bill of lading. This custom arises from the practice of airmailing two identical sets of documents to the issuing bank or importer in two mails, each a day apart, to ensure that one set would get through if something happened to one of the airplanes.

On Board. This written notation on the bills of lading indicates that the goods have actually been put on board the named vessel.

Ocean Bills of Lading. Airlines, trucks, and railroads also issue bills of lading. The designation of "ocean" confirms that the shipment is by sea.

To Order Shipper, Blank Endorsed. This provides protection to the bank that issues the letter of credit during the time between the bank's payment to the exporter and the repayment to the bank by the buyer. The bill of lading can indicate that the goods are to be shipped and delivered to a designated party. However, by requiring that the consignee be the shipper and by requiring the shipper to endorse the bills of lading in blank, the document becomes a negotiable instrument wherein the title to the merchandise goes with possession of the bills of lading. The shipping company agent at the receiving port can deliver the goods only when someone presents an endorsed bill of lading. In the interim, the bank retains possession of the bills of lading. If the buyer goes into bankruptcy, the bank takes possession of the merchandise. In this way, it has a source of repayment for the extension of credit.

The letter of credit specifies the latest date, the expiration date, on which the documents can be presented. The shipment may take place at any time prior to that, but as soon as it does, the shipper must assemble the documents promptly and forward them to the bank. If he delays, the documents can be considered stale, and the bank can refuse to pay him.

Once the seller has made the shipment, he assembles the documents, prepares the draft drawn on the issuing bank, and presents it for payment.

The issuing bank examines the draft and documents upon receipt, to ensure that the documents conform to the letter of credit. If anything is wrong, the discrepancies are subject to acceptance by the buyer.

Once the documents are verified, the bank pays the sight draft presented by the seller and then notifies its customer, the buyer, that the documents have been successfully negotiated and that he must pay the bank in accordance with his application. After the payment has been completed, the bank releases the documents to the buyer, retaining only such copies as are needed for its files. The buyer now has the bill of lading, which he can present to the shipping company to receive his goods.

After-Class Study

(I) *Names of Parties Concerned*

1. opener 开证人
   applicant 开证人（申请开证人）
   principal 开证人（委托开证人）
   accountee 开证人
   accreditor 开证人（委托开证人）
   for account of Messrs 付（某人）账
   at the request of Messrs 应（某人）请求
   on behalf of Messrs 代表某人
   by order of Messrs 奉（某人）之命
   by order of and for account of Messrs 奉（某人）之命并付其账户
   at the request of and for account of Messrs 应（某人）得要求并付其账户
2. beneficiary 受益人
   in favor of 以（某人）为受益人
   in one's favor 以……为受益人
   favor yourselves 以你本人为受益人
3. drawee 付款人（或称受票人，指汇票）
   to drawn on/upon 以（某人）为付款人
   to value on 以（某人）为付款人
   to issued on 以（某人）为付款人
4. rawer 出票人
5. advising bank 通知行
   the notifying bank 通知行
   advised through…bank 通过……银行通知
   advised by airmail/cable through…bank 通过……银行航空信/电通知
6. opening bank 开证行
   issuing bank 开证行
   establishing bank 开证行
7. negotiation bank 议付行
8. paying bank 付款行
9. reimbursing bank 偿付行
10. the confirming bank 保兑行

(II) Kinds of L/C 信用证的形式

1. irrevocable Letter of Credit   不可撤销信用证
2. revocable Letter of Credit   可撤销信用证
3. confirming Letter of Credit   保兑信用证
4. non-confirming Letter of Credit   不可保兑信用证
5. transferable Letter of Credit   可转让信用证
6. non-transferable Letter of Credit   不可转让信用证
7. documentary Letter of Credit   跟单信用证
8. clean Letter of Credit   光票信用证
9. sight Letter of Credit   即期信用证
10. usance Letter of Credit   远期信用证
11. revolving Letter of Credit   循环信用证
12. without recourse Letter of Credit   无追索权信用证
13. with recourse Letter of Credit   有追索权信用证
14. divisible L/C   可分割信用证
15. indivisible L/C   不可分割信用证
16. deferred payment L/C   延付信用证
17. anticipatory L/C   预支信用证
18. revolving L/C   循环信用证
19. back to back L/C   对背信用证
20. reciprocal L/C   对开信用证
21. traveler's L/C   旅行信用证

(III) Amount of the L/C（信用证金额）

1. amount RMB…   金额：人民币
2. up to an aggregate amount of HKD…   累计金额最高为港币……
3. for a sum/sums not exceeding a total of GBP…   总金额不得超过英镑……
4. to the extent of HKD…   总金额为港币……
5. for the amount of USD…   金额为美元……
6. for an amount not exceeding total of JPY…   金额的总数不得超过……日元的限度

(IV) The kinds of drafts （汇票种类）—Draft (Bill of Exchange)

1. available by drafts at sight   凭即期汇票付款
2. draft(s) to be drawn at 30 days sight   开立30天的期票
3. sight drafts   即期汇票
4. time drafts   远期汇票

(V) Drawn clauses（出票条款）（注：即出具汇票的法律依据）

1. all drafts drawn under this credit must contain the clause "Drafts drawn Under Bank of… credit No.…dated…"
   本证项下开具的汇票须注明"本汇票系凭……银行……年……月……日第……号信用证下开具"的条款

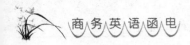

2. drafts are to be drawn in duplicate to our order bearing the clause "Drawn under Malayan Banking Corp. Irrevocable Letter of Credit No ….dated July 12, 2010"

汇票一式两份，以我行为抬头，并注明"根据马来西亚银行 2010 年 7 月 12 日第……号不可撤销信用证项下开立"

3. draft(s) drawn under this credit to be marked："Drawn under…Bank L/C No ….Dated (issuing date of credit)"

根据本证开出得汇票须注明"凭……银行……年……月……日（按开证日期）第……号不可撤销信用证项下开立"

4. drafts in duplicate at sight bearing the clauses"Drawn under…L/C No ….dated…"

即期汇票一式两份，注明"根据……银行信用证……号，日期……开具"

5. draft(s) so drawn must be in scribed with the number and date of this L/C

开具的汇票须注上本证的号码和日期

6. draft(s) bearing the clause："Drawn under documentary credit No ….(shown above) of…Bank"

汇票注明"根据……银行跟单信用证……号（如上所示）项下开立"

(VI) The Stipulations for the Shipping Documents（装运单据的规定）

1. available against surrender of the following documents bearing our credit number and the full name and address of the opener   凭交出下列注名本证号码和开证人的全称及地址的单据付款

2. drafts to be accompanied by the documents marked(×)below   汇票须随附下列注有(×)的单据

3. accompanied against to documents hereinafter   随附下列单据

4. accompanied by following documents   随附下列单据

5. documents required   单据要求

6. accompanied by the following documents marked(×)in duplicate   随附下列注有(×)的单据一式两份

7. drafts are to be accompanied by…   汇票要随附（指单据）……

(VII) Kinds of Payment （支付的种类）

terms of payment = payment terms	支付条款
payment in cash = cash payment	现金付款
payment by / in installment	分期付款
payment in lump sum	一次付清，整笔支付
payment in part	部分支付
payment in full	全部付清
payment on credit	记账付款
payment on arrival	货到付款
payment on demand	即期付款
payment on delivery	交货付款
deterred payment	延期付款
payment by remittance	汇付

in payment for / of sth.　　　　　　　偿付某物，用于支付某物

(VIII) Kinds of Sales（销售的种类）

have a great / ready sale	畅销
make a sale	达成交易
sale as per origin	凭产地买卖
sale as seen	看货买卖
sale by bulk	成批出售
sale by catalogue	凭目录买卖
sale by description	凭说明买卖
sale by sample	凭样品买卖
sale by trade mark and brand	凭商标或标牌出售
sale on arrival	货到销售
sale on commission	委托销售
sale on consignment	寄售
sale on monthly installment	按月（分期）付款销售
sale on trial	试销
sales department	销售部
sales contract	销售合同

(IX) *The Detailed Procedures of D/P at sight, D/A and L/C*

1. D/P at sight

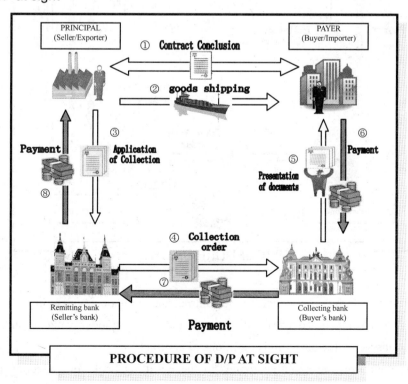

(1) The buyer and the seller conclude the contract and agree on payment in D/P at sight.

(2) After conclusion of contract, the exporter makes the goods available and effects the shipment of goods as per the terms and conditions of contract.

(3) After shipment, the exporter applies to the remitting bank for collecting the invoice value by sending an application, a sight draft and shipping documents to the remitting bank.

(4) The remitting bank draws up a collection order and transfers it as well as the sight draft and shipping documents to the collecting bank.

(5) The collecting bank presents the draft and shipping documents to the importer according to the instructions in the collection order.

(6) The importer pays the purchase price at sight to the collecting bank.

(7) The collecting bank transfers the funds (proceeds) to the remitting bank.

(8) The remitting bank transfers the funds to the principal (seller/exporter).

2. D/A

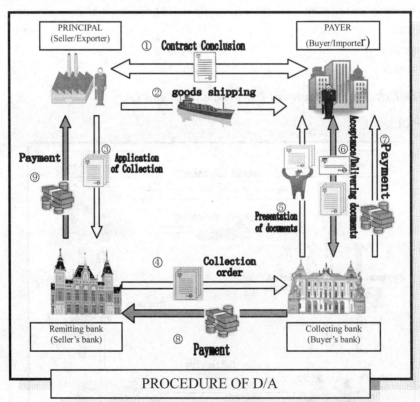

PROCEDURE OF D/A

(1) The buyer and the seller conclude the contract and agree on payment in D/A.

(2) After conclusion of contract, the exporter makes the goods available and effects the shipment of goods as per the terms and conditions of contract.

(3) After shipment, the exporter applies to the remitting bank for collecting the invoice value by sending an application, a time draft and shipping documents to the collecting bank.

(4) The remitting bank draws up a collection order and transfers it as well as the time draft and shipping documents to the collecting bank.

(5) The collecting bank presents the draft and documents to the importer.

(6) The importer accepts the draft. So the bank will deliver the shipping documents to the importer while taking back the accepted draft.

(7) The importer pays the purchase price at the maturity of accepted draft.

(8) The collecting bank transfers funds to the remitting bank.

(9) The remitting bank transfers funds to the principal.

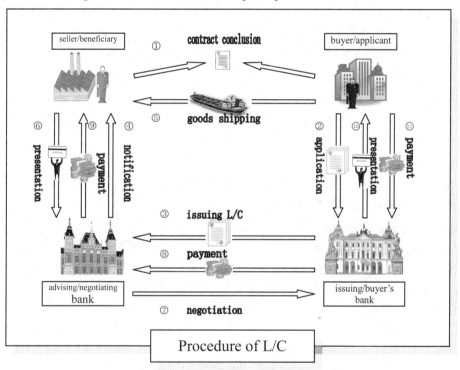

Procedure of L/C

3. L/C

(1) The buyer and the seller agree to conclude the contract providing payment by a documentary credit, and the contract is the basis for the buyer to apply for a credit.

(2) The importer/buyer/applicant applies to his bank (issuing bank) for issuing a L/C in favor of the exporter (seller/ beneficiary), and provides a certain amount of posit and formality fees.

(3) The issuing bank sends a L/C opened to the advising bank.

(4) The advising bank authenticates L/C and transfers it to the exporter.

(5) After examining the L/C, the exporter effects the shipment according to the stipulations of L/C. After shipment, the exporter makes out a draft and draws up the documents in accordance with the L/C.

(6) The exporter delivers documents as well as shipping documents to the negotiating bank within its validity.

(7) If the documents are in conformity with the L/C, the negotiation or the negotiating bank presents the documents to issuing bank for negotiation.

(8) The negotiating bank will pay to the exporter.

(9) The issuing bank informs the applicant and asks him to make payment so as to get hold of the shipping documents.

(10) The applicant makes payment to get hold of shipping document and takes delivery of the goods against documents at the port of destination.

(X) The Content of L/C

1. the parties involved   信用证的当事人

2. the nature of L/C and number of L/C   信用证的性质和号码

3. the amount of the L/C   信用证的金额

4. the draft terms   汇票条款

5. the documents (bill of lading; insurance bills; commercial invoices; inspection certificate; origin certificate) terms   单据条款

6. the shipping terms   装运条款

7. the expiry terms   信用证的有效期和到期的时间

8. the presentation date   交单的日期

9. the confirming terms   保证条款

10. special terms   特殊条款

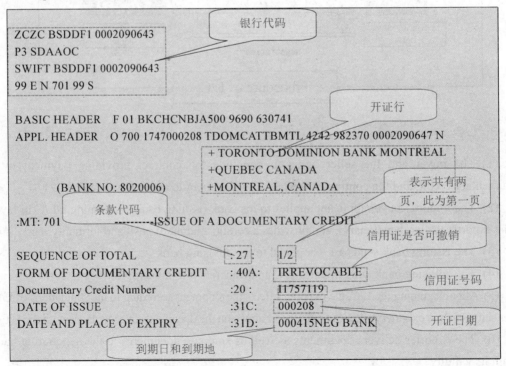

Unit 7 Terms of Payment

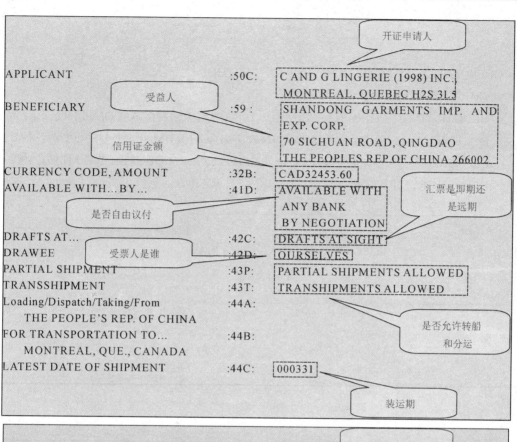

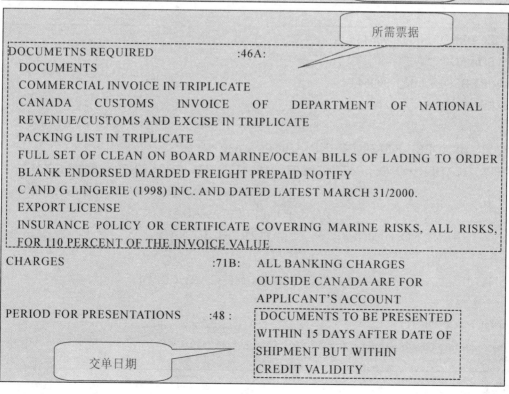

CONFIRMATION INSTRUCTION :49 : WITHOUT   是否需要保兑

INSTRUCTION TO BANK :78 :

NEGOTIATING BANK TO AIRMAIL (1) DRAFT(S) AND COMPLETE SET OF DOCUMENTS (2) REMAINING DOCUMENTS BY NEXT MAIL TO US

ON RECEIPT OF DOCUMENTS IN ORDER AT OUR COUNTER WE SHALL PAY A DEPOSITORY OF NEGOTIATING BANK'S CHOOSING

TRAILER

    MAC: 4678C676   CHK:982922E807BA

NNNN

表示第一页结束

ZCZC BSDDF1 0002090643

P3 SDAAOC

SWIFT BSDDF1 0002090643

99 E N 701 99 S

BASIC HEADER   F 01 BKCHCNBJA500 9690 630741

APPL. HEADER   O 700 1747000208 TDOMCATTBMTL 4242 982370 0002090647 N

                        + TORONTO DOMINION BANK MONTREAL

                        +QUEBEC CANADA

(BANK NO: 8020006)   +MONTREAL, CANADA

:MT: 701   ----------ISSUE OF A DOCUMENTARY CREDIT   ----------

SEQUENCE OF TOTAL   :27 : 2/2   表示共有两页，此为第二页

Documentary Credit Number   :20 :   I175119

DESCRPT OF GOODS/SERVICES   :45B:
    16/84 PCT COTTON/POLYESTER WOVEN SATIN FLEECE, LADIES SLEEPWEAR, S/C 20SGC5102
    1020 PCS PYJAMA STYLE 1539 AT CAD8.90 PER PC.
    240 PCS NIGHT SHIRT STYLE 1540 AT CAD5.40 PER PC.
    600 PCS HOUSECOAT STYLE 1541 AT CAD8.90 PER PC.
    964 PCS PYJAMA STYLE 1542 AT CAD8.90 PER PC.
    420 PCS NIGHT SHIRT STYLE 1543 AT CAD6.40 PER PC.
    240 PCS NIGHT SHIRT STYLE 1544 AT CAD5.00 PER PC.
    480 PCS HOUSECOAT STYLE 1545 AT CAD8.90 PER PC.
    C.I.F. MONTREAL

ADDITIONAL CONDITIONS   :47B:
    SPECIAL CONDITIONS
    CONTAINER SHIPMENT ALLOWED
    INSURANCE TO BE COVERED BY SHIPPER
    SHIPMENT ONLY ON ANY ONE OF THE FOLLOWING FOUR SHIPPING LINES IS ACCEPTABLE   1. MITSUI O.S.K.,   2. SEALAND,   3. AMERICAN PRESIDENT   4. KASE SHIPPING ENTERPRISE LTD.

BENEFICIARY'S CERTIFICATE ADDRESED TO ISSUING BK CONFIRMING THEIR ACCEPTANCE AND/OR NON-ACCEPTANCE OF ALL AMENDMENTS MADE UNDER THIS LC QUOTING THE RELEVANT AMENDMENT NO.,
IF THIS LC IS NOT AMENDED SUCH STATEMENT IS NOT REQUIRED.
ALL DOCUMENTS CALLED FOR UNDER THIS CERDIT, EXCEPT THOSE WHICH THE CREDIT SPECIFICALLY STATES CAN BE 'COPIES', MUST BE CLEARLY MARKED ON THEIR FACE AS 'ORIGINAL'.
A DISCREPANCY HANDLING FEE OF
CAD45.00
IS PAYABLE BY THE BENEFICIARY ON EACH DRAWING PRESENTED WHICH DOES NOT STRICTLY COMPLY WITH THE TERMS AND CONDITIONS OF THIS VREDIT AND HAS TO BE REFERRED TO THE APPLICANT.

TRAILER
        MAC:233E646C   CHK: 50198DC6F8D2

NNNN

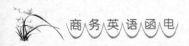

Chinese Version of Specimen Letters

<例信 1> 要求开立信用证

敬启者：

我方愿意确认贵公司订单，订购本公司 600 台数码相机，总额为 18,000 美元。按照贵公司要求，我方准备在 10 月底前装运，请尽快开出 9 月 15 日前有效的不可撤销信用证。一经接到贵公司信用证，我们将立即装运此货。

谨上

<例信 2> 通知信用证

敬启者：

有关第 369 号订购确认书项下货款，兹已委托伦敦中国银行于 2011 年 6 月 12 日开出以贵公司为受益人的不可撤销的第 567 号跟单信用证，总金额 8,768 美元。请即按照确认书内规定的交货期准时发运为盼。

谨上

<例信 3> 催开信用证

敬启者：

事由：我方第 C215 售货确认书

关于我方第 R3369 号售货确认书项下两千打衬衫，拟提请注意交货期日益迫近，但至今我们仍未收到有关信用证。请尽速开立信用证，以便我方顺利执行这项订单。

为了避免随后的修改，务请注意（做到）信用证内的规定事项与合同条款完全一致。

盼佳音。

谨上

<例信 4> 要求对方注意信用证期限

敬启者：

我方很高兴与你方达成交易，签订第 123 号销售确认书。现特函请你方注意确认书中关于你方信用证到达我处限期的规定。希望你们遵守双方所同意的条款，于 2011 年 6 月 20 日前将信用证开到。

一经收到来证，我们当即安排装船。同时，希望你方继续新的订单。对此我方定当给予认真考虑。

谨上

<例信 5> 修改信用证（1）

敬启者：

信用证修改事项说明如下：

我方现收到的信用证，其付款规定为见票 90 天付款。但是我方所需要的是见票即付信用证。此项规定已经贵方同意并在贵方订购书上明确记载。因此，请贵方按订购书内的说明对信用证加以修改。货物将于本月 10 日交运。

敬请贵方依照我方要求立即修改。

谨上

<例信 6> 修改信用证（2）

敬启者：

贵公司经由德意志银行开出的第 3368 号信用证已收悉。

本公司核查后发现该信用证列明不容许转运或部分装运有关货品。

直航你方港口的班次很少，往往需经鹿特丹转运。若要等候全部货品一次装运，而不先行装运库存货会拖延速度。故此，转运和部分装运是必要的。

有鉴于此，今天电传贵公司，请求将信用证有关条目修改为"准许转运和部分装运"。

我们相信该项修改当能获贵公司同意，并请电复你方的最终决定。

谨上

<例信 7> 信用证展证（1）

敬启者：

事由：你方第 1211 号信用证
10 公吨粗红糖

有关你方订货 10 公吨粗红糖的第 1211 号信用证收到，谢谢。由于供方延误，该货不能在本月底前备妥，甚歉。

此货可望在 10 月初备妥待装，现我方正安排由"东风"轮装运，该轮将于 10 月 10 日左右从上海起航。

盼传真延期你方信用证装船期到 10 月 15 日，有效期至 10 月 30 日，以便我方装运上述货物。

谢谢你方的合作。

谨上

<例信 8> 信用证展证（2）

敬启者：

感谢贵方 9 月 16 日的电报，通知我方第 18 号订单的第 517 号信用证已延期至 11 月 5 日。

由于中东战争，此地银行非常谨慎，除非具有保证函，否则就不接受装船文件。在信用证延期有效期间，我方将尽力装运。

但是，根据装运前的情形，修改后的信用证恐怕也会到期，因此烦请贵方向顾客说明我方处境，并设法争取他们同意再度延长信用证。第 18 号订单货物现储存在青岛货棚内，请立即将第 517 号信用证延期至 11 月 15 日，以利我方装运

谨上

<例信 9> 拒绝展证

敬启者:

收到你方 7 月 30 日来函,要求把第 1027 号信用证的装运期和议付期分别延至 9 月 31 日和 9 月 15 日一事收悉。

我方知道第 3369 号确认书证明的条款,即如果所购货物在 8 月份装运,有关信用证最迟在 7 月 15 日到达你方。然而,由于我方须办理申请进口许可证的必要手续,我方不能再早开证。该许可证在 7 月 17 日才领到,并且有效期只到 8 月 31 日。

凡是能与你合作的事,我方都愿意去做,但由于目前进口规章规定许可证不准延期,很遗憾无法满足你方要求的上述信用证展证一事。

请尽最大努力及时把货物装运,谢谢你方的合作。

谨上

<例信 10> 付款交单

敬启者:

你方 10 月 2 日所定货物已于今日由"红龙"号装出,该轮定于 11 月 5 日抵达洛杉矶。

这批货物是由我们精心挑选,均适销北美,希望你方对此满意,并希望你方的首批订货将导致双方业务的进一步开展。

从所附发票,你方将看到,货价 30,000 美元仍在你方指定的最高货价范围之内。我方已通过花旗银行向你方开出上述金额的汇票,并指示该行在你方兑付汇票时交出单证。由于你方订货要得急,没有足够时间按惯例征询意见,无奈只得按我们同新客户的一般做法,把这笔交易作为现金交易,请见谅。

我们盼望你方继续来定单,并愿以你方提供合格的资信证明并经常订货为条件,准备考虑与你方做赊账交易,每季度结算一次。

谨上

<例信 11> 承兑交单

敬启者:

兹欣然通知,你方 10 月 22 日所订购的无绳电话已作好装运安排,该货将由"虹桥"轮在上海装出,预定于 11 月下旬到达巴生港。

我们已按通常的付款条款,向你方开具 60 天期汇票,并将汇票及装运单证交给我方银行。该单证将在你方按惯例承兑汇票时,由渣打银行递交你方。

谨上

<例信 12> 拒绝接受承兑交单付款

敬启者:

你 11 月 15 日来函已到。如我方在前信中指出的,我方已同厂方接洽,今后尽可能准时交货。我方将注意你方利益随时得到保护。

至于付款方式，我方想重申，我方通常以保兑的不可撤销信用证为付款方式，在一般情况下应保持不变，因此，我方很抱歉与国外客户的一切交易中，时下无法接受以承兑交单方式付款。

对于今后的装运，我方将尽全力在规定的时间内履行你方订单。如万一不能做到，我方当以付款交单的方式发运货物，以免因展证而给你方带来不便。

相信贵方会理解我方的合作。

谨上

Unit 8　Packing

Learning Aims

After you finish learning this unit, you are requested to:
(1) understand some basic knowledge about packing, marking and packing list in foreign trade;
(2) master how to choose proper containers[1] for different exported commodities;
(3) acquire how to write good and effective packing letters according to the requirements.

Unit 8 Packing

Background Knowledge

(I) *About Packing*

Nowadays, non-price competition factors are playing vital roles to influence the import and export of commodities in modern international trade. Good packing will not only protect commodities against damage in the process of storage and transportation but also beautify commodities for sales. Hence, package is regarded as one of the 5P key elements[2] (i.e. Product, Promotion, Price, Place and Package) in international marketing theory.

According to the different functions, packing can be divided into two types: the transport packing (outer packing) and sales packing (inner packing). As we all know, the former is for protecting the goods against damage or losing while the latter is for prettifying the goods.

(II) *The Classification of Commodities in Foreign Trade*

In general, all cargoes for import and export mainly fall into the following three categories:

✧ **Bulk Cargo**[3]: It refers to the cargo that is unpacked (un-bundled or un-bound) and is of the same or a similar kind or nature, it is characterized as large quantities, usually dropped or poured with a spout or shovel bucket into bulk carrier. Bulk Cargoes are classified as liquid (such as crude oil) and dry (such as wheat, grains, mineral ore, coal etc.)

✧ **Nuded Cargo**: It refers to the cargo that is unnecessary or difficult for packing. For example, planks, vehicles, bronze, steel plates, rubbers are nude cargoes.

✧ **Packed Cargo**: All the other cargoes except bulk cargo and nude cargo.

Bulk cargoes and nude cargoes don't need packing while packed cargoes need.

(III) *Division of Packing and Its Application*

Transport packing can be divided into unit outer packing and assemblage outer packing[4]. Containers for unit outer packing mainly consist of the following:

✧ **Crates and Baskets.** They are usually featured as metal or wood, open, wrapped with protective materials, used for machinery.

✧ **Drums, Barrels and Casks.** They are usually featured as wood, plastic or iron materials; they are waterproof, airtight and sealed; used for liquids, chemicals, powder etc.

✧ **Cases.** It includes wooden cases, iron cases, cartons, plastic cases etc. They are usually strengthened with metal bands, wire or battens; used for fruit, perishable food, paper, flowers etc.

✧ **Bags and Sacks.** They include paper bags, cloth bags, gunny bags, plastic bags, kraft paper bags etc. They are usually enclosed, wrapped with protective materials; used for grains, vegetables etc.

✧ **Bales and Bundles.** They are usually featured as cloth, wrapped with protective material; used for carrying textiles.

✧ **Bottles.** Like Cylinder, flask, carboy, bomb, jar, demijohn etc., they are all bottle containers, which are usually made of glass or metal, enclosed; used for dangerous chemicals, liquids, medicines or gas etc.

Containers for assemblage outer packing include containers, flexible containers and pallets. Flexible containers are bags made of fiber, featured as moisture-proof, dust-proof and usually used for holding powdery cargoes like cement, flint etc. Pallets are a kind of movable platforms, used for moving, storing, loading and unloading cargoes and packages.

(IV) Marking[5]

Marking means to have some designs, letters, words or numbers stenciled on the transportation packing of cargoes. The primary function of marking is to clearly identify material for a shipment. In foreign trade, marking can be mainly classified into three types:

✧ **Shipping Marks.** Shipping marks identify the shipper (exporter) and the consignee[6] (importer) of a shipment. The names and addresses of the two parties may be shown on the outer packages. Shipping marks also include the indications of weight and volume so that shipment itself can be matched more easily to the bill of lading issued by a forwarding agent[7] or carrier. It is recommended that the exporter indicate the country of origin on each export package, "Made in China", for instance. This will decrease the likelihood that customs will open the packages for inspection which delay clearance and delivery of the shipment. A simple shipping mark is supplied below for illustrating.

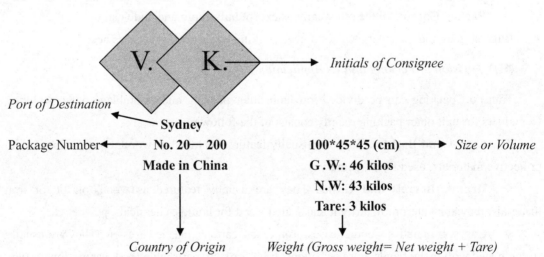

✧ **Indicative Marks.** Indicative marks are stenciled in order to remind the carriers that improper handling might cause damage to the cargoes. The following pictures are some commonly-used indicative marks in international trade.

THIS SIDE UP　　　　FRAGILE　　　　KEEP DRY　　　　USE NO HOOKS

HANDLE WITH CARE　　　KEEP FROZEN　　　PROTECT FROM HEAT　　　PERISHABLE

✧ **Warning Marks**. Warning marks are used to warn the carrier or importers to be very careful for those dangerous cargoes like fertilizer, petroleum, chemicals etc. The following pictures are some commonly used warning marks in international trade.

POISONOUS　　　　　　EXPLOSIVE　　　　　　STOW AWAY
　　　　　　　　　　　　　　　　　　　　　　FROM FOODSTUFF

INFLAMMABLE　　　　　RADIOACTIVE　　　　　CORROSIVE

(V) Packing List

What is packing list[8]? It is a special itemized list of articles usually included in each shipping package, giving the quantity, description and weight of the contents. Packing list is prepared by the shipper and sent to the consignee for accurate tallying[9] of the delivery goods. Here is an example of packing list.

浙江省机械设备进出口责任有限公司
Zhejiang Machinery & Equipment Imp. & Exp. Co., Ltd.

Address: No.111 Jie Fang Rd, Hangzhou City, Zhejiang Province, P.R. China
Tel: (86)-0571-87828909   Fax: (86)-0571-87828900   E-Mail: info@zmec.com

---

装 箱 单
Packing List

Invoice No. <u>BK-1101</u>
S/C No. <u>TS-1502</u>
Date <u>March 7, 2012</u>

Messrs: <u>No.223 Foster Rd, Agimi Imp. & Exp. Co. Ltd., , San Fransico, CA, U.S.A.</u>
Under mentioned goods from <u>Shanghai</u> to <u>New York</u>

Marks & Nos.	Description of Goods	QTY (PC)	Weight (MT) N.W.	Weight (MT) G.W.	Meas. (CBM)
LFZ 20120387 ZMEC C/No:22 Made in China	Hydraulic Pressure Jack (STJ-2000 Series)	20	0.9	1.1	3.6
	Water Pump (CJC-1001B Series)	10	0.6	0.7	8.5
	Air Compressor (BQ-127A Series)	10	6.6	7.9	16.6
	Fork Lift (ST-5230 Series)	20	40	42.5	30.2
	Computerized Gloved Knitting Machine (AN-2009 Series)	20	5	5.9	64.8
	Fuse Machine (TD-800B Series)	5	4.5	5.2	12.5
	Total:	75	57.6	63.3	136.2

Zhejiang Machinery & Equipment
Imp. & Exp. Co., Ltd.

Writing Tips

In letters of packing, negotiations between the importer and the exporter mainly focus on the details of packing such as the choice of packing containers, the quantity or weight of package, the instructions of marking, the presentation of packing list etc. Therefore, packing letter in foreign trade usually consists of the following three parts:

(1) At the beginning part, mention the previous contacts and express thanks for the concern

of your counterpart.

(2) In the message part, seller usually introduces their customary packing mode for his clients; while buyer states his specific requirements of packing for the goods ordered. If necessary, both parties had better give the reasons why they insist on choosing such kind of packaging in their correspondences.

(3) Hopes are expressed in the closing part with a view to receiving a favorable and prompt reply from the addressee.

Sentence Patterns & Examples

【Pattern 1】be packed in…　　用某种容器/方式包装

The Commodities should in no case be packed in cartons.
这批货物无论如何都不能用纸箱包装。
Porcelains are fragile goods, so they must be packed in shock-proof[10] cardboard boxes as per our previous instruction.
瓷器属于易碎品，因此必须按照我们先前的指示装入防震的纸盒内。
Wool is usually packed in bales before export.
羊毛在出口前一般先打包。

【Pattern 2】be packed in … of … each = be packed in … each containing　　用某种容器包装，每件容器装若干

Pliers will be packed in boxes of 20 dozen each.
钳子将用盒子包装，每箱20打。
The goods are to be packed in wooden cases, each containing 10 dozen.
货物用包装，每箱装10打。
Peanuts should be packed in double gunny bags, each containing 50 kilos.
花生应用双层麻袋包装，每袋装50公斤。

【Pattern 3】be packed in… , (and) … to …　　用某种容器包装，若干数量再装入另一更大容器

Chalks are packed in box, 100 boxes to a carton.
粉笔装入纸盒，每100盒再装入一纸箱。
Each T-shirt is packed in a polythene bag and 8 to a box.
每件T恤衫装一个塑料袋，8袋装一盒。
Beer is packed in can, 24 cans to a carton.
啤酒装入易拉罐，24罐装入一纸箱。

【Pattern 4】be lined with…　　内衬……

Each case should be lined with foam plastics in order to protect the goods against press.

每个箱子都应内衬泡沫塑料，以便保护货物不受挤压。

The packing for blouses should be double bags lined with kraft paper.
女式衬衫包装应为双层袋子并内衬牛皮纸。

The cartons for packing eggs should be lined with corrugated paper board.
包装鸡蛋的纸箱必须内衬波纹瓦楞纸。

【Pattern 5】be reinforced / secured by…　　用……加固（包装）

Before export, those cases must be nailed, battened and reinforced by metal strapping[11].
那些箱子必须在出口前钉上钉子，用木板固定，并用铁箍加固。

All the cartons will be secured by overall strapping so as to prevent possible damage in transit.
所有的纸箱将用皮带加固以避免（货物）在转运过程中可能受到的损坏。

【Pattern 6】protect…from / against　　使（货物）免受……

Statistics show that proper packaging and marking can prevent nearly 70% of all cargos from damage or loss.
统计数据表明，正确的包装和刷唛能使70%的货物免受损失。

Our cartons for canned food are not only seaworthy but also strong enough to protect the goods against damage.
我包装罐头食品的纸箱不仅适合海运而且很结实，能防止货物受损。

【Pattern 7】see to it that…　　务必，注意，保证

Please see to it that all the packages are suitable for a long sea voyage.
请保证所有包装均适合长途海运。

We trust you will see to it that the order is executed within the stipulated time, as any delay would cause us much inconvenience.
我们相信你方会保证在规定时间内执行订单，因为任何延误都会给我们带来诸多不便。

【Pattern 8】be susceptible to…　　易于……（受损）

The cartons are so thin that they are susceptible to breakage by heavy pressure.
这些纸箱太薄，因此极易受重压后破损。

Metal tools are susceptible to damage by rust in such humid environment.
金属工具在如此潮湿的环境中很容易生锈。

【Pattern 9】be assorted　　被搭配

In order to facilitate selling, it should be better to pack the towels with equally assorted colors.
为了便于销售，最好将各色的毛巾进行平均搭配包装。

As requested, we pack the seafood in cartons, each containing 20 with yellow croakers, squids, sardine and ribbonfish equally assorted.
根据要求，我们将海鲜产品装入纸箱，每箱20条，并按黄鱼、鱿鱼、沙丁鱼和带鱼均

量搭配。

【Pattern 10】be marked / stenciled / printed with...　　被（印）刷上……的标记

All the goods exported should be marked with "passed-quality" by the local commodity inspection bureau.

所有出口的商品均须刷上当地商检局标示的"品质合格"的标记。

According to our usual practice, every case should be stenciled shipping mark with our initials in a diamond.

根据我们的惯例，所有的箱子上都要刷上菱形的运输标志，内标明我们公司的首写字母。

Indicative marks like "FRAGILE", "USE NO HOOK" and "DO NOT DROP" should be printed clearly on the outer packing.

像"易碎品"、"请勿挂钩"、"轻搬轻放"的指示性标志应当被清楚地印刷在外包装上。

Specimen Letters

<Letter 1> Seller's Packing Descriptions

Dear Sirs,

We thank you for your order No. 253 of October 31, for 1,500 solar water heaters (AN-2011 series) and we are glad to inform you that we are in a position[12] to supply all the products from stock. We are now ready to effect shipment by M.V.[13] Blue Bird, which can sail from Ningbo to Singapore directly by the early of October.

With reference to our Sales Confirmation No. 2472, each solar water heater should be packed in standard export cartons which are lined with foam plastics. On the outer packing, consignee's initials, port of destination and warning marks should be marked by the seller before export. In addition, by calculating, one FCL[14] can hold 500 sets and therefore the whole shipment will comprise 3 containers, each weighing 12.6 tons(G.W).

We would like to remind you that the relevant L/C must reach us not later than September 15 so that we can arrange shipment in good time.

Your prompt reply will be highly appreciated.

Yours sincerely,

<Letter 2> Buyer's Packing Instructions

Dear Sirs,

We wish to refer you to our order No. C-186 for 30,000 pieces LED tubes and 20,000 LED bulbs which should be shipped before May 20. In order to avoid possible future troubles, we would like to make clear our packing requirements beforehand[15] as follows:

As the goods are susceptible to breakage, please see to it that the above mentioned must be packed in shock-proof cardboard boxes of 10 pieces each, 50 boxes to a carton. Each carton should be lined with polythene sheet[16] and reinforced by overall strapping so as to prevent the goods from dampness. In a word, we hope your export packages can withstand rough handling and long distance ocean transportation.

Please mark the cartons with our initials FLD in a diamond, under which the port of destination and package number should be stenciled as well. Besides, warning marks like HANDLE WITH CARE, USE NO HOOK, FRAGILE should be printed on the outer packing.

We are looking forward to your kind cooperation.

Yours faithfully,

<Letter 3> Seller's Suggestions for Replacing Packing

Dear Sirs,

We are in receipt of[17] your repeat order[18] for 8,000 pieces bamboo-fiber T-shirts and have the pleasure to inform you that we will pack the commodities in cartons instead of wooden cases. The reasons why we plan to adopt this packing method are as follows:

(1) Cartons lined with plastic sheet can protect goods against moisture better than wooden case;

(2) T-shirts are not fragile goods and cartons are comparatively light in weight and easy to handle, and moreover it will reduce the freight greatly;

(3) It can prevent skillful pilferage[19] effectively because cartons breakage is easily detected;

(4) Carton packing is more suitable for long-distance ocean transportation.

We assure you that the above way of packing has been widely accepted by other clients and we haven't received any complaints so far. We hope you will accept carton packing and look forward to your confirmation.

Yours faithfully,

<Letter 4> Buyer's Acceptance of New Packing Method (Reply to Letter 3)

Dear Sirs,

Thank you for your letter of December 5, suggesting us to replace the packing container for 8,000 pieces bamboo fiber T-shirts. After discussing this matter with our clients, we find your proposal is reasonable, therefore we write to inform you that we are ready to accept your new packing method mentioned in your previous letter.

If the result of substituting cartons for wooden cases proves to be satisfactory, you may continue using this packing method in our future transaction. Otherwise, we deem[20] it your responsibility to compensate for[21] any damage or loss might sustain on account of[22] your using such cartons in transportation. We think you will understand our statement is for the sake of[23] our mutual benefit as packing is a sensitive subject which often leads to trade disputes.

We look forward to receiving the consignment in good condition and give our clients complete satisfaction.

Sincerely yours,

<Letter 5> Buyer's Requirements for Improving Packing Method

Dear Sirs,

On July 10, we received your consignment of 100 cartons of ball bearing. We regret to inform you that 12 cartons were delivered damaged and the contents had spilled, leading to some losses.

We accept that the damage was not your fault but feel that you must improve your packing methods to avoid future losses, otherwise we have rights to reject taking your delivery. We think the goods under the captioned contract should be packed in international standard ball bearing cardboard boxes, 50 boxes to one seaworthy wooden case. Make sure all the cases must be nailed, battened and secured by overall metal strapping before shipment.

Please let us know whether these methods can be met by you and whether they will lead to an increase in your prices.

We anticipate your early reply.

Yours sincerely,

Notes

1. container   *n.*   包装容器的统称（广义）；集装箱（狭义）
   Now, the port has 80 berths and the annual container throughput has reached 2.8 million TEU.
   目前现在该港口已拥有80个泊位，年集装箱吞吐量达280万20尺柜。
   Please keep salt in an airtight container in a dry place.
   请将盐保存在密封的容器内并放置在干燥处。
   常见搭配：
   flexible container   集装袋
   dry container   干货集装箱
   air container   空运集装箱
   tank container   罐状集装箱；液体集装箱
   bulk container   散装货箱
   container ship   货柜船；集装箱运货船
   container terminal   集装箱码头

2. 5P 要素：国际市场营销学术语，即 Product（产品）、Promotion（促销）、Price（价格）、Place（市场）与 Package（包装）。产品包装属于价格因素以外的一种非竞争性策略，在现代国际市场营销活动中的地位和作用越来越令人关注。

3. bulk cargo　　　散装货物（如：煤、矿砂、谷物、水泥、石油等）
   nuded cargo　　裸装货物（如：钢材、铝锭、木材、橡胶等）

4. unit outer packing　　单位外包装
   assemblage outer packing　　集合外包装

5. marking　　n.　　唛头
   外贸中"唛头"的作用是为了便于识别货物，防止错发货。它通常由带有几何图形的收件人（公司）简称、目的港、包装编号、产地等组成。
   shipping mark　　运输标志
   indicative mark　　指示性标志
   warning mark　　警告性标志

6. consignee　　n.　　收货人，收件人
   consignor　　n.　　发货人，发件人
   consignment　　n.　　寄售的货物
   consignment note　　托运单，寄售通知书

7. forwarding agent　　货运代理人（包括空运、陆运、海运）
   shipping agent　　海运代理人

8. packing list　　装箱单
   装箱单是发票的补充单据，一般列明信用证（或合同）中买卖双方约定的有关包装事宜的细节，便于买方在货物到达目的港时供海关检查和核对货物。
   外贸中跟"list"搭配的常见单据有：
   weight list　　重量单
   measurement list　　尺码单
   price list　　价格单
   assortment list　　花色搭配单
   specification list　　规格单

9. tallying　　n.　　明细记录

10. shock-proof　　a.　　防震的
    英语中"-proof"后缀表示"防……"，如：fire-proof（防火的）、water-proof（防水的）、burglar-proof（防盗的）、dust-proof（防尘的）、heat-proof（防热的）等。

11. strap　　n.　　皮带
    metal strapping　　铁箍

12. be in a position to…　　能够……
    By the end of this year, we will be in a position to double the turnover.
    到今年年末，我们能使营业额翻一番。

13. M.V. (Motor Vessel)　　机动轮
    S.S. (Steamer Ship)　　蒸汽轮

14. FCL (Full Container Load)　　整箱（货）
    LCL (Less Than Container Load)　　拼箱（货），散货

15. beforehand　　*adv.*　　预先，事先
    Shipping space should be booked beforehand in busy season.
    在旺季，船位应该提前预订好。
    类似的表达还有 ahead of time, in advance。

16. polythene sheet　　俗名 plastic sheet，聚乙烯（薄膜），塑料纸

17. be in receipt of…　　已收到……
    We are in receipt of your reply letter on May 10.
    贵方 5 月 10 日的回复信函我们已经收到。
    区别：upon / on receipt of…　　一俟收到……
    The total amount must be paid in full upon receipt of the shipping documents.
    全部款项在收到装船单后全额付清。

18. repeat order　　续（购）订单
    外贸中常见的订单类型有：
    first order / initial order　　首次订（购）单
    trial order　　试（购）订单
    substantial order　　大宗订单
    regular order　　定期订单
    provisional order　　临时订单

19. pilferage　　*n.*　　偷窃
    在国际贸易中，买方或卖方经常投保 T.P.N.D. (Theft, Pilferage and Non-Delivery)，即"偷窃提货不着险"险种以避免因此所蒙受的损失。

20. deem　　*v.*　　认为，相信
    We deem it necessary to make clear the packing method in advance.
    我们认为事先明确包装方式是有必要的。

21. on account of…　　由于……
    The shipment was delayed on account of typhoon.
    由于台风这次装运被延迟了。

22. for the sake of…　　为了……
    I stopped smoking for the sake of my health.
    为了自己的健康，我戒烟了。

Exercises

I. *Translate the following terms into English*:

1. 装箱单　　　　　　　　　　　　2. 铁箍
3. 指示性标志　　　　　　　　　　4. 散装货
5. 板条箱　　　　　　　　　　　　6. 收货人

7. 易燃液体   8. 塑料纸
9. 请勿挂钩   10. 毛重

II. Translate the following terms into Chinese:

1. forwarding agent
2. country of origin
3. radioactive
4. equally assorted
5. assemblage outer packing
6. flexible container
7. seaworthy packing
8. neutral packing
9. corrugated cardboard box
10. fragile goods

III. Choose the best answer to complete the following sentences:

1. We usually pack the water pumps in wooden case _____ with soft materials.
   A. supported   B. surrounded   C. padded   D. full
2. We will not be responsible for any damage which results _____ rough handling.
   A. from   B. off   C. in   D. to
3. Please indicate the initials of the consignee on the _____.
   A. inner packing   B. outer packing   C. products   D. vessel
4. Each case should be _____ with a polythene sheet and secured by overall metal strapping.
   A. lining   B. lined   C. line   D. to line
5. We are in a position to supply all the commodities you required _____ stock.
   A. in   B. to   C. against   D. from
6. Seaworthy cartons are not only easy to handle, but also well protected _____ moisture.
   A. against   B. for   C. through   D. by
7. The goods are packed in cartons lined with _____ materials.
   A. water-proved   B. water-protected
   C. water-proof   D. water-tight
8. _____, we are faxing you our latest packing method for the export cargo.
   A. As requesting   B. At request   C. As requested   D. At requested
9. 100 cases arts and crafts you sent us were found to be badly damaged due to _____ packing.
   A. faulty   B. large   C. outer   D. rough
10. The goods under L/C No. 561 left here _____.
    A. in a good condition   B. in prime condition
    C. in the good condition   D. in sound conditions

IV. Fill in the following blanks with the words and expressions in the box, change the form when necessary:

cover	accept	observe	facilitate	put up with
comparative	secure	novel	ensures	customary

Unit 8 Packing

1. The cartons are too thin to _____ heavy pressure.

2. We propose the use cartons with hinged to _____ opening for customs examination.

3. The crates must be _____ by overall metal strapping.

4. The goods should be packed in a manner that _____ safe and sound arrival of them at the destination.

5. Our way of packing has been widely _____ by other clients.

6. Full details regarding packing and marking must be strictly _____.

7. It is our _____ practice to pack this kind of goods into gunny bags.

8. The outer packing of the digital photo frame looks _____.

9. We'd like to remind you that the _____ shipping documents must reach us before August 10th.

10. Cartons are _____ light and compact than wooden cases.

V. Translate the following sentences into Chinese:

1. The dimensions of TEU container are 5.69 meters long, 2.13 meters wide and 2.18 meters high, therefore the volume of one TEU container is about 26.42 cubic meters.

2. Foam plastics are applied to protect the goods against press.

3. We have no objection to the stipulations about the packing and shipping mark.

4. Please send us the packing list in triplicate promptly, indicating the gross weight, net weight, length, height, width of each case and the total number of cases.

5. It is necessary to take precautions since these silk garments are liable to be spoiled by moisture or rain in transit.

VI. Translate the following sentences into English:

1. 包装必须适合海运，并且坚固承受得起粗鲁搬运。

2. 所有纸箱都必须衬防震的波纹瓦楞纸板，外用牛皮纸包裹。

3. 毛笔要用木盒包装，每盒装5支。

4. 请务必在外包装上刷上"易碎"、"小心轻放"、"请勿挂钩"的警示性标志。

5. 我们采用的新包装不但便于搬运而且适合橱窗展销。

VII. Simulated writing:

Now you are required to write a letter to Evergreen Trading Co., Ltd. of Canada, to inform them the following details:

敬启者：

贵公司寄来的编号为TK-223对5,000台GPS导航仪（GPS navigator）产品的首次订单我方已于10月13日收悉。由于库存充足，因而我们能够现货供应。现将此次出口产品的包装细节告知于你：

所有导航仪均装入内衬防震的塑料泡沫纸板盒，每 100 台装入一大纸箱，纸箱用塑料薄膜密封。每个大纸箱毛重 70 千克。此外，我们已在外包装上刷上了运输标志：椭圆形，内有收件人缩写 ETC，图形下方标明了目的港（Vancouver）、包装编号和原产国。同时还刷上了"小心轻放"、"请勿挂钩"的警示性标志。

我们随信附寄以下装运单据：

装箱单一式两份，原产地证明书与商业发票各一式三份。

希望这批货物能完好运达你处。

Dear Sirs,

Yours faithfully,

Supplementary Reading

Strategy for Export Packing

In deciding what method of packing to use, the exporter must take into account, for each shipment, the following factors:

(1) The type of goods;
(2) Can they be easily damage in transit or in storage;
(3) Do they require temperature control or other special protection.

Type of Carrier

What are the various types of carriers to be used before the goods arrive at their foreign destination? Usually, truck and ship are used.

Types of Hazard

For each type of carrier, what hazards are the shipment likely to encounter? For ocean shipping, this would include the type of storage, loading and unloading facilities, route, time of year (summer, winter, monsoon, etc.) port reputation, etc.

Cost Factors

As well as ensuring maximum protection for the goods being shipped, the exporter should minimize transportation costs by using lightweight, least bulky materials etc.

In some importing countries, import duties are based on the gross weight of the item, including the interior and exterior containers and packing material.

An allowance for tariff purpose is given for "tare" (the difference between the gross and net weights) and so both weights should be shown on the commercial invoice.

7. Legal Restrictions

The exporter should ensure that he complies in his choice of packing materials, with the legal restrictions that some countries, such as Australia and New Zealand, have imposed.

8. After-sale Recycle Usage

Some products have their sales appeal enhanced by being packed in cotton sacks, special boxes, etc. that can even be sold as recycled products in their own right.

After-Class Study

(I) *List of Commonly-Used Packing Containers in Foreign Trade*

bag	袋子	bale	包件
barrel	琵琶桶	basket	篓
bomb	钢桶	bottle	瓶
box	盒子	can	罐/听
canvas	帆布	carboy	酸瓶
cardboard box	纸箱	carton	纸板箱，纸盒
case	箱	cask	桶
casket	小箱	chest	大箱
container	集装箱	crate	板条箱
cylinder	钢筒	demijohn	细颈大坛
drum	圆桶	fiber board case	纤维板箱
flexible container	集装袋	foam plastic bag	泡沫塑料袋
glass jar	玻璃瓶装	gunny bag	麻布袋
iron drum	铁桶	jar	瓮
jute bag	麻袋	keg	小桶
kraft paper	牛皮纸	kraft paper bag	牛皮纸袋
metal strap	铁箍	packet	包裹，封套
paper bag	纸袋	plastic bag	塑料袋
plywood case	三合板箱	polythene bag	聚乙烯袋
sack	布袋	skeleton case	漏孔箱
straw bag	草包	tin	听
tub	木桶	veneer case	胶合板箱
wooden box	木箱	wooden case	木箱

wooden cask　　木桶

(II) List of Packing Terms in Foreign Trade

durable packing　　耐用包装
economical packing　　经济型包装
faulty/poor/inferior/inadequate packing　　劣质包装
blister packing　　起泡包装
neutral packing　　中性包装
skin packing　　吸塑包装
hanging packing　　挂式包装
unlabelled packing　　无牌包装
in bulk, in loose packing　　散装
nude packing　　裸装
bulk packing　　整批包装
consumer packing　　零售包装
large packing　　大包装
inner/internal/end packing　　小包装
shrunk packaging　　压缩包装
foam-spray packaging　　喷泡沫包装
gift-wrap　　礼品包装
free packing / packing included　　免费包装
waterproof packing　　防水包装
seaworthy packing　　海运包装
Gross Weight (G.W.)　　毛重
Net Weight (N.W.)　　净重
Tare　　皮重

(III) List of Commonly-Used Export Marks in Foreign Trade

Indicative Marks

Keep Away Heat　　切勿受热
Keep Away From Moisture/Dampness　　切勿受潮
Keep Dry　　保持干燥
Keep Upright　　切勿倒置
Keep Flat; Stow Level　　注意平放
This Side Up　　此端吊起
Open This End　　此端打开
Handle With Care　　小心轻放
Don't Crush　　切勿挤压

Don't Turn Upside Down　　切勿倾斜
Protect From Cold　　防冻
Not To Be Laid Flat　　不可平放
Not To Be Stowed Below Another Cargo　　不可重叠
No Dumping　　切勿抛掷
With Care　　小心谨慎
Porcelain With Care　　当心瓷器

Warning Marks

Explosive　　易爆品　　　　Perishable　　易腐品
Fragile　　易碎品　　　　　Inflammable　　易燃品
Poisonous　　有毒品　　　　Dangerous　　危险品
Radioactive　　放射品　　　Oxidizer　　氧化品

(IV) List of Commonly-Used Measurement Units in Foreign Trade

Gram（g）克　　　　　　　　Kilogram（kg）公斤
Quintal（q）公担　　　　　　Metric Ton（MT）公吨；
Pound（lb）磅　　　　　　　Ounce（oz）盎司
Meter（m）米　　　　　　　Kilometer（km）公里
Centimeter（cm）厘米　　　　Millimeter（mm）毫米
Yard（yd）码　　　　　　　　Foot（ft）英尺
Inch（in）英寸　　　　　　　Square Meter（sqm）平方米
Gallon（gal）加仑　　　　　　Liter（l）升
Milliliter（ml）毫升　　　　　Cubic Meter（CBM）立方米
Kilowatt（kw）千瓦　　　　　Carat（car）克拉
Bushel（bu）蒲式耳　　　　　Horse Power（hp）马力

Chinese Version of Specimen Letters

<例信1> 卖方包装描述

敬启者：

　　感谢贵公司8月31日编号为253的订单，向我方订购1,500台太阳能热水器（AN-2011系列），我们非常高兴的通知贵公司这批货我们能够进行现货供应。目前，我们正准备安排"蓝鸟"号机动轮装运这批货，该轮将于10月上旬从宁波港直达新加坡港。

　　根据双方签订的编号2472的销售确认书，每台太阳能热水器均应装入内衬泡沫塑料的出口纸箱内；货物出口前，卖方应在货物外包装刷上收件人（公司）缩写、目的港名称和警示性标识。此外，经计算，一整集装箱能装此类热水器500台，因此这批货总计需三个集装箱，每个毛重12.6吨。

我方提醒贵公司请最迟于9月15日前将现相关的信用证寄达我方以便我们及时安排装船。

希望贵方早日回复。

谨启

<例信 2> 买方包装指示

敬启者：

我方希望贵公司参阅编号为 C-186 的订单，订单所述 30,000 件 LED 灯管和 20,000 个 LED 灯泡应在 5 月 20 日是前装运。为避免日后可能出现的麻烦，我方想事先明确一下这次的包装要求，具体如下：

由于此类货物易破损，请务必注意上述货物必须先每 10 件装入防震的纸盒，50 盒装入纸箱。每个纸箱须内衬塑料纸并用皮带安全加固以避免货物受潮。总之，我们希望你方的出口包装能够承受粗鲁的搬运与长途远洋运输。

请在纸箱上刷上菱形的几何图形并在里面标明我们公司首字母的缩写 "FLD"，图形下方还要刷上目的港与包装编号。此外，请在外包装上刷上 "小心轻放"、"请勿挂钩"、"易碎" 的警示性标志。

我方期盼贵公司的倾力合作。

谨启

<例信 3> 卖方建议更换包装

敬启者：

贵公司订购 8,000 件竹纤维 T 恤衫的续购订单我方已经收悉，我们非常高兴地告知贵公司我们此次准备使用纸箱来代替先前使用的木箱包装。以下是改用纸箱包装的理由：

（1）内衬塑料布的纸箱比木箱防潮能力更好；

（2）T 恤衫不是易碎商品，且纸箱相对（木箱）重量更轻，搬运方便，还有纸箱包装将大幅减少运输费用；

（3）由于纸箱破损易被查验出来，因此可有效防盗；

（4）纸箱包装更适合长途海运。

我们向贵公司保证上述包装已在我方其他客户交易中广泛使用且至今未受到投诉。我们希望贵方能接受该类包装和相关确认（信函）。

谨启

<例信 4> 买方接受新包装（例信 3 回复函）

敬启者：

感谢贵方 12 月 5 日的来函,建议我方替换 8,000 件竹纤维 T 恤衫的包装容器。经与我方客户协商，我们认为贵方的建议有理，因此致函告知我们愿意接受贵方在上次信函中提及的新包装方式。

倘若使用纸箱替换木箱包装结果满意，你方可继续在我们将来的贸易中使用。

反之，我们认为贵方有义务对使用此类纸箱包装在运输过程中所可能造成的损失承担责任。我们认为贵方能够理解我们的声明是出于双方共同利益考虑的，因为包装是个敏感问题，经常会带来贸易争端。

我们期望货物收到时能完好无损并让我们的客户完全满意。

谨启

<例信 5> 买方要求改进包装方式

敬启者：

7月10日收到贵公司100纸箱装滚珠轴承货物。然而，我们非常遗憾地告知贵公司货物中有12个纸箱于运送途中破烂，令货物散落，造成损失。

本公司谅解到此非贵公司之过失，但希望贵方能改进包装方法，以避免同类事件日后再次发生，否则我方在权拒收货物。我方认为标题合同项下的滚珠轴承商品应装入国际标准的滚珠轴承纸板盒中，每50盒装入一个适合海运的木箱，并务必在装船前将所有木箱用钉子钉牢，加上板条，并用整条的铁箍加固。

烦请确认上述方法是否可行，并告知新方法会否引致价格上涨。

盼望早日赐复。

谨启

Unit 9 Insurance

Learning Aims

After you finish learning this unit, you are requested to:

(1) understand some knowledge about insurance in foreign trade;

(2) know how to negotiate in written form about insurance;

(3) master how to write the letters concerning insurance arrangement and its reply.

Unit 9 Insurance

Background Knowledge

(I) *About Insurance*

In international trade, goods traveling long distances to another country, out of the direct physical control of both the buyer and the seller, may face all kinds of risks or losses and therefore must be insured against loss or damage at each stage of their journey. In this way, whatever mode of transport is being used, neither the exporter nor the importer suffers any loss. Obviously, cargo insurance is a contract whereby the insurer (i.e. insurance company), on the basis of a premium[1] paid, undertakes to indemnify the insured against loss from certain risks or perils to which the cargo insured may be exposed. It is an indispensable adjunct of international trade. Without adequate insurance and protection of the interests of those with goods in transit, international trade can not be guaranteed.

(II) *Application of Insurance*

Import and export cargoes are subject to damage or loss incurred by a variety of risks in the course of transit, loading and unloading, storage, etc. Therefore, before shipment and transportation, people (buyers or sellers) usually insure their goods with a certain insurance company against such risks, so that they can be compensated in time by the insurance company after the damage or loss. The sales and purchase contracts generally have the stipulation as to who (the buyer or the seller) should cover[2] insurance and bear the expenses. If the goods are sold on FOB or CFR terms, the buyer shall arrange insurance and bear the expenses. Provided the goods are sold on CIF terms, the seller is under obligation to take out insurance and bear the expenses.

Usually insurance is arranged by the exporter (under CIF terms etc.) or the importer (under FOB, CFR terms etc.) approaching an insurance company which has a department specializing in cargo insurance. They may start by inquiring and choosing the right coverage[3] and then negotiate insurance premium rates[4]. Sometimes, brokers may be utilized whose assistance can be of enormous benefit they are highly skilled specialists and can obtain sound and reliable coverage together with competitive premium rates. In export trade, who will affect insurance depends on the particular trade term adopted. Under CIF terms, it is the seller who arranges insurance with an insurance company. Under the terms as FOB, CFR, etc., the buyer effects insurance, but he may ask the seller to arrange insurance on behalf of the buyer. An insurance policy is issued when goods are insured, but it is also usual for a certificate of insurance to be issued for documentary purposes. Meanwhile insurance policy is actually a contract, serving as evidence of the agreement between the insurer and the person taking out insurance. It forms part of the shipping documents.

The amount insured must be at least the invoiced value of the goods. Under a CIF contract, it is common practice for the exporter to insure the goods for 10% above the invoice value. In return for payment of a premium paid by the insured, the insurer agrees to pay the insured a sum

when the event insured occurs. In the sales contract, insurance clause should be expressly stipulated, including the insurer, the insured, the criterion for the insurance clause, insured value and so on.

The marine insurance policy forms part of the shipping documents. When goods are sold on CIF basis, the seller is under obligation to present a marine insurance policy or an insurance certificate at the time of negotiation. Moreover, the risks covered under the policy should be strictly in accordance with the terms of the contract and with those of the letter of credit, if the shipment is made under it.

(III) *Categories of Basic Risks*

✧ Free from Particular Average(F.P.A.)

Under a "Free from Particular Average" Policy, the goods are insured against total or constructive total losses due[5] to natural calamities or other fortuitous accidents. The insurer will also be responsible to claim for losses incurred in the course of loading or unloading.

✧ With Particular Average (W.P.A.) or With Average (W.A.)

Under a "With Particular Average" policy, the insurer is responsible to pay the claims for partial losses of the insured goods due to risks caused by natural calamities mentioned under F.P.A. insurance cover.

✧ All Risks (A.R.)

Under an "All Risks" policy, goods are insured against all risks. For example, from natural calamities, fortuitous accidents at sea, general extraneous risks, irrespective of percentage of loss, total or partial. While natural deterioration of perishable goods, delay, loss or damage caused by inherent vice nature of the subject matter are not covered.

An insurance claim, if any, should be submitted to the insurance company or its agent as soon as possible.

(IV) *Insurance Documents*

✧ Insurance Policy

This is the most commonly used document which contains all the details concerning the goods, coverage, premium and the insurance amount.

✧ Insurance Certificate

This is the simplified version of the insurance policy serving the same functions in the trade.

✧ Open Policy[6]

It is recommended dealers who make considerable large quantities of trades. An open policy provides coverage for all goods shipped by the insured while the policy is valid.

Unit 9 Insurance

Writing Tips

In letters of insurance, negotiations between the importer and the exporter mainly focus on the articles of insurance such as the coverage, premium, insurance period and place etc. Therefore, insurance letter in international trade usually consists of the following three parts:

(1) At the beginning part, mention the previous contacts and express thanks for the concern of your trade partner.

(2) In the message part, state which kind of insurance is desired and provide the reader with convincing and specific reasons.

(3) In the end part, the concerned party should express the hope with an aim to receiving a favorable and prompt reply from the addressee.

Sentence Patterns & Examples

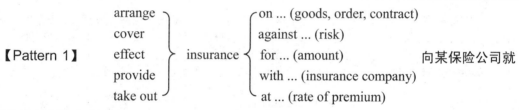

【Pattern 1】 arrange / cover / effect / provide / take out insurance on ... (goods, order, contract) / against ... (risk) / for ... (amount) / with ... (insurance company) / at ... (rate of premium)   向某保险公司就某货物投保某金额某种保险

We have covered insurance on the 1,000 cartons of Chinese black tea for 110% of the invoice value against All Risks with PICC.

我们已将1,000箱中国红茶向中国人民保险公司按发票金额110%投保了一切险。

In compliance with your request, we have taken out the insurance on the table-cloths against All Risk for 110% of the invoice value with the PICC.

根据你方要求，我们已对这批台布按发票金额的110%向中国人民保险公司投保一切险。

【Pattern 2】 charge ... to one's account   将……（费用）记在某人的账上

近似的表达方法还有：

to record ... to one's account

to be for one's account

be borne by somebody

Please charge the samples to our account this time.

这次可将样品费记在我方账上。

The extra premium will be for your account.

额外费用将由你开支（负担）。

The extra premium is to be borne by you.

额外费用将由你方负担。

【Pattern 3】file a claim with the insurance company　　向保险公司提出索赔

类似的表达还有：

file / lodge / raise a claim against / with / on …

apply to … for compensation

Since the goods have been covered by insurance, you should lodge your claim against the insurance company concerned.

由于货物已经投保，你方应向有关保险公司提出索赔。

We have filed a claim against you for the short delivery of 15 cases.

我们已向你方提出索赔短交货 15 箱。

【Pattern 4】as per　　依据……条款

As per the contract, the seller should effect shipment not later than May, 15th.

依据合同，卖方须最迟在 5 月 15 日前装货启运。

We usually insure our goods with the PICC as per their Ocean Marine Cargo Clause, Jan 1, 1981 revision.

我们通常按照中国人民保险公司 1981 年 1 月 1 日的《海洋运输货物保险条款》向他们投保。

【Pattern 5】subject to　　以……为准，以……为有效，受……约束

The offer is subject to your final confirmation.

该报盘以你方的最终确认为准。

All orders will be subject to our written acceptance.

所有订单均以我方书面接受为有效。

【Pattern 6】in excess of　　超出

Commodity Weight in excess of 30 kilos is charged at a higher rate.

重量超过 30 公斤货物的要按更高的费率收取费用。

The insurance policy should be in triplicate, covering All Risks and War Risk including W. A. and breakage in excess of 5% on the whole consignment.

保险单须一式三份，投保一切险和战争险，包括水渍险和整批货物破损的 5% 绝对免赔率。

Specimen Letters

<Letter 1> Insurance Arrangement

Dear Sirs,

　　In reply to your letter of the 1st December enquiring about the insurance on our CIF offer for the consignment[7] of 50 cases of women's down jackets made to you on the 20th November, we wish to give you the following information.

　　For transactions concluded on CIF basis, we usually cover insurance with The

People's Insurance Company of China against All Risks, as per[8] Ocean Marine Cargo Clauses. Should you require the insurance to be covered as per Institute Cargo Clauses[9] we would be glad to comply but if there is any difference in premium between the two it will be charged[10] to your account.

We are also in a position to insure the shipment against any additional risks if you so desire, and the extra premium is to be borne by you. In this case, we shall send you the premium receipt issued by the relative underwriter[11].

Usually, the amount insured is 110% of the total invoice value. However, if a higher percentage is required, we may do accordingly but you will have to bear the extra premium as well.

We hope our above information will provide you with all the information you wish to know and we are now looking forward to receiving your order.

Yours faithfully,

<Letter 2> **Seller's Insurance Advice for Buyer**

Dear Sirs,

We thank you for your Order No.636 for 3,000 sets of cameras, which is placed on CIF basis. In reply, we would like to inform you that most of our clients are placing their orders with us on CIF basis. This will save their time and simplify procedures. May we suggest that you would follow this practice[12]?

For your information, we usually effect insurance[13] with the People's Insurance Company of China for 110% of the invoice value. Our insurance company is a state-operated enterprise enjoying high integrity[14] in settling claims promptly and equitably and has agents in all main ports and regions of the world. Should any damage occur to the goods you might file your claim with the agent at your end, which will take up the matter without delay.

We insure the goods against the usual risks and in the present case we will take out All Risks. Should broader coverage be required, the extra premium is for the buyer's account.

We hope you will agree to our suggestion and look forward to your favorable reply.

Yours faithfully,

<Letter 3> **Buyer's Insurance Request**

Dear Sirs,

We wish to refer you to our Order No. 1027 for 300 sets of PDA[15], from which you will see that this order was placed on a CFR basis.

As we now desire to have the shipment insured at your end[16], we shall be much pleased if you will kindly arrange to insure the same on our behalf against All Risks at invoice value plus 10%, i.e. amount to[17] USD 3,300.

We shall of course refund the premium to you upon receipt of your debit or not, if you like, you may draw on us at sight for the same.

We sincerely hope that our request will meet with your approval.

Yours sincerely,

<Letter 4> Seller's Reply to Buyer for Insurance Covering

Dear Sirs,

This is to acknowledge receipt of your letter dated November 15, 2011, requesting us to effect insurance on the captioned shipment for your account.

We are pleased to confirm having covered the above shipment with the People's Insurance Company of China against All Risks for USD 3,300.00. The policy is being prepared accordingly and will be forwarded[18] to you by the end of the week together with our debit note[19] for the premium.

For your information, this parcel will be shipped on S.S. "Shenzhou", sailing on or about the eleventh of next month.

Yours truly,

<Letter 5> Buyer's Insurance Claim

Dear Sirs,

<u>**Our Order No. 1027**</u>

When the S.S. "shenzhou" arrived at Singapore on 16 December, it was noticed that one side of case No.7 containing the PDA was split. We therefore had the case opened and the contents examined by a local insurance surveyor[20] in the presence of the shipping company's agents. The case was invoiced as containing 30 PDA, 12 of which were badly damaged.

We enclose the surveyor's report and the shipping agent's statement. As you hold the insurance policy we should be grateful if you would take the matter up for us with the insurers. 12 replacements[21] PDA will be required. Please arrange to supply these and charge to our account.

We hope no difficulty will arise in connection with the insurance claim and thank you in advance for your trouble on our behalf.

Yours faithfully,

Notes

1. premium   n.   保险费
   extra premium = additional premium   额外保费
2. cover   n.   =insurance cover   保险
   We have arranged the necessary insurance cover.
   我们已安排了必要的保险。

Does your policy provide adequate cover against breakage?
你们的保单提供足够的破碎险吗？

    cover   vt.   保险，投保

We wish to cover the goods against All Risks.
我们想投保一切险。

You're requested to cover War Risk in addition to All Risks.
除一切险外，请加保战争险。

Insurance is to be covered by the buyers.
由买方办理保险。

This insurance policy has covered us against All Risks and War Risk.
这份保单给我们保了一切险和战争险。

We usually cover 110% of the invoice value.
我们通常投保发票金额的110%。

    insure   v.   保险

We normally insure this item against All Risks and TPND.
这种货我们通常投保一切险和偷窃、提货不着险。

This insurance policy insures us against All Risks.
本保险单为我们投保了一切险。

We usually insure for 10% above the invoice value.
我们通常按发票金额的110%投保。

    underwrite   vt.   承保，给……保险，签单

Insurers here will not underwrite this risk.
此间的保险商不承保这种险。

3. coverage   n.   保险；承保险别；保险范围（包括险别、保值、保险起讫地等）

What types of coverage do you usually underwrite?
你们公司通常承保什么险？

If the business is concluded on CIF terms, what coverage will you take out?
如果以 CIF 价成交，你们将投保什么险？

4. rate   n.   =insurance premium rate   （保险）费率

rate 还有"价格"的意思。

We agreed to a rate with the vendor for the item.
我们与小商贩商定了一个价格，购买这个商品。

What's the going rate for this type of machine tool?
这种机床的现价是多少？

5. due   adj.

（1）适当的，按时的

After due consideration, we have decided to allow you a 2% discount on this article.
经过适当考虑，我们决定对这种商品给你2%的折扣。

We trust the shipment will reach you in due course.
我们相信这批货将按时到达你处。

（2）到期

The time of shipment falls due next month.
装船期于下月到期。

（3）预定的，应到的

The steamer is due next Monday.
该船应于下星期一到达。

Fresh supplies are due to arrive early next month.
新货应于下月初到达。

（4）所欠的

The remittance is in payment of all commissions due to you up to date.
这笔汇款支付迄今为止欠你方的各项佣金。

（5）overdue / past due   逾期

The shipment of 10 sets of machines is rapidly becoming overdue (past due).
10 台机器的装船期很快就要过了。

6. open policy   预约保（险）单，船名未确定保单（即流动保单）

7. consignment   n.   = shipment   （一批）货物

The most recent consignment of cloth was lost in transit.
最近一批布料在运输途中丢失。

A new consignment of goods has just arrived.
一批新货刚到。

consignment   n.   （一种贸易方式）寄售；寄售的货物

consignment goods   寄售商品

consignment business   寄售业务

on consignment   （以）寄售（方式）

Generally, we do not sell goods on consignment terms.
通常，我们不以寄售方式出售货物。

consign   v.   运送；寄售

The goods under Contract No. 12 will be consigned to you per S.S. "Red Star".
12 号合同项下的货物将由红星轮运抵你方。

We do not agree to consign the goods.
我们不同意寄售此货。

8. as per   按照，根据

近似的表达方法有：according to

You are requested to pack the goods as per details on the attached list.
请按附单上的具体要求将货物包装。

9. I.C.C.   协会货物条款

As to the coverage of Marine Insurance, the Institute of London Underwriters（英国伦敦保险业者协会）has a set of universally accepted stipulations—the Institute Cargo Clauses (ICC)—which are adopted by most countries in the world in their marine insurance business. There are six coverages in the latest revised ICC:

(1) ICC(A)　　　协会货物条款（A）
(2) ICC(B)　　　协会货物条款（B）
(3) ICC(C)　　　协会货物条款（C）
(4) Institute War Clause—Cargo　　　协会战争险条款（货物）
(5) Institute Strike Clause—Cargo　　　协会罢工险条款（货物）
(6) Malicious Damage Clauses　　　恶意损害险条款

ICC (A), ICC (B), and ICC(C) are three principal perils. The other three are additional risks.

10. charge　　*v.*　　收取费用；记账

    You may charge us the expense incurred.
    所产生的费用可向我们索取。
    We charge RMB5,000 for storage.
    我们收存储费 5,000 元。
    Shall we charge the flowers to your account?
    我们可以把这些花记到你的账上吗？

    charge　　*n.*　　费用

    Is there a charge for children or do they go free?
    对孩子是收费的还是免费的？
    There's an admission charge of £5.
    要收 5 英镑的门票费。
    They fixed my watch free of charge.
    他们免费为我修了手表

11. underwriters　　保险商（指专保水险的保险商）；保险承运人
12. practice　　*n.*　　惯例 / 习惯做法

    usual practice　　习惯做法
    international practice　　国际惯例
    follow the practice　　遵循惯例

13. to cover / insure　　投保，办理保险

    国际贸易中与办理保险常见的介词搭配如下：
    (1) cover / insure on　　+ 保险的标的物，如：
    cover on 1,000 sets electric fans　　为 1,000 台电风扇投保
    (2) cover / insure for　　+ 保险金额，如：
    insure for 110% of the invoice value　　按发票金额的 110%投保
    (3) cover / insure against + 保险险别，如：
    cover against All Risks and War Risk　　投保一切险和战争险
    (4) cover / insure at + 保险费，如：
    cover / insure at a premium of 5%　　按 5%的保险费投保
    (5) cover / insure with + 保险公司，如：
    insure with PICC　　在中国人民保险公司投保

    We have insured on your order with PICC for 110% of the invoice value against All Risks and War Risk.

我们已在中国人民保险公司对你们的订货按发票金额的 110%投保了一切险和战争险。

14. integrity   n.   信誉，资信

    It is our trade policy to abide by contract and keep commercial integrity.
    我们的交易原则是"重和同，守信用"。
    No one doubted that the president was a man of the highest integrity.
    没有人怀疑总统是一个有至高诚信的人。

15. PDA(Personal Digital Assistant)掌上电脑

16. at this end   在此地，在我地

    There is no problem for us to obtain an import license at this end.
    我们在此地获得进口许可证毫无问题。
    at our end   在我处
    at your end   在你处
    We exceptionally accept your proposed payment terms to encourage sales of our products at your end.
    我们破例接受你们提出的支付条款以促进你方在你地销售我方产品。

17. amount to   合计，共计；等于

    Their investment amounts to USD 10 million.
    他们的投资总额达一千万美元。
    Their annual spending on R&D amounted to £7 million in that year.
    他们那年的研发支出高达 700 万英镑。
    Your reply amounts to a refusal of our request.
    你方答复等于拒绝了我们的请求。
    His behavior amounted to serious professional misconduct.
    他的行为严重地破坏了职业道德。

18. forward   v.   寄送，运送

    Two sample books have been forwarded by air.
    已空邮两本样品本。
    The 50 tons of iron nails will be forwarded in a few days.
    50 吨铁钉日内运出。
    forwarder, forwarding agent   货运代理

19. debit note   借方通知

20. surveyor   n.   检查员，鉴定人
    survey   v.   调查，检查；观察，鉴定
    Please survey the business possibilities and advise your findings.
    survey   n.   调查，检查；观察，鉴定
    survey report   调查报告，检查报告

21. replacement   归还，复位，交换，代替者
    the replacement of conventional weapons by nuclear weapons   用核武器取代常规武器

Unit 9 Insurance

Exercises

I. Translate the following terms into English:

1. 发票金额
2. 海洋运输货物保险条款
3. （伦敦保险协会）协会货物条款
4. 平安险
5. 水渍险
6. 综合险
7. 投保
8. 险别
9. 保险费
10. 保险人

II. Translate the following terms into Chinese:

1. insurance amount
2. insurance policy
3. insurance certificate
4. debit note
5. total loss
6. insurance clause
7. Marine Losses
8. partial loss
9. insurance coverage
10. insurance endorsement

III. Choose the best answer to complete the following sentences:

1. Since most of the voyage is in tropical weather and the goods are liable to go moldy, we think it advisable to have the shipment _____ the risk of mould.
   A. covered insurance   B. taken out insured
   C. covered against   D. insured for

2. Buyer's request for _____ to be covered up to inland city can be accepted on condition that such extra premium is for buyer's account.
   A. loss   B. shipment   C. insurance   D. risks

3. Since the insurance policy taken out by you does not include such a risk, you naturally have no right to claim _____ the insurance company _____ loss caused by it.
   A. on, to   B. to, against   C. with, against   D. on, for

4. Since we have entered _____ a long-term contract with the PICC, _____ which all our imports and exports are to be insured with them, we have to request you to send us another quotation on CFR terms.
   A. /, under   B. into, under   C. into, with   D. into, /

5. We know that according to your usual practice, you insure the goods only _____ 10% above invoice value, therefore the extra premium will be for our account.
   A. for   B. in   C. over   D. above

6. Will you please arrange to _____ all risks insurance on the following consignment of Electric Pumps from our warehouse at the above address to Boston.
   A. take out   B. take in   C. take away   D. take into

7. The package is stenciled ABC London and _____ FPA for 10% over the invoice amount.
   A. insure   B. cover   C. insured   D. coverage

8. We thank you for your instructions to arrange the shipment of special paper. We take it that you wish us to insure the goods against the usual risks, for the _____ of the goods plus freight.

    A. costs   B. value   C. cost   D. values

9. The premium varies _____ the extent of insurance. Should additional risks be covered, the extra premium is for buyers' account.

    A. to   B. as   C. at   D. with

10. We have to invite your attention to your L/C No.789 _____ shipment of 100 tons of Peanuts.

    A. cover   B. covering   C. coverage   D. covered

IV. Fill in the following blanks with the words and expressions in the box, change the form when necessary:

| insurance | additional | stated | lower | covering |
| forward | franchise | insured | cover | refer |

Dear Sirs,

    We have received your letter dated April 22 __(1)__ Chinaware.

    We would like to __(2)__ you to the __(3)__ clause in your letter. We usually do not __(4)__ Breakage for this item.

    Breakage is an __(5)__ risk, and for the goods as porcelain, glassware, wall tiles, etc., even if they have been __(6)__, the cover is __(7)__ to a 5% __(8)__. That means if the breakage is inspected to be __(9)__ than 5%, the losses will not be compensated.

    We are looking __(10)__ to your reply.

                                                Yours faithfully,

V. Translate the following sentences into Chinese:

1. We have insured all future shipments of hand tools made by you from your warehouse in Tianjin to our warehouse in Hamburg under an open policy for the total amount of $50,000. If the value of any shipment exceeds this number, we shall make adjustment accordingly.

2. Our clients would like you to quote CIF New York price because they think it simpler to have the insurance arranged by you. They wish to know what risks will be covered, for what amount and with which underwriters the insurance will be effected.

3. We usually insure the goods against All Risks for 110% of the full invoice value. Should you have specific requirements for the insured amount or insurance coverage, please let us know and we will do everything within our power to meet your requirements. However, the additional premium involved will be for your account.

4. Please see to it that the above-mentioned shipment should be covered for 120% of invoice value against All Risks. We know that according to your usual practice, you insure the

goods only for 10% above invoice value; therefore the extra premium will be for our account.

5. As insurance brokers are generally more familiar with the technicalities of the business of insurance than the average businessmen, the latter usually use the former's service in securing their insurance policy.

6. If you prefer to have CFR price instead of CIF price as quoted by us, you may deduct 0.3% from the quoted price; then the resultant figure will be the CFR price requested by you.

7. Insurance of the goods shall be effected by us for 110% of their CIF value, and any extra premium for additional insurance, if required, shall be borne by the buyers.

8. If any loss or damage occurs to the goods, you may file a claim supported by a survey report, an insurance policy, a statement of claim and other necessary documents with our insurance company's agent at your end within 60 days after arrival of the shipment.

9. Would you please insure our ordered goods for 30% above the invoice value in order to cover some possible costs that may happen in case of accident?

10. The Peoples Insurance Company of China has surveyors and agents in practically all main ports all over the world. In case there is any loss or damage to the goods, the insurance claim can be collected at your end.

VI. *Translate the following sentences into English*:

1. 请注意（做到）上述货物必须在 7 月 15 日装出。保险须按发票价格的 130%投保综合险。我们知道按照你方一般惯例你们只按发票价格加 10%投保，因此额外保费由我方负担。

2. 请你方立即告诉我们对你方该批货物要投保的详细险别。在我们没有收到客户明确通知的情况下，我们一般投保水渍险和战争险。

3. 由于损坏的原因属于保险单的保险范围之内，你们应该向有关的保险公司要求赔偿。

4. 按贵方电文指示，我方今日按惯例向被认可的保险业者安排投保。

5. 我们已将你方第 55 号订单项下的货物按发票价另加 15%投保至目的港。

6. 有关被损坏货物的索赔诉讼通常涉及三个方面：即被保险人、承运人和保险人。

7. 第 66 号合同项下的货物已备好待运，请贵方把想给货物投保的险别详细情况立即告诉我们。

8. 由保险公司签发的保险单应按发票总金额另加 10%投保水渍险。

VII. Simulated writing:

Now you are required to write a letter to Mr. Jones of J. B. Samson & Company, 2816 St. Susan Street, Los Angeles, CA 030012, U.S.A., to inform them the following details:

敬启者：

感谢收到你方 8 月 29 日电邮，要求我方记你方账目投保以 CFR 销售的标题下的货物。

我方很高兴通知你方我们已经将货物向中国人民保险公司上海分公司投保了

一切险，金额为 650,000 美元，相关保单与借记通知单已随函寄去。

你方货物预计由神风号轮于 10 月 20 日左右到达纽约，我们将电传通知确切的装运时间。

敬上

August 30, 2011

Mr. Jones
J. B. Samson & Company
2816 St. Susan Street
Los Angeles, CA 030012
U.S.A.

Dear Mr. Jones,

Yours sincerely,

Enclosures: (1) Insurance Policy
　　　　　　(2) Debit Note

Supplementary Reading

Marine Loss

In cargo insurance practice, loss is generally known as average, which actually has nothing to do with its normal meaning. It refers to any loss or damage due to natural calamities and fortuitous accidents and the related costs incurred in the process of transit. Marine insurance defines its coverage in terms of the nature of the loss or damage, the extent of the loss or damage and the conditions under which it occur. Loss hence can be classified into two types according to the level of loss. One is total loss and the other is partial loss.

Total Loss

Total loss refers to the loss of the entire value of the subject matter to the insured, normally involving the maximum amount for which a policy is liable. Most insurance policies provide for the payment of total loss up to the insurance amount. According to the situation of losses, total loss can be actual or constructive.

Actual total loss, as its name indicates, means that the cargo has been totally lost or, has been damaged to the extent that it has lost its original usage. For example, that the peanuts under one contract all went moldy and cannot be used any more is a kind of actual total loss even if the peanuts arrived at the final destination.

Constructive total loss is different from actual total loss in that the cargo is not totally lost, but the actual total loss shall be unavoidable or the restoration fees together with other miscellaneous expenses will exceed the anticipated amount of profit when the cargo is delivered to the destination. In other words, when a ship or a cargo is so badly damaged that the cost of repair or the effort of rescue would be greater than the market value of the ship or cargo, they are treated as totally lost.

Under the circumstance of a constructive total loss, a concept known as abandonment shall be clarified here. If a claim is made for total indemnity of the cargo lost or damaged under constructive total loss or actual total loss, the claimant must declare the abandonment of all the fights concerning the cargo. This is "notice of abandonment." If the abandonment is found to be valid, after indemnity has been made, the insurer is entitled to take over the interest of the insurant in whatever may remain of the insured subject matter and all proprietary rights thereto.

Partial Loss

Partial loss means a partial damage to or the total loss of part of the insured cargo. Partial loss can be further divided into general average and particular average.

General Average is defined as a partial and deliberate sacrifice of the ship. Freight, cargo, or the additional expense incurred to rescue a ship and its cargo from impeding danger or for the common safety of the adventure under a peril of the sea or some other hazards.

General average is based upon a relationship between the ship-owner and all the shippers who have cargo aboard the same vessel on a particular voyage. All these parties are bound together in the "adventure" When the whole ship was threatened by a peril of the sea or some other hazards, in order to save the ship and cargo, part of the cargo or vessel has to be sacrificed, then an act of general average would be declared. According to marine law, those parties whose property was saved must contribute proportionally to cover the losses of those whose property was voluntarily sacrificed.

The idea of general average liability is to spread the losses suffered by some parties among all parties to the voyage. For instance, whilst a vessel is in danger of sinking in a storm or in a collision, some of the cargo would have to be thrown out of the vessel. Such a case, termed as jettison, shall be one of the typical circumstances of general average.

Particular average refers to a partial loss of the subject matter insured proximately caused by an insured peril, other than a general average loss, i.e. the loss which should be borne by the party who suffers.

Although both general average and particular average belong to the category of partial loss, there are still some distinctions between them.

(1) Particular average is a kind of cargo loss usually caused directly by sea perils, but general average is a kind of cargo loss caused by intentional measures taken;

(2) Partial loss is often borne by the party whose cargo is damaged, but general average should be contributed by all the benefited parties proportionately.

Expenditures

Expenditures refer to the charges incurred in rescuing the insured cargo, including sue and labor charges and salvage charges.

(1) Sue and labor charges are any reasonable expense incurred by the insured or his agent or his employees in preventing or minimizing a loss when the subject matter insured is endangered. The insurer will reimburse the insured for such expense if the loss so minimized or prevented is proximately caused by an insured peril.

(2) Salvage charges is an award payable to a third party for services rendered to preserve maritime property from perils at sea and is payable only when the property has been saved.

After-Class Study

(I) *List of Insurance Terms in Foreign Trade*

insurance company　　保险公司
insurance agent　　保险代理人
insurance amount　　保额
insurance certificate　　保险凭证
insurance claim　　保险索赔
underwriters　　保险商（指专保水险的保险商）保险承运人
insurance broker　　保险经纪人
insurance underwriter　　保险承保人
insurance applicant　　投保人
insurant, the insured　　被保险人，受保人
marine insurance　　水险，海上保险
ocean marine cargo insurance　　海洋运输货物保险
air transportation insurance　　航今运输保险
overland insurance　　陆运保险
overland transportation insurance　　陆上运输保险
insurance cover　　保险
insurance coverage　　保险范围
insurance endorsement　　保险批单
insurance policy　　保（险）单
insurance slip　　投保单
insured amount　　保险金额
insurance clause　　保险条款
insurance instruction　　投保通知
insurance premium　　保（险）费
insurance declaration　　保险产明书　保险通知书

average 海损
Particular Average（P.A.） 单独海损
General Average（G.A.） 共同海损
Marine Losses 海损
partial loss 部分损失
total loss 全部损失

(II) *List of Extraneous Risks in Foreign Trade*

常见的附加险有：
Theft, Pilferage & Non-Delivery Risks（T.P.N.D.） 偷窃、提货不着险
Fresh and / or Rain Water Damage Risks 淡水雨淋险
Total Loss Only（T.L.O.） 全损险
Strike, Riots and Civil Commotion（S.R.C.C.） 罢工、暴动、民变险
Leakage Risk 渗漏险
Breakage of Packing Risk 包装破裂险
Storage Risk 短量险
Intermixture & Contamination Risks 混杂、沾污险
odour Risk 串味险
Sweating & Heating Risks 受潮受热险
Hook Damage Risk 钩损险
Rust Risk 锈损险
War Risk 战争险
Mould Risk 发霉险
Risk of Natural Loss or Normal Loss 途耗或自然损耗险
Risk of Failure to Delivery 交货不到险
Risk of Import Duty 进口关税险
Risk of Aflatoxin 黄曲霉素险
Survey in Customs Risk 海关检验险
Institute War Risk 学会战争险
Overland Transportation All Risks 陆远综合险
Risk of Spontaneous Combustion 自燃险
Erection All Risks 安装工程一切险
Construction All Risks 建筑工程一切险
Parcel Post Risk 邮包险

(III) *List of Insurance Documents in Foreign Trade*

policy 保单，保险单
insurance policy 保（险）单
open policy 预约保（险）单，船名未确定保单（即流动保单）
general open policy 预约总保单
floating policy 流动保单

voyage policy　　航程保单
marine insurance policy　　海上保险单
specific policy　　单独保单，船名确定保单（以别于船名未确定的流动保单）
time policy　　定期保险单
transferable policy　　可转让的名单

(IV) *List of Other Insurance Words and Phrases*

health insurance　　疾病保险，健康保险
sickness insurance　　疾病保险
insurance for medical care　　医疗保险
"major medical" insurance policy　　巨额医药费保险
insurance during a period of illness　　疾病保险
life insurance　　人寿保险
endowment insurance　　养老保险
insurance on last survivor　　长寿保险
to purchase health insurance　　购买健康保险
to have a health insurance policy　　购买健康保险
Additional Words and Phrases
policy-holder　　保险客户
extra premium　　额外保险费
additional premium　　附加保险费
insurance law　　保险法
insurance act　　保险条例
insurance division　　保险部
insurance treaty　　保险合同
cover note　　保险证明书
guarantee of insurance　　保险担保书
premium rebate　　保险费回扣
insurance claim　　保险索赔
ceding, retrocession (for reinsurance)　　分保
reinsurance　　分保（再保险）
ceding (insurance) company　　分保公司
co-insurance company　　共同保险公司
insurance document　　保险单据
certificate of insurance　　保险凭证
increasing coverage / extending coverage　　加保
renewing coverage　　续保
insurance commission　　保险佣金
social insurance　　社会保险
personal property insurance　　个人财产保险
insurance of contents　　家庭财产保险

Chinese Version of Specimen Letters

<例信 1> 安排保险

敬启者：

兹复你方 12 月 1 日来信，就信中你们询问我方在 11 月 20 日向你方报女式羽绒衣 CIF 价的保险一事，我们向你方提供如下信息：

对于以 CIF 价格条款成交的交易，我们通常是按照中国人民保险公司 1981 年 1 月 1 日颁布的海洋运输货物保险条款，向中国人民保险公司投保一切险。如你方要求按协会货物条款投保，我们也会将十分高兴满足你方的这一要求，但两者费用上的差额应由你方负担。假如你方需要，我们也能够给货物投保任何附加险，但额外费用将由你方负担。如果这样的话，我方将把有关保险公司开立的费用收据寄给你方。一般情况下投保的金额是发票总金额的 110%。但是，如果需要投保更高的金额，我们也可以照办，但你方还得承担额外的费用。

希望上述正是你方所需了解的信息，并望早日收到你方订单。

谨上

<例信 2> 卖方给买方的投保建议

敬启者：

感谢你方按 CIF 价格订购 3,000 台相机的第 636 号订单。

我们想要告知你方，大部分客户都是按 CIF 价格向我们订货的，这样能简化手续，节约时间。我们建议你方也能按这一做法向我们订货。

我们一般是按发票金额的 110%向中国人民保险公司办理保险的。我们的保险公司是一家国有企业，享有理赔迅速、处理公平的盛誉，并在全世界各主要港口和地区都有代理。如果货物发生损坏，你们可向他们在你处的代理人提出赔偿，他们的保险代理人将会迅速地进行解决。

我们一般将货物投保一些常用险别对本交易来说，我们将投保一切险。如果你方要求投保更多一些险别，额外的保险费将由买方承担。

望你方能同意我们的建议。盼答。

谨上

<例信 3> 买方的保险要求

敬启者：

我方第 1027 号订单内 300 箱 PDA 是按 CFR 订购的。

我们现在想在你方投保，故请将上述货物按发票金额外加 10%，即 3,300 美元代我方投保一切险。收到你借方结账单后，我方即将保险费汇付给你们。若你方愿意，亦可开具即期汇票，向我方收款。

诚挚希望你方的认可。

谨上

<**例信 4**> **卖方回复买方投保范围**

敬启者:

你方 2011 年 11 月 15 日函,要我方对标题项下第 1027 号合同货代办保险已悉。

我们已按你方要求,为上述船货向中国人民保险公司投保了一切险,投保金额为 3,300 美元。可望周末前将保险单与保险费的借方结账单一并寄你。该货物将装"神舟号"轮,约在下月 11 日起航。

谨上

<**例信 5**> **买方保险索赔**

敬启者:

订单第 1027 号

"神舟"轮于 12 月 16 日抵达新加坡时,发现第七号货箱有一边开裂。因此在船公司代理人监察下,我们请当地一家保险验货行开箱检查。按发票所列明,该箱装 PDA30 台,其中 12 台严重受损。现附上保险验货行的报告书和船公司代理人的报告书。由于你公司持有保险单,希望你公司就此事与保险公司接洽。现需补进 12 台 PDA,请安排供应。货款请借记我公司账户。

希你公司向保险公司索赔时顺利,预致谢意。

谨上

Unit 10 Shipment

> **Learning Aims**

After you finish learning this unit, you are requested to:
(1) understand some basic knowledge about shipment in foreign trade;
(2) know the different means of transport in foreign trade and their characteristics;
(3) know some common shipping documents and their application;
(4) grasp how to write good and effective letters concerning shipment.

Background Knowledge

(I) *About Shipment*

Shipment is an indispensable part in foreign trade because the goods have to be delivered from the seller's country to the buyer's country by various means of transport, such as by road, rail, air, sea etc., to fulfill the whole transaction successfully.

Before shipment, the buyers generally send their shipping requirements to the sellers to inform them in writing of the packing and mark, mode of transportation, etc., known as the Shipping Instruction. On the other hand, the sellers usually send a notice to the buyers immediately after the goods are loaded on board the ship, advising them of the shipment, especially under FOB or CFR terms. Such a notice, known as the shipping Advice, may include the following: Contract number, L/C number, name of commodity, number of packages, total quantity shipped, name of vessel and its sailing date and sometimes even the total value of the goods, as the requirements may be.

(II) *Means of Transport*

The main means of international transport for cargo consignment include the ocean cargo transport, railway transport, air transport, inland road transport, parcel delivery, pipeline for oil transportation and the combination of over any two of the above methods.

Ocean Cargo Transport. Among all types of transport, ocean cargo transport is most frequently used owing to its two major advantages i.e. huge capacity and low cost. In addition, it is unrestricted by such facilities and conditions as railways and pipelines demand. The disadvantages of ocean cargo transport are slow voyage speed, long time taken for the voyage, unpredicted sailing schedule and it is easily influenced by bad weather and some other force majeure. Ocean cargo transport occupies 80% of the total international cargo transportation volume. Two types of ocean cargo transport are most commonly used: liner transport and chartered transport.

Railway Transport. It is less subject to weather influence and can run on the rails all the year round. Besides, the features of railway transport are large capacity, fast speed, continuity of transport and fewer risks during transportation. There are two major types of railway transport namely, the domestic railway cargo transport and international railway cargo transport.

Road Transport. It is a flexible but low capacity method of transportation. Road transport usually can offer door-to-door service and is suitable for general merchandise and selective bulk cargos. However, when crossing frontiers, there are a lot of complicated procedures to conduct such as customs examinations, duty payment etc.

Airway Transport. It is one of the modern means of transportation. Except for its expensive freight rate, airway transport is characterized as fast delivery, simplified packing procedure, low insurance premium and low cost of storage, and it is unrestricted by the geographical conditions in traveling. Most international traders choose airway transportation for the perishable goods, live and fresh goods and seasonal commodities.

Container consignment is one of the modern transport methods using containers as an unit for international cargo transport. It is widely used in not only ocean cargo transport, but also in railway and inland road or river. If cargos need to be shipped across borders to a destination through more than one transportation way, the international through consignment can be the best choice for its unique advantages in its simplified procedures, fast delivery, low cost and less subject to inspections than through other means of transport.

(III) *Shipping Documents*

Shipping documents indicate the goods have been loaded on board the vessel or have been delivered to the custody of the carrier. The main function of shipping documents are for the seller to prove that he has fulfilled the duty of delivery, as well as for the buyer to pay the purchase price. However, different shipping documents are required by different modes of transport as illustrated in the following table:

Modes of Transport	Shipping Documents
Ocean Transport	Bill of Lading (B/L)
Air Transport	Airway Bill
Rail Transport	Railway Bill / Consignment Note
Road Transport	Road Bill / Consignment Note
Inland River	Waterway Bill
Multimodal Transport	Multimodal Transport Document

Among the above shipping documents, B/L is the most commonly used form in foreign trade. When export goods are loaded on board a ship or they are delivered to places in the shipping company's custody, the shipping company or its agent issues a bill of lading (B/L) to the shipper, acknowledging that the goods are shipped on board or received for shipment. The bill of lading is an important sea transport document, together with insurance policy and commercial invoices, constitutes the chief shipping documents indispensable to foreign trade.

Writing Tips

Letters regarding shipment in foreign trade are usually written for the purpose of urging an early shipment or advising shipment. Generally speaking, letters for urging shipment is usually written by the buyer containing the following parts:

(1) Remind or urge the seller of when and how to ship the goods;

(2) State the necessity and reasons of punctual shipment or immediate shipment is required;

(3) State the consequences of the seller's action for shipment (Usually, the buyer will mention the harm to business if shipment is delayed and wish the seller to ship the goods as soon as possible).

While letters for advising shipment is usually written by the seller and contain the following parts:

(1) Inform the buyer the details of the shipment for the ordered goods;
(2) Advise the buyer what shipping documents have been sent;
(3) Wish the goods to arrive in good condition;
(4) Thank the buyer for his order and wish to receive his repeat orders in the future.

Sentence Patterns & Examples

【Pattern 1】effect / arrange shipment   安排装运

We will open an L/C if you promise to effect shipment one month earlier.
如果你方答应提前一个月交货，我们将开立信用证。

Regarding your Order No.1753, please open the L/C by cable so as to enable us to arrange shipment.
关于你方第1234号订单，请即电开信用证，以便我们安排装运。

【Pattern 2】be ready for shipment   备妥待运

The goods are being prepared for immediate delivery and will be ready for shipment tomorrow.
该货可以立即交付，准备明日装船。

Please advise us when the articles are ready for shipment so that we can arrange the shipping space and insurance in time.
请告知这批货物何时能备妥装运，以便我方及时安排舱位和保险事宜。

【Pattern 3】prompt shipment   即期装运

For this lot, could you consider prompt shipment?
我们这批货，贵方能不能考虑即期装运？

Silks are seasonal goods in North America, so can you make a prompt shipment?
在北美丝绸是季节性物资，因此贵方是否能够安排即期装运？

【Pattern 4】advance / postpone shipment   提前 / 推迟装运

We can't advance shipment of your order owing to heavy commitments.
由于承约过多，我方不能将你方订货提前装运。

We consider it advisable to postpone shipment.
我们认为推迟装运为宜。

【Pattern 5】partial shipment   分批装运

Please note in the L/C "Partial Shipment Allowed".
请在信用证中注明"允许分批装运"。

To make it easier for us to get the goods ready for shipment, we hope that partial shipment is allowed.
为了便于准备货物，我们希望允许分批装运。

Unit 10 Shipment

【Pattern 6】transshipment　　转船

All the transshipment charges should be borne by the seller.
所有的转船运费用均应由卖方承担。

You are kindly requested to have your L/C issued early next month allowing partial shipment and transshipment.
请务必于下月初开出信用证，准许分批装运和转船。

【Pattern 7】ship... by...　　由……(轮)装运货物

It is our customary practice to ship our commodities by motor vessel.
我们通常使用机动轮来装运我们的货物。

As per the S/C, all the goods should be shipped by S.S. "Dongfang" which is due to arrive at Lagos on June 15.
根据售销合同，所有货物应通过"东方号"汽轮装运，该轮预计在6月15日抵达拉各斯。

【Pattern 8】book shipping space　　预订舱位

In order to book the shipping space at an earlier date, we request you to open the relevant L/C immediately.
为了尽早预订船期，请你方速开有关信用证。

Please book the necessary shipping space in advance to insure timely dispatch of the goods ordered.
请预订所需的舱位以保证及时装运所订购的货物。

【Pattern 9】few and far between　　稀少

Direct steamers to your country are few and far between.
去贵国的直达班轮稀少。

Please consider allowing transshipment since direct steamers are few and far between now.
直达班轮目前稀少，请考虑允许转船。

Specimen Letters

<Letter 1> Giving Shipping Instructions to the Seller

Dear Sirs,

　　We are pleased to receive your Sales Contract No. 1732 in duplicate against our Order No. 878 for 1,000 dozen "Universe" brand men's shirts.

　　Although the price is quoted on FCA[1] basis, we wish to request that you sign the contract of carriage with the carrier on usual terms at our risk and expense[2].

　　When you have booked the shipping space, please advise us of the name and voyage number of the vessel, B/L No., estimated time of departure (ETD), estimated time of arrival (ETA), and any other information necessary for us to arrange insurance at our end.

As the cartons are easily broken, please pack them in specially made cases capable of withstanding rough handling[3].

Your close cooperation in the above respects is highly appreciated.

Yours faithfully,

<Letter 2> Urging Shipment[4]

Dear Sirs,

Referring to the Contract No. 1732 covering 1,000 dozen "Universe" brand men's shirts, we wish to remind you that we have had no news from you about shipment of the goods.

As we mentioned in our last letter, we are in urgent need of[5] the goods and may be compelled to seek an alternative source of supply if you can't provide the goods. Your delay has caused us much inconvenience, as the goods are urgently required by our customers.

Under these circumstances, it is impossible for us to extend our letter of Credit No. 2192 further, which expires on August 20. Please understand how serious and we must now ask you to do your utmost to solve this matter.

We look forward to receiving your shipping advice by fax, within the next seven days.

Yours faithfully,

<Letter 3> Advising Shipment

Dear Sirs,

Contract No. 1732-1000 dozen Universe brand Men's Shirts

Thank you for your letter of May 12 enquiring about the shipment of the caption goods.

Please accept our apology for the delay that has been caused by the unavailability of shipping space from Qingdao to London. However, we are now pleased to inform you that we have shipped the mentioned goods by S.S. Pand which was sailed for your port yesterday directly.

Enclosed you will find one full set of shipping documents covering this consignment, which comprises:

(1) One non-negotiable[6] copy of the bill of lading;
(2) Commercial invoice in duplicate[7];
(3) One copy of the certificate of quality;
(4) One copy of the certificate of quantity;
(5) One copy of the insurance policy;
(6) Weight Memo[8] in duplicate.

We are glad to have been able to execute your order as contracted and trust that the goods will reach you in good time and prove to be entirely satisfactory.

We avail ourselves of this opportunity to assure you that any further order from you will receive our prompt attention.

Yours faithfully,

<Letter 4> Asking for Transshipment

Dear Sirs,

Re: SWC Sugar

We are in receipt of your L/C No. B-503 for amount of USD 1,050,000 opened in our favor through the Hong Kong & Shanghai Banking Corporation to cover the FAS cost of 10,000 metric tons of the subject sugar and thank you for it.

With regard to[9] shipment, we regret very much to inform you that, despite strenuous efforts having been made by us, we are still unable to book space of a direct vessel sailing to Jakarta. The shipping companies here told us that, for the time being, there is no regular boat sailing between ports in China and Jakarta. Therefore, it is very difficult for us to ship these 10,000 metric tons of sugar to Jakarta directly.

In view of[10] the difficult situation faced by us, you are requested to amend the L/C to allow transshipment of the goods in Hong Kong where arrangements can easily be made for transshipment. Please be assured that we will ship the goods to Hong Kong right upon receipt of the L/C amendment. Your agreement to our request and your understanding of our position will be highly appreciated.

We are anxiously awaiting the amendment to the L/C.

Yours faithfully,

<Letter 5> Proposing Partial Shipment

Dear Sirs,

Your Order No.5718 for Safety Pin Machines[11]

We are in receipt of your letter of July 20 requesting us to ship all the 20 sets of Safety Pin Machines in one lot in September. Unfortunately we are unable to comply with[12] your wishes.

When we offered the machines it was especially stated that shipment would be effected in October. If you desire early delivery, we can only make a partial shipment of ten machines in September and the remaining ten in October. We hope this arrangement will be agreeable to you. Should this be so, please amend the covering credit to allow partial shipment and inform us.

Please cable us your confirmation so that we can request the manufactures to expedite delivery.

Yours faithfully,

Notes

1. **FCA (Free Carrier)**　　货交承运人

   货交承运人是国际贸易术语解释通则中的 13 种贸易术语之一。根据《2000 年国际贸易术语解释通则》的规定，它是指卖方只要将货物交在指定的地点交给买方指定的承运人，并办理出口清关手续，即完成交货。需要说明的是，交货地点的选择对于在该地点装货和卸货的义务会产生影响。若卖方在其所在地交货，则卖方应负责装货，若卖方在任何其他地点交货，则卖方不负责卸货。该术语可使用于任何运输方式，包括多式联运。若卖方指定承运人以外的人领取货物，则当卖方将货物交给此人时，即视为已经履行了交货义务。

2. **at our risk and expense**　　费用和风险由我方承担

3. **rough handling**　　野蛮装卸，粗暴搬运

4. **shipment**　　*n.*　　装运，装船；装运的货物；装运期

   ship　　*v.*　　装船

   shipping　　*n.*　　装运

   shipping advice　　装船通知

   shipping agents　　装运代理人

   shipping company　　轮船公司

   shipping marks　　装船唛头

   shipping order　　装货单

   shipping space　　船位，载位，舱位

5. **be in urgent need of = be urgently in need of**　　急需

6. **non-negotiable**　　*adj.*　　不可议付的，不可转让的

   non-negotiable bill of lading　　不可转让的提单

7. **in duplicate = in two folds / in two copies**　　一式两份

   in triplicate　　一式三份

   in quadruplicate　　一式四份

   in quintuplicate　　一式五份

   in sextuplicate　　一式六份

8. **weight memo**　　重量单，磅码单

9. **with regard to**　　关于

10. **in view of**　　鉴于

    注意区别：词组 with a view to，意为"希望……，为了……"，to 为介词，后接动名的现在分词。例如：

    (1) He has bought land with a view to building a house.
    他买地为的是要盖房子。

(2) In view of your previous substantial orders, we will give a special discount for this transaction.

鉴于贵公司以前大量的订购，此次交易我方将给你们特别优惠。

11. Safety Pin Machines 　　 安全别针机
12. comply with = conform to 　　 与……一致

Exercises

I. *Translate the following terms into English*:

1. 安排装船
2. 备妥待运
3. 启运港
4. 目的港
5. 预订舱位
6. 运费
7. 散装货
8. 分批装运
9. 转船
10. 即期装运

II. *Translate the following terms into Chinese*:

1. shipping instruction
2. shipping advice
3. nude cargo
4. air waybill
5. E.T.A.
6. M.V.
7. E.T.D.
8. S.S.
9. in duplicate
10. shipping documents

III. *Choose the best answer to complete the following sentences*:

1. The use of containerization in transportation greatly _____ carriage of goods.
   A. facilitate   B. facilitates   C. speed   D. speeds

2. Time of shipment refers to the time limit for loading the goods on board the vessel at the port of _____ .
   A. destination   B. transhipment   C. loading   D. unloading

3. In our letter of October 20, we made _____ clear that shipment is to be effected in November.
   A. you   B. them   C. it   D. that

4. Please tell us _____ the goods will be transsshipped.
   A. where   B. what   C. which   D. why

5. Although we have been making great efforts to book shipping space on time, but _____ our regret, we were told there were no shipping container before July 20.
   A. much for   B. many for   C. much to   D. many to

6. We request you to have the validity of the L/C _____ in later than Dec. 10.
   A. extend   B. extended   C. expand   D. expanded

7. We trust this transaction will bring you a good profit and _____ your future order.

    A. result from   B. result in   C. bring out   D. bring in

8. _____ transport is undoubtedly the most economical means of transportation particularly when bulk commodities are involved.

    A. Inland   B. Air   C. Sea   D. Road

9. It has to be stressed that shipment must be made _____ the prescribed time limit, as a further extension will not be considered.

    A. at   B. in   C. on   D. within

10. As you have failed to deliver within the specified tome, we have no alternative but _____ our order.

    A. to cancel   B. cancel   C. canceling   D. canceled

IV. Fill in the following blanks with the words and expressions in the box, change the form when necessary:

sets	assurance	overdue	obliged	dispatched
consignment	facilitate	punctual	proceed	utmost

Dear Sirs,

    Referring to our order No. 529 for 5,000 electronic calculators, we wish to remind you that the time of shipment has long been ___1___.

    When we placed the order we pointed out that ___2___ shipment was of ___3___ importance because this order was secured from the largest dealers here and we had given them a definite ___4___ that we could supply the goods by the end of June. Your delay has caused us much inconvenience and we must now ask you to do your utmost to dispatch the first 2,000 ___5___ under this order by air as the goods are urgently required by our customers.

    We suggest the use of cartons with hinged lids to ___6___ opening for customs examination. You will no doubt ___7___ with your arrangements of the shipment of the remaining 3,000 set of the ___8___ by sea without further delay, and we would ask you to be particularly careful to seal each box into a watertight bag before packing into the case.

    We should be ___9___ if you would send us by air a copy of the packing list for the shipment to be ___10___ by sea, and also duplicates of the insurance policy, certificate and the commercial invoice. This will enables us to arrange speedy passage through customs on arrival of the consignment.

V. Translate the following sentences into Chinese:

1. We are sorry that we cannot allow you extra days for shipment, since our customers in urgent need of the goods, any delay of your shipment shall put us in a rather difficult position.

2. In order to catch up with the selling season, please arrange for shipment upon receipt of

our L/C and cable us the shipping advice.

3. As our client is urgently in need of the goods, we hope you will advance the time of delivery from June to May.

4. We are pleased to inform you that order No. 7246 has been shipped today per S.S. "Sunshine", which is leaving for your port on December 12.

5. We are advised by the shipping company that because direct vessels, either liner or tramp, sailing for your port are few and far between, the shipping space has been fully booked up to the end of November.

VI. *Translate the following sentences into English*:

1. 货已备妥待运多时，请告知所派船名、航次及预计抵达时间，以便我方及时安排装运。
2. 货物将由"东风号"轮183次航次装运，该轮预定于10月31日抵达哥本哈根港，请速订仓。请确认货物将按时备妥。
3. 意外的情况迫使我们寻求你方配合，请将123号合同下的货物装期由8月份提前到7月份。
4. 我们理解你方的处境，但很遗憾，我们无法提前发货，因为工厂订单太多。
5. 兹通知你方已由"黄河"轮029航次将200箱闹钟运往你处。此货物将在新加坡转船，预定于下月初到达你方港口。

VII. *Simulated writing*:

Now you are required to write a letter to Evergreen Trading Co., Ltd. of Canada, to inform them the following details:

敬启者：
　　我方在上述地点有50箱化工试剂（chemical reagents）准备发往任一欧洲主要港口，若蒙贵方安排船运集装箱运此货物，我方将感到十分高兴。每箱重60公斤。
　　因我方客户要求不得迟于7月15日装运此货，请在最后期限前向我方报价从香港到达上述口岸的船运集装箱。
　　若蒙贵方早日报价则不胜感激。

×××谨上

Dear Sirs,

Yours faithfully,

Supplementary Reading

提单式样：

装货单号　　　　　　　　　　　　　　　　　　　　提单号
S/O No _____　　　　　　　　　　　　　B/L No _____

BILL OF LADING
提　　单

DIRECT OR WITH TRANSSHIPMENT
直运或转船

船名　　　　　　　航次　　　　　　　　　卸货港
Vessel _____　Voy _____　　　　Port of Discharge _____

国籍　　　　　　　　　　　　　　　　　　装货港
Nationality _____　　　　　Port of Loading _____

托运人
Shipper _____

收货人　　　　　　　　　　　　　　　　　　　　　　　　　　　　　或受让人
Consignee _____or assignee

通知
Notify _____

　　下列外表情况良好的货物（另有说明者除外）已装在上列船上并应在上列卸货港或该船所能安全到达并保持浮泊的附近地点卸货。

　　Shipped on board the vessel named above in apparent good order and condition (unless otherwise indicated) the goods or packages specified herein and to be discharged at the above mentioned port of discharged or as near thereto as the vessel may safely get and be always afloat.

　　重量、尺码、标志、号数、品质、内容和价值是托运人提供的，承运人在装船时并未核对。

　　The weight, measure, marks, number, quality, contents, and value, being particulars furnished by the Shipper, are not checked by the Carrier on loading.

　　托运人、收货人和本提单的持有人兹明白表示接受并同意本提单和它背面所载的一切印刷、书写或打印的规定、负责事项和条件。

　　The Shipper, Consignee and the Holder of this Bill of Lading hereby expressly accept and agree to all printed, written or stamped provisions, exceptions and conditions of this Bill of Lading, including those on the back hereof.

Unit 10 Shipment

托运人所提供的详细情况
Particulars Furnished by the Shipper

标志和号数 Marks & Number	件数 No. of Packages	货　　名 Description of Goods	毛　重 Gross Weight	尺　码 Measurement

合计件数（大写）
Total Packages (in words) _____

运费和其他费用
Freight and Charges:

运费在_____支付
Freight payable at_____

请托运人特别注意本提单内与该货保险效力有关的免责事项和条件。

Shippers are requested to note particularly the exceptions and conditions of this Bill of Lading with reference to the validity of the others to stand void.

为证明以上各节，承运人或其代理人已签署本提单一式份，其中一份经完成提货手续后，其余各份失效。

In witness whereof, the Carrier or his agents has signed Bills of Lading all of this tenor and date, one of which being accomplished, the insurance upon their goods.

签单日期　　　　在
Dated ----------at ----------------------------

　　　　　　　　　　　　　　　　船长
---------------------------- For the Master

After-Class Study

(I) *Terms Used in Shipment*

inland transportation　内陆运输
sea transportation　海运
air transportation　空运
through transportation　联运
multi-modal combined transport　多式联运
transfer transportation　中转运输
drop and pull transportation　甩挂运输
containerized transportation　集装运输
container transportation　集装箱运输
door-to-door　门到门

full container load (FCL)　整箱货
less than container load (LCL)　拼箱货
prompt shipment　即期装运
timely shipment　及时装运
express shipment　快速装运
direct shipment　直接装运
partial shipment　分批装运
shipping documents　装运单据
shipping agent　装运代理商
shipping advice　装运通知
shipping instruction　装运指示
shipping mark　唛头
shipping order / permit　装船通知单，装货单，装运单
shipping space　舱位
time of shipment　装运期
date of delivery　交货日期
immediate delivery　立即交货
punctual delivery　按期交货
delivery in instalments　分批交货
transshipment　转运
partial shipment　分装
liner　班轮，定期轮船
tramp　非定期轮船
motor vessel (M.V.)　机动轮
steamship / steamer ship (S.S.)　（蒸）汽轮
direct steamer　直达汽轮
optional port　任意港
port of shipment　装运港
port of destination　目的港
port of loading　装货港
port of unloading / discharge　卸货港
freight charge　运费
loading charge　装货费
storage charge / cost　仓储费用
additional charge / fee　额外费用
dead freight　空舱费
dispatch　速遣费
demurrage　滞期费
freight prepaid　运费付至

freight paid　运费已付
freight collect　运费到付
forwarding agent / forwarder　货运代理人 / 运输行
estimated time of arrival (ETA)　预抵期
estimated time of departure (ETD)　预离期
lay days　受载日期
document title　物权凭证
berth　泊位
port congestion　港口拥挤
weight ton　重量吨
measurement ton　尺码吨
freight ton　运费吨
weight memo　重量单 / 磅码单
RoRo = roll on / roll off　滚装船，驶上驶下船
voyage charter　定程租船
time charter　定期租船

(II) *Main Ports*

Name of Port	Chinese Equivalent	Country
Aden	亚丁	民主也门
Alexandria	亚历山大	埃及
Amsterdam	阿姆斯特丹	荷兰
Antwerp	安特卫普	比利时
Auckland	奥克兰	新西兰
Baltimore	巴尔的摩	美国
Bangkok	曼谷	泰国
Barcelona	巴塞罗那	西班牙
Beirut	贝鲁特	黎巴嫩
Bordeaux	波尔多	法国
Boston	波士顿	美国
Bremen	不莱梅	德国
Buenos Aires	布宜诺斯艾利斯	阿根廷
Calcutta	加尔各答	印度
Chittagong	吉大港	孟加拉国
Colombo	科伦坡	斯里兰卡
Gdansk	格但斯克	波兰
Genoa	热那亚	意大利
Glasgow	格拉斯哥	英国
Hamburg	汉堡	德国

Name of Port	Chinese Equivalent	Country
Hong Kong	香港	中国
Honolulu	火鲁努努（檀香山）	美国
Houston	休斯顿	美国
Istanbul	伊斯坦布尔	土耳其
Jeddah	吉达	沙特阿拉伯
Karachi	卡拉奇	巴基斯坦
Kobe	神户	日本
Lisbon	里斯本	葡萄牙
Liverpool	利物浦	英国
London	伦敦	英国
Los Angeles	洛杉矶	美国
Manila	马尼拉	菲律宾
Marseilles	马赛	法国
Melbourne	墨尔本	澳大利亚
Montreal	蒙特利尔	加拿大
Nagoya	名古屋	日本
Naples	那不勒斯	意大利
New Orleans	新奥尔良	美国
New York	纽约	美国
Osaka	大阪	日本
Philadelphia	费城	美国
Quebec	魁北克	加拿大
Rangoon	仰光	缅甸
Rijeka	里耶卡	南斯拉夫
Rio De Janeiro	里约热内卢	巴西
Rostock	罗斯托克	德国
Rotterdam	鹿特丹	荷兰
San Francisco	旧金山	美国
Singapore	新加坡	新加坡
Southampton	南安普顿	英国
Stockholm	斯德哥尔摩	瑞典
Sydney	悉尼	澳大利亚
Tokyo	东京	日本
Tripoli	的黎波里	利比亚
Valparaiso	瓦尔帕莱索	智利
Vancouver	温哥华	加拿大
Venice	威尼斯	意大利
Wellington	惠灵顿	新西兰
Yokohama	横滨	日本

Chinese Version of Specimen Letters

<例信 1> 买方给卖方发出装运指示函

敬启者：

很高兴收到 878 号订单项下的 1,000 打宇宙牌男士衬衫的编号为 1732 的销售合同一式两份。

尽管所报的是"货交承运人"价格，我们想请你方按照通常条件与承运人签订运输合同，而风险和费用则由我方承担。

当你方锭到舱位的时候，请通知我方船名及航次、提单号、预计离开时间、预计抵达时间，以及其他一些对我方在我地办理保险所必需的信息。

由于一般纸箱容易破损，请用特别制作的箱子包装，以经得起野蛮装卸。

如蒙你方在上述方面的密切合作，我方不胜感激。

谨启

<例信 2> 催促装运安排

敬启者：

有关第 1732 号合同订购 1,000 打宇宙牌男士衬衫的事宜，至今未收到贵公司装运通知。

上次已经致函贵公司，表示急需此货物。如贵公司不能供应此货，我们也许可以寻求其他货源。由于我们客户急需此货，所以你方延迟给我们带来了很多不便。

在这种情况下，8 月 20 日到期的信用证已经无法再作延期。还望贵公司体察，尽快解决此问题。

烦请于 7 天内将贵公司的装运通知传真给我方。

谨启

<例信 3> 装运通知

敬启者：

1732 号合同项下 1000 打宇宙牌男士衬衫

5 月 12 日询问有关标题货物转运情况的来信收悉。

因为未能订到从青岛到伦敦的舱位而造成的延误，我方深表歉意。但是，该货已于昨日装运上潘迪号汽轮，直接驶往伦敦。

随函敬附下列全套装运单据：

（1）不可转让的提单副本一份；

（2）商业发票一式两份；

（3）质量证书副本一份；

（4）数量证书副本一份；

（5）保险单副本一份；

（6）重量单一式两份。

能够按照合同订明的要求为贵公司效劳，我们深感殊荣，相信此货将及时运抵贵公司，符合订购的要求。

借此机会向你方承诺，如有任何需要我方乐意效劳。

谨启

<例信 4> 要求转船

敬启者：

关于特级白糖

贵方经由香港汇丰银行开立的、以我方为受益人的第 B-503 号信用证收悉，谢谢。该信用证包括以船边交货计算的 10,000 公吨上述白糖，金额为 1,050,000 美元。

关于装运之事，今歉告，尽管我方做了极大的努力，但仍未预定到直达雅加达的轮船仓位。我处船运公司告知，中国港口与雅加达之间暂无定期船只，因而我方很难将此 10,000 公吨白糖直运雅加达。

鉴于我们所面临的困难，请修改信用证，允许在香港转船，因为在香港很容易转运。我方保证，一旦受到你方修改的信用证，我方即将装货，贵方若能统一我方要求，并能理解我方所处的情况，当不胜感激。

急盼修改后的信用证。

谨启

<例信 5> 建议分批装运

敬启者：

你方第 5718 号安全别针机订单

你方 7 月 20 日要求 9 月份一次装运的 20 台安全别针机的来函收悉，但歉告，我方无法满足你方的要求。

我方报盘时已经特别指出，10 月份方能办理装运。如你方要求提前交货，我方只能分批装运，即 9 月份 10 台，其余 10 月份装运。我们希望此种安排你方能接受。若同意这样安排，请修改有关信用证，允许分批装运，并通知我方。

请电报确认，以便我方要求厂家尽快交货。

谨启

Unit 11 Complaints and Claims

Learning Aims

After you finish learning this unit, you are requested to:
(1) acquire some basic knowledge concerning complaints[1] and claims[2] in foreign trade;
(2) master how to write good and effective letters to lodge[3] a claim for compensation.

Background Knowledge

(I) *Brief Introduction of Complaints and Claims*

In international trade, complaints and claims do not happen in every transaction but often occur because of some personal or non-personal factors. When troubles and conflicts in trade happen between the importer and exporter in different countries, the letters of complaint or claims (LOC) are commonly used in practice.

If the loss is not serious, the party suffered the loss may write a complaint letter to call the other party's attention to avoid this matter happening again. If the loss is serious, the party suffered the loss may lodge a claim for compensation.

(II) *The Main Reasons for Complaints and Claims in Foreign Trade*

Complaints and claims are usually raised by buyers for the following reasons:
- the delivery of wrong goods;
- the delivery of short weight or shortage of quantity;
- the loss caused by non-delivery or delay of delivery;
- the inferior[4] quality and improper packing;
- the discrepancy between the previous samples and the goods received;
- a breach[5] of contract, etc.

On receiving complaints or claims, the seller should make investigations and settle the problem. This is called the adjustment[6].

On the contrary, sellers may also raise claims against buyer for non-establishment of L/C or a breach of contract, etc.

Writing Tips

In order to achieve your final aims to make a successful **complaint or claim**, we might as well adopt the following steps:

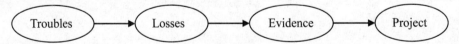

(1) During the claim period as stipulated in the contract, the buyer should present the problem suffered in detail. The presentation should include in the dates, the name and quantity of goods, the contract number or any other specific information that will make a recheck easier for the readers.

(2) Present the inconvenience or loss that is caused by the error.

(3) Present the evidences such as the survey report issued by CCIB[7] to support your complaints or claims.

(4) Try your best to stimulate prompt investigation and action by the seller. Meanwhile, present the way you wish to settle the problem.

In order to achieve your final aims to **adjust the complaint or claim** you received, we might as well adopt the following steps:

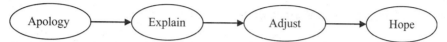

(1) Regret for the inconvenience caused to the buyer as soon as receiving the complaints or claims. In case the sellers are the first to discover that a mistake has been made, they should not wait for a complaint, but should write, telex or fax at once to let the buyers know, and either put the matter right or offer some compensation.

(2) Explain the reasons of the problem on the ground of investigation. There is no need for the sellers to go into a long story of how the mistake was made. A short explanation may be useful but, generally speaking, the buyers are not interested in hearing how or why the error occurred but only in having the matter put right.

(3) Express the wish to grant the claim and present the adjustment methods in detail.

(4) Wish to cooperate with the buyer again.

In order to achieve your final aims to **reject the complaint or claim** you received, we might as well adopt the following steps:

(1) Regret for the inconvenience suffered by the buyer.

(2) Explain the reasons of the problem on the ground of investigation.

(3) Express your position to refuse the complaint or claim directly and clearly. Moreover, you can suggest some possible settlement.

(4) Wish to cooperate with the buyer again.

Sentence Patterns & Examples

【Pattern 1】regret to inform you that...　　非常遗憾地通知贵方……

We regret to inform you that your shipment for our Order No. 680303 has been found short in weight.

我们非常遗憾地通知贵方，贵方装运来的我方第680303号订单项下的货物短重。

We regret to inform you that our order for Christmas Decorations arrived today, two days after the Christmas Day.

我们非常遗憾地通知贵方，我方订购的圣诞装饰品在圣诞节过了两天之后的今天才抵达。

【Pattern 2】lodge / file / make / put / submit / forward / raise / register / a claim　　提出索赔

We lodge a claim for USD 8,000, together with a survey report by the Shanghai Commodity Inspection Bureau.

我们提出索赔8,000美元，并附上上海商检局的检验报告。

We have to forward a claim against you for a short-weight of 5 tons.
由于短重5吨，我们必须向你们提出索赔。

【Pattern 3】be not in conformity with…　　与……不一致

It is obvious that the quality of your products is not in conformity with the samples you sent us previously.
很明显，你方产品的质量与先前寄送给我们样品的质量不符。

After checking, we find the consignment is not in conformity with the original sample.
经检验，我们发现这批货与原样本不一致。

【Pattern 4】be liable for…　　对……负责

The shipping company will be liable for damage.
运输公司将对损坏负责。

The seller is liable for the refund of the extra cost because of the discrepancy in weight.
卖方应负责退还因重量差异而多收的货款。

【Pattern 5】find there is a shortage of… / be (found) short by…　　发现……短量（重）

We are sorry to find that there is a shortage of 1,605 kilos, though the packing remains intact.
很遗憾，虽然包装原封不动，但短重1,605公斤。

Your shipment of our order No.635 has been found short by 15 cases.
现发现你方所发送的我方第635号订单货物少了15箱。

【Pattern 6】compensate for　　赔偿，补偿

The buyer strongly demands that the seller should compensate for the damage.
买方强烈要求卖方赔偿损失。

If we were at fault, we should be very glad to compensate for your losses.
如果责任在我方，我们当然愿意赔偿你方的损失。

【Pattern 7】make up for　　赔偿，补偿

We employ part-timer to make up for staff shortage.
我们雇佣临时工以弥补人员不足。

Hard work can often make up for a lack of ability.
努力工作经常可以弥补能力的不足。

【Pattern 8】settle the claim　　理赔

We hope you will settle the claim as soon as possible and bring the case to a satisfactory close. We trust that there will be no repetition of this kind of trouble.
希望贵方尽快解决此事，并期望类似麻烦不再发生。

The insurance company refused to settle his claim for storm damage.
保险公司拒绝对风暴造成的损坏进行理赔。

【Pattern 9】a survey report issued by…　　由……签发的调查报告

We should require a survey report issued by your local insurance agent, with which we may

Unit 11 Complaints and Claims

know the extent of the damage.

我们要求出具一份由你方当地保险代理商签发的检验报告，以便我们能了解损坏的程度。

According to the survey report issued by CCIB, we regret to tell you that the quality of your shipment for our Order No.990630 is far from the agreed specifications.

根据中国商品检验局出具的检验报告，我们很遗憾地告知贵方，贵方装运来的我方第990630号订单项下的货物的品质与我方认可的规格相去甚远。

【Pattern 10】accept / entertain a claim   接受索赔

We are not in a position to accept your claim.
我们不能接受你们提出的索赔要求。

We won't entertain your claim as we cannot bear the responsibility for unforeseen circumstances.
对于贵方的索赔我们不会接受，因我们不能对无法预测的情况承担责任。

Specimen Letters

<Letter 1> A Complaint about Short Delivery of MP5

Dear Sirs,

We have received the documents and taken delivery of the Order No. 0630 that arrived at Qingdao on the M.V. Victoria.

On checking the goods we found that carton No. 16 contains only 400 sets of Samsung MP5, although 500 sets of it had been entered on both the packing list and the invoice.

The full consignment is urgently required to complete orders for three of our major customers, so it is absolutely essential that you ship the additional 100 sets of Samsung MP5 on the earliest possible flight from Seoul[8] at your expense.

This is the third time in the last year that you have short-shipped one of our orders. If there is any further repetition of this we will be forced to look for an alternative supplier[9].

Yours faithfully,

<Letter 2> About Short Delivery of MP5 (Reply to Letter 1)

Dear Sirs,

Thank you for your Letter of 20 January. We are extremely sorry to learn that an error was made in carton No. 16 of your Order No. 0630.

The missing 100 sets of Samsung MP5 were sent this morning by the Southern Airway and the documents have been forwarded to you.

We greatly regret the inconvenience caused by this and the previous two errors and offer our sincere apologies. We will try our best and can assure you that similar errors will not occur again. We wish to be able to serve you in future business.

Yours sincerely,

<Letter 3> A Complaint about Wrong Laser Printer[10]

Dear Sirs,

We would refer to your consignment of the laser printer of our Order No. 0303 which arrived this morning.

On opening the cases we found that we had received the wrong goods. We received LP-868 instead of LP-888 laser printers that we ordered. Please advise us when we can expect to receive our order, as some of our customers have been waiting for up to one month. Besides, please also let us know what we are to do with the laser printers now in our possession[11].

Yours faithfully,

<Letter 4> About Wrong Laser Printer (Reply to Letter 3)

Dear Sirs,

We thank you for your letter of 10 September informing us of the wrong delivery of the laser printers.

On going into the matter, we find that a mistake was indeed made in packing, through a confusion of number[12]. We have arranged for the right goods to be dispatched to you at once. Relative documents will be mailed as soon as they are ready.

Do you think you might sell the LP-868 Laser Printer? If so, you may wish to keep them a while and if they don't move you can return them to us. In any event, we'll pay all shipping charges.

Yours sincerely,

<Letter 5> A Complaint about Delay Delivery of Two HERCULES Excavators[13]

Dear Sirs,

Last November we signed a contract to build a large school in Pudong. As the work was due to start in March, we placed an order with you for two HERCULES excavators immediately.

On placing the order, we were told that they would be delivered in site about the middle of March. Today is 18 March and these excavators have not yet to be delivered! At the end of March we will begin work on the site and these machines will be needed from the first day. Until they arrive, we can do nothing. The direct and indirect economic loss may add up to million.

Please tell us as soon as possible when you intend to deliver these excavators.

Yours truly,

<Letter 6> About Delay Delivery of Two HERCULES Excavators (Reply to Letter 5)

Dear Sirs,

We have received your letter of 18 March, and regret the delay delivery of the two

HERCULES excavators you have ordered. We are now trying our best to deliver them. You will have both excavators by 28 March at the latest.

The HERCULES is the most successful excavator we have produced by now. It gets an instant success at its first appearance at the Hong Kong Building Exhibition at last year and we were soon inundated with orders[14]. Your order was received in November. It was not due for delivery until April according to the waiting list we had then. Nevertheless, we put the delivery date forward so that you would have the machines in March. In February, our production was slightly set back by the late arrival of some special parts and this has been responsible for the delay in the present case.

We trust that you will not be unduly inconvenienced by having to wait a few more days. The performance of the HERCULES excavators will amply compensate you.

Yours sincerely,

<Letter 7> A Claim for the Low Quality Fax Machine[15]

Dear Sirs,

For the first time in my memory, I lodge a claim for one of your office products—fax machine. The quality of our order No.268 I received from you at last week is very bad. It does not satisfactorily print the letters.

As this lot of fax machines is of no use at all to us, we require you refund[16] the invoice amount and inspection fee of the goods amounting to USD3,000. We trust you will promptly settle this claim. As soon as the settlement is accomplished, we will send the goods back to you. All the expenses will be for your account.

In support of our claim, we are sending you a survey report issued by CCIB.

If we can settle the problem smoothly, we will order from you in the future.

Yours faithfully,

<Letter 8> About the Quality of Fax Machine (Reply to Letter 7)

Dear Sir,

I couldn't agree with you more when you say that the fax machine of your Order No.268 you received from us are not satisfactory. We have telephoned the manufacturer and looked into the matter of your claim for the low quality fax machine. All is a mistake by their staff at the warehouse.

But our proposal of settlement is that we will immediately send you replacements[17] of which the quality is guaranteed. As to the low quality goods you received, please send back at our expense.

We believe that the solution we have made will satisfy you and look forward to receiving your further orders.

Yours sincerely,

Notes

1. complaint   *n.*   投诉；申诉；抱怨，不满

   Complaint means statement about things being dissatisfactory.
   申诉的含义是对事情不满意的陈诉。

   My customers are driving me to distraction with their complaints and return.
   顾客的投诉和退货搞得我焦头烂额。

2. claim   *n.*   索赔

   Claim means lodging a demand for compensation.
   索赔的含义是提出赔偿的要求。

   His claim for money cannot be considered.
   他提出的金钱赔偿不予考虑。

3. lodge   *v.*   提出（申诉、抗议等）

   He lodged a complaint against the seller with the authorities concerned.
   他向有关当局对卖方提出控诉。

   I lodge a claim for one of your office products—Fax Machine for the first time.
   这是我第一次对你方所供应的办公用品——传真机提出索赔。

4. inferior   *adj.*   （质量等）劣等的，差的，次的

   I couldn't agree with you more when you say that the fax machine of your Order No. 268 you received from us are inferior goods.
   你来信指出传真机的品质堪虑，这点我完全同意。

5. breach   *n.*   破坏；违反；不履行

   A breach of contract means an act of breaking or not fulfilling a promise.
   违反合同是指破坏或不履行承诺的行为。

6. adjustment   *n.*   理赔，（保险业中）评定（赔偿要求）

   Adjustment means the act of settling complaints.
   理赔是指处理申诉的行为。

   On receiving the complaint or claim, the seller will make investigations and settle the problem. This is called the adjustment.
   当收到申诉或索赔时，卖方将进行调查并解决问题，这就是理赔。

7. CCIB (China Commodity Inspection Bureau)   中国商品检验局

8. Seoul   首尔（韩国首都）

9. an alternative supplier   替代供货商，新的供货商

10. laser printer   激光打印机

11. in our possession   我方手头的货

12. a confusion of number   由于数字混淆

13. HERCULES Excavators   "大力神"牌挖掘机

14. we were soon inundated with orders   我方订单很快就应接不暇

15. fax machine   传真机
16. refund   v.   偿还，归还（款项）

    We will refund the invoice amount and inspection fee of the goods.
    我方将偿还发票金额和检验费。

    The seller promised to refund the buyer the full invoice value of the goods.
    卖方答应按货物发票金额的全额偿还买方。

    We will refund the transportation expenses.
    我们会退回运费。

17. replacement   n.   替代物，替代品

    We will send you the replacement as soon as possible.
    我们会尽快给你发寄去换货。

Exercises

I. Translate the following terms into English:

1. 短重
2. 调查
3. 理赔
4. 提出索赔
5. 赔偿
6. 质量较差
7. 违约
8. 迟交货物
9. 调查报告
10. 争端

II. Translate the following terms into Chinese:

1. entertain a claim
2. in conformity with
3. slip-up
4. replacement
5. color deviation
6. faulty goods
7. ask for compensation
8. the party suffered the loss
9. discrepancy
10. force majeure

III. Choose the best answer to complete the following sentences:

1. We suffered a great loss resulted _____ your oversight.
   A. in   B. to   C. from   D. for

2. We have lodge a claim _____ your company _____ the delay of the goods we ordered.
   A. with, on   B. against, for   C. against, on   D. with, against

3. The buyer made a _____ against us for the poor quality of the educational instruments.
   A. claim   B. communication
   C. discount   D. apology

4. In the case, we have to _____ the buyers the full invoice value of the goods.
   A. pay   B. grant   C. offer   D. refund

5. In view of the above, we regret that we have to return the defective goods to you for replacement_____ your expense.

  A. at   B. for   C. on   D. under

6. _____ this reason, we cannot accept your claim for a replacement.

  A. By   B. For   C. With   D. As to

7. Please return the wrongly delivered goods to us for _____ as soon as possible.

  A. claim   B. service   C. replacement   D. sale

8. We are extremely sorry about the mistake we have made. However, _____ you will realize was due to circumstances beyond our control.

  A. that   B. what   C. where   D. then

9. Your claim for the damage is to be _____ with the insurance company.

  A. met   B. filed   C. satisfied   D. compensate

10. All the claim terms were agreed _____ by the two companies.

  A. to   B. with   C. for   D. on

IV. Fill in the following blanks with the words and expressions in the box, change the form when necessary:

regret	investigation	convenience	complaint	evidence
claim	compensation	inconvenience	re-inspection	report

1. We regret to inform you that the goods shipped per S.S. Shunfeng arrived in such an unsatisfactory condition that we cannot but lodge a _____ against you.

2. We have been put to considerable _____ by the long delay in delivery.

3. After_____, we found that the quality of the goods was not in conformity with the contract stipulation.

4. On the basis of the CCIB's survey _____ we lodge you a claim for the short-weight.

5. Our _____ shows that damage was cause by improper packing. Therefore we have to refer this matter to you.

V. Translate the following sentences into Chinese:

1. We regret to know that you did not receive the ten sets of 6-hp Sailing outboards you wanted, and I guess both of us share the blame.

2. We are sorry to inform you that your claim can't be entertained as it is raised far beyond the time limit stipulated in the contract.

3. As the goods are inferior in quality, we will return the whole of the 100 cases and must ask you to replace them as soon as possible.

4. As stipulated in the contract, minor color deviation is permissible. That's why the case you brought up is still a normal phenomenon.

5. The only reasonable explanation for the damaged goods is that cartons have been crushed as a result of rough handling at the port of transshipment.

Unit 11　Complaints and Claims

VI. *Translate the following sentences into English*:

1. 经检查，我们发现短重 100 公斤。
2. 请退回 10 台问题打印机，费用由你方承担。
3. 我们希望你方设法弥补我们所蒙受的损失。
4. 我们别无选择，只能向你方提出索赔。
5. 我们将作出一切努力确保类似事件不再发生。

VII. *Simulated writing*:

Now you are required to write a letter to Evergreen Trading Co., Ltd. of Canada, to claim for short delivery and with the following details:

敬启者：
　　编号为 TK-223 号订单项下 GPS 导航仪（GPS navigator），由"永丰"号机动轮于 12 月 3 日运抵温哥华（Vancouver），提货时我们发现少了 10 箱货。轮船公司告诉我们只有 40 箱装上船。
　　由于短少数量较大，请在交付最后三个品种时，将这 10 箱货补交（make up a deficiency），并请你们核对一下，当初 50 箱货物是否一并在启运港全都装上了船。
　　请尽快电复。

Dear Sirs,

Yours faithfully,

Supplementary Reading

Claims in Foreign Trade

Disputes and Causes

The following are the possible causes of disputes between the parties of an Imp. & Exp. contract:

(1) The parties have different understandings of the formation of the contract, or different laws and common practices have different interpretations on the formation of the contract.

(2) The terms in the contract are not clear and definite, leading to different interpretations of the parties.

(3) Some events unforeseeable and beyond the parties' control have occurred during the execution of the contract, and the parties have different understandings of the effects of such events.

(4) The importer failed to fulfill his contractual obligations of making payment, timely establishing the L/C, duly taking delivery of goods, duly arranging shipment, etc.

(5) The exporter failed to fulfill his contractual obligations of making timely delivery of the contracted goods, duly arranging shipment, duly arranging insurance, timely presenting the prescribed documents, etc.

Breach of Contract and Its Effect

In British laws, contract terms are classified as either conditions（要件）or warranties（担保）and breach of contract is classified as either breach of conditions or breach of warranties.

American laws classify breach of contract into major breach of contract and minor breach of contract.

The Convention classifies breach of contract into fundamental breach and non-fundamental breach and stipulates that "a breach of contract committed by one of the parties is fundamental if it results in such detriment to the other party as substantially to deprive him of what he is entitled to expect under the contract, unless the party in breach did not foresee and a reasonable person of the same kind in the same circumstances would not have foreseen such a result." It also stipulates that on one party's fundamental breach of the contract, the other party is entitled to terminate the contract as well as to claim for compensation, otherwise, he can not terminate the contract but claim for compensation.

Claims and Settlement

Such request the affected party makes for compensation is called "claim."

The party held in breach of the contract and responsible for the losses or damages has to take measures to deal with the claim one way or another. His handling of the affected party's claim is called "settlement of claim."

There may be four ways used to settle disputes between the parties:

(1) Friendly Consultation（友好协商）

(2) Mediation（调解）

(3) Arbitration（仲裁）

(4) Litigation（诉讼）

When handling claims and disputes the following points should be observed:

(1) Generally speaking, the parties involved in a claim should first try to settle it through friendly negotiation. Failing to do so, they should then try to settle it by mediation or arbitration, and try to avoid litigation.

(2) Generally an Imp. & Exp. contract will stipulate a period for either party to file a claim. The claim should be filed within the time limit.

The party responsible for the claim should take immediate action to make investigations, send prompt reply to the affected party and solve the problem in accordance with relevant international laws, conventions, or common practices.

(3) The affected party should give a clear description of the loss or damage incurred, and also tells the reason why the other party should be responsible for the loss or damage. It is more convincing if the affected party can provide the relevant evidences, a certificate of inspection for example, to support his claim or request.

(4) Despite that dealing with a claim is no pleasant a matter, we should be calm and reasonable in negotiating for a settlement. Being rude and emotional does not help to resolve a dispute.

After-Class Study

(I) *List of Beach of Contract in Foreign Trade*

inferior quality　　劣质
defective goods　　有瑕疵的货物
improper packing　　不当包装
leakage　　渗漏
delayed shipment　　迟装
non-delivery　　提货不着
short delivery　　短交，缺交
short-shipped　　短装
short loading　　装运短重
short weight　　短重
short shipment　　短装，装载不足
short-invoice　　发票少开
short-paid　　少付
short-calculated　　少算
non-establishment of L/C on time　　没有按时开立信用证
damage during loading　　在装船时发生损坏
not adequately reinforced　　没有很好加固
the case was broken　　箱子破裂
the color unsatisfactory　　颜色不令人满意
not up to the usual standard　　不符合原来标准
the goods do not agree with the original sample　　发现货物与原样品不一致
the quality is not in conformity with the agreed specification　　质量与规格一致
sent the wrong goods　　发错了货

(II) *List of Some Commonly-Used Evidence of Claim in Foreign Trade*

inspection report　　检验报告
survey report　　调查报告
Inspection Certificate of Quality　　质量检验证书

| Inspection Certificate of Quantity | 数量检验证书 |
| Inspection Certificate of Weight | 重量检验证书 |

(III) *List of How to Express Claim in Foreign Trade*

accept a claim	同意索赔
reject a claim	拒绝索赔
settle a claim	理赔
waive our claim	放弃索赔
claim for	后接索赔原因或金额
claim on goods	后接索赔的货物对象
claim against somebody	向某人索赔

Chinese Version of Specimen Letters

<例信 1> 关于短装 MP5 的投诉

敬启者：

  我们已经收到 0630 号订单项下的单证，并已经提取经由维多利亚号机动轮运抵青岛的该批货物。

  检查货物后发现 16 号货箱内只装了 400 台三星牌 MP5，而装箱单和发票上均显示的是 500 台。

  这批货是我们为我方的三位大主顾订购的急需货物，因此务必将另外的 100 台三星牌 MP5 尽快从首尔空运过来，费用由你方负担。

  这已是一年以来短装我方订货。如果类似情况再有发生，我方将寻求新的供货商。

谨启

<例信 2> 关于短装 MP5（例信 1 的回函）

敬启者：

  感谢贵方 1 月 20 日来函。获悉贵方 0630 号订单项下的第 16 号货箱发生差错，深感抱歉。

  漏装的 100 只三星牌 MP5 已于今天早晨由南方航空公司出运，单证也已经寄给贵方。

  对于三次差错给贵方造成的不便我方深感歉意。我方会尽一切努力使错误不再发生。我方希望能够在将来的生意上为你方提供服务。

谨启

<例信 3> 关于激光打印机型号不对的投诉

敬启者：

  兹谈及今天上午收到的我方 0303 号订单项下的激光打印机。

开箱时我们发现货物不对。我方收到的是LP-868型而不是我方订购的LP-888型。请告知我方何时可以收到订货,我们的顾客有等候已达一个月以上者。除此之外,也请告知我方手头的激光打印机如何处置。

谨启

<例信4> 关于型号不对的激光打印机(例信3的回函)

敬启者:

感谢贵方9月10日来函告知激光打印机发错了货。

经过调查我方发现,由于数字混淆,包装中确实出现差错。我方已经安排立即出运正确货物。相关单证缮制妥当后将尽快寄给贵方。

贵方认为已收到的LP-868激光打印机有机会出售吗?如果有的话,不妨先搁置一阵子,若卖不出去再退货也不迟。无论如何,我们都会负担所有运费。

谨启

<例信5> 关于延迟出运两台"大力神"牌挖掘机的投诉

敬启者:

我方于去年11月份签署了一份在浦东建造一家大型学校的合同。由于要在今年3月份开土动工,我方立即向贵方订购了两台"大力神"牌挖掘机。

发订单时,你方承诺将在3月中旬运抵货物。今天已是3月18日,但挖掘机连影子都没有。3月底,我们破土动工时就得使用这两台机械。没有这两台机械,我们只能坐等。由此造成的直接经济损失和间接经济损失将逾百万。

请尽快告知我方贵方何时能出运货物。

盼望早日赐复。

谨启

<例信6> 关于延迟出运的两台"大力神"牌挖掘机(例信5的回函)

敬启者:

贵方3月18日的来函收悉,对贵方订购的两台"大力神"牌挖掘机的延迟发货深表歉意。我方竭尽全力立即出运货物,最迟在3月28日到货。

"大力神"牌挖掘机是我公司至今生产出的最成功的产品。自去年在香港建筑机械展览会首次亮相即大获成功后,订单就应接不暇。贵方订单11月收悉,若按当时的交货时间表得等到4月份才可能交货。尽管如此,我方仍将交货日期提前到3月。我方2月份的生产由于一些专门部件迟到而影响了进度,这也是我方延迟发货的主要原因。

请贵方不厌其烦再等几天。相信"大力神"牌挖掘机将足以弥补贵方的受损进度。

谨启

<例信7> 关于低质传真机的索赔

敬启者:

就我记忆所及,这是我第一次对你方所供应的办公用品—传真机提出索赔。

上周收到的268号订单项下传真机的品质实在是太差了，没有办法传真信函。

由于这批货物对我方毫无用处，我方向贵方提出3000美元的损失赔偿，包括发票金额和检验费用。希望贵方能及时理赔，一俟贵方理赔，我方将把货物退还贵方，相关费用由贵方负担。

随信附上（国家质量监督检验检疫总局）中国商检局的商检报告一份，作为我方索赔的依据。

如果问题能顺利解决，我们将来还会继续向贵方订货。

谨启

<例信8> 关于低质传真机（例信7的回函）

敬启者：

你来信指出传真机的品质问题堪忧，这点我完全同意。我们已经打电话给制造商调查了你方的索赔事件。这完全是由于厂家仓库工作人员失误所致。

但我方建议的解决方式是，我方立即发运质量保证的替代物。至于贵方已经收到的劣质货，请退还，相关费用由我方负责。若同意上述意见，请电传告知我方。

但愿我方的处理意见能使贵方满意，并期望得到贵方更多的订单。

谨启

Unit 12　Agency

Learning Aims

After you finish learning this unit, you are requested to:
(1) know about agents and types of agents;
(2) know the main clauses in an agency agreement;
(3) know how to write an application for sales agency and how to answer such application letters;
(4) know how entrust a client with sole agency.

Background Knowledge

(I) *About Agency*

Agency is a kind of common practice in foreign trade. It is a means of business in which an agent does buying and selling for his principal abroad. For example, a seller authorizes a person or a firm as a selling agent to act for him, in order to sell his products to some middlemen or other clients. An agent obtains a commission at certain percentage of sales as the remuneration for his service. It is more convenient and economical for some firms of smaller scale to do their business through some agencies abroad.

There are mainly two types of agents i.e., general agent and sole agent.

A general agent may be a firm or a person who acts under instructions from his principal to sell or buy on the best terms obtainable, charging a commission under an agreement concerned.

A sole agent may be a firm or a person who acts exclusively for one foreign principal with exclusive agency rights to sell certain kinds of commodities in a certain area contracted between the two parties.

(II) *Relations between Principal and Agent*

The relation between the principal and the agent is a legal one through signing a contract or an agreement, which is a relationship of rights and duties. In commercial practice, it is a must for the principal to know clearly about the relevant laws and regulations of the country concerned prior to choosing an agent and signing of the contract because the word "agent" or "agency" may have different meaning in different countries.

The following principles concerning the relationship between the principal and the agent are universally accepted.

(1) The relationship between a principal and an agent is one in which the agent is being entrusted by the former to buy or sell on his behalf. The agent himself is not involved as one party in a transaction;

(2) Therefore, the agent is not entitled to sign his own name on any such contract of buying or selling;

(3) The agent needn't share the risks of business;

(4) The agent has no right, either, to share any profit from a transaction. What he can get is but a prearranged commission as his remuneration for his work done. Usually, the commission rate varies 5% to 10%.

Writing Tips

When you are ready to act as an agent for a foreign firm, you will write to ask for sole agent. The following elements should be included:

(5) Express your wishes to represent as their sole agent;

(6) State why you think an agent is needed;

(7) Give out your advantages serving as an agent;

(8) What terms you can accept.

If you are a firm who are seeking for sole agent to expand your business, the letter should be written like this:

(1) Why you want to appoint an agent;

(2) Why you choose this company to represent for you;

(3) The terms of agency you can provide.

Sentence Patterns & Examples

【Pattern 1】be conversant with　　懂得，熟谙

After years of business in this trade, he is conversant with the sources of supplies.
在这个行当做了几年之后，他对货源情况非常了解了。

Acting as an import agent for more than twenty years, he is fully conversant with the import rules.
做了20多年的进口代理，他熟谙进口规则。

【Pattern 2】commit oneself to　　答应，承诺；使自己负有责任

We are heavily committed now and could not accept any new orders.
我们现在承约过多，不能接受新订单了。

You commit yourselves to help us promote the sale of this new product.
你们承诺帮助我们推销新产品的。

【Pattern 3】in particular　　特别，尤其

We manufacture carpets of various patterns in wool, silk, cotton and fabric, among which the hand-made woollen ones are in particular of great fame.
我们生产毛织、丝织、棉织以及化纤的各式地毯，其中手工编织的毛地毯特别出名。

Please advise us your price and delivery terms of this article, the payment term in particular.
请告诉我方该货品的价格和交货条件，特别是付款方式。

【Pattern 4】settle the account, clear the account　　结清款项

We were under the impression that payment was the end of this month, when we would have had no difficulty in settling our account.
我公司本以为直到月底才到付款期，届时我们付清款项是没有问题的。

Not having received any reply to our letter of 15 June requesting settlement of your account, we are writing again to remind you that amount still owing is USD 5,800.
我公司于6月15日去函催告付款，迄今未获复函，故特此再催告你方应付账款为5,800美元。

【Pattern 5】draft　　起草；草案

We will draft a sole agency agreement for you to confirm.

我方将起草一份独家代理协议,请你方确认。
We are pleased to receive the draft agreement stating the terms and conditions of the agency.
很高兴收到贵方关于代理条款的代理协议草案。

【Pattern 6】 entitle sb. to a discount; give / allow / offer sb. a discount   给某人打折

This coupon will entitle you to a 20% discount on any purchase of our products.
使用此券购买任何我公司的产品,将享受八折的优惠。

We will give you 10% discount in view of the previous substantial orders.
鉴于过去的大量订购,我公司将给予贵方10%的折扣。

【Pattern 7】 renew   展期;更新;恢复

We can renew the agreement of agency on its expiry.
我们可以再代理协议期满时续订。

I've come again to renew our sole agency agreement for another 5 years.
我们这次再访是想把我们之间的独家代理协议延长5年。

【Pattern 8】 connection   联系;客户;生意关系

We have established business connection with them.
我们和他们建立了业务关系。

We have many connections all over the world.
我们在世界各地都有业务往来客户。

【Pattern 9】 represent   代理,代表

Our firm is represented by ABC Company in Japan.
本公司在日本的代理商是ABC公司。

We are the agent for Textiles in this city and wish to represent another firm.
我们是本市纺织品的代理人,愿意为其他公司代理。

【Pattern 10】 put into   投入生产(使用)

More buses are to be put into service.
更多的公共汽车将投入使用。

A variety of new machines have been put into production.
有好些新机器投产了。

Specimen Letters

<Letter 1> Asking to be Sole Agent

Dear Sirs,

    We would like to inform you that we act on a sole agency basis for[1] a number of manufacturers[2].

    We specialize in finished cotton goods for the European market: Our activities cover all types of household³ linen⁴. Until now, we have been working with your textiles department and our collaboration⁵ has proved to be mutually beneficial. Please refer to⁶ them for any information regarding our company.

We are very interested in an exclusive arrangement with your factory for the promotion of your products in Europe.

We look forward to your early reply.

Yours faithfully,

<Letter 2> Rejecting to be Sole Agent

Thank you for your letter of 15 September suggesting that we grant⁷ you a sole agency for our household linens. I regret to say that, at this stage, such an arrangement would be rather premature⁸. We would, however, be willing to engage in⁹ a trial collaboration with you company to see how the arrangement works.

It would be necessary for you to test the market for our products at your end. You would also have to build up a much larger turnover to justify¹⁰ a sole agency.

We enclose price lists covering all the products you are interested in and look forward to hearing from you soon.

Yours truly,

<Letter 3> Agreeing to be Sole Agent

Dear Sirs,

Thank you for your letter of 18 May proposing a sole agency for our office machines.

We have examined our long and, I must say, mutually beneficial collaboration. We would be very pleased to entrust you with the sole agency for Canada.

We have drawn up¹¹ a draft agreement that is enclosed. Please examine the detailed terms and conditions and let us know whether they meet with your approval.

On a personal note, I must say that I am delighted that we are probably going to strengthen our relationship. I have very pleasant memories of my last visit to Toronto when you entertained¹² me so delightful. I look forward to reciprocating¹³ on your next visit to Shanghai.

Yours sincerely,

<Letter 4> Looking for Agent

Dear Sirs,

Our company manufactures a range of¹⁴ printing presses that are used successfully by companies in over 20 countries. A product specification brochure is enclosed.

We are considering expanding¹⁵ our products to new markets and we would appreciate you assistance. In particular¹⁶, we would like to identify the best agents who are currently serving the printing industry in your region. We are looking for organizations which conduct their business in a truly professional[17] manner. They must be fully conversant with the technical side of the printing industry and have a comprehensive understanding of all the features of the lines they represent.

We would be very grateful if you could take a few moments to send us the names of three or four organizations that match our requirements. We shall then contact them to explore the possibility of establishing a mutually acceptable business relationship. Thank you very much for your time and consideration in this matter.

Yours faithfully,

<Letter 5> Welcoming the New Agent

Dear Sirs,

I would like to welcome you to our organization.

We are very pleased to have you on our team. I know that you will be equally proud of our products. Our European sales Representative, Antoine Gerin, will be in touch with you at regular intervals[18].

Please feel free to call him any time you have a problem. If I can ever be of service, please call me. I am planning a trip to France next month, and I am looking forward to meeting you.

In the meantime[19], the best of luck with our product line.

Yours truly,

Notes

1. on a basis of   以……为基础
   Rates of work are calculated on a weekly basis.
   工资是以周为计算基准的。
   Your attention should be drawn to the fact that the price we quote is on FAS Seattle basis instead of on FOB Seattle basis.
   请贵方注意，我们所报的价格是西雅图 FAS 价而不是西雅图离岸价。

2. manufacturer   制造商
   Another manufacturer has bitten the dust.
   又有一家厂商倒闭了。
   Prices are laid down by the manufacturer.
   价格是由厂商制定的。

3. household   家庭的，家用的
   household electric appliance   家用电器
   household setout   家用设备
   household wares   家用器具

Unit 12　Agency

　　She runs the household herself.
　　她亲自操持家务。

　　Telephone is now a household necessity.
　　现在电话是一种家庭必需品。

4. linen　　亚麻布

　　unbleached linen　　本色的亚麻布

　　This linen launders well.
　　这亚麻布经洗。

　　The worker is starching the linen.
　　这名工人正在给亚麻布上浆。

5. collaboration　　合作　协作

　　Our collaboration is over.
　　我们的合作结束了。

　　This collaboration is important because it brings different perspectives.
　　这种协作是十分重要的，因为它给我们带来了各种发展前景。

6. refer to　　提到，参考

　　Don't refer to the matter again.
　　不要再提这件事了。

　　You should refer to the dictionary.
　　你应该查查字典。

　　I refered to your invoice numbered 1234.
　　我查阅了你们编号为 1234 的发票。

7. grant　　授予；允许；承认

　　We regret our inability grant your request.
　　我们很遗憾不能同意您的要求

　　I grant that your explanation is reasonable.
　　我承认你的解释是合理的。

　　Congress may not grant titles of nobility.
　　国会可以不授予贵族的头衔

8. premature　　不成熟的；比预期早的

　　Though we intend to make investment in your country, we think premature to take any action now.
　　虽然我们打算在贵国投资，但觉得现在采取行动时机还不成熟。

　　The baby was four weeks premature.
　　那个婴儿早产了 4 星期。

9. engage in　　参加　从事　忙于

　　engage sb in conversation　　使某人参加谈话

　　engage sb in　　让某人从事于

　　engage oneself in　　正做着；从事于

Much of the behavior we engage in is, in fact, very predictable.
我们做出的许多行为实际上在很大程度上都是可以预测的。

The State applies a system of permit to the distribution of publications. Without a permit, no entity or individual may engage in the activity of distributing publications.
国家实行出版物发行许可制度，未经许可，任何单位和个人不得从事出版物发行活动。

10. justify　　证明合法；证明……是正当的；替……辩护

But the cost of the recent financial crisis makes that policy hard to justify.
但是最近的金融危机消耗让这个政策难以实行。

By the president's own account, health reform is his proudest achievement, one that would justify his election on its own.
对总统自己而言，医疗改革是他最自豪的成功，这会证明他的当选当之无愧。

11. draw up　　草拟，起草；停住；使靠近

We must draw up a contract.
我们必须起草一份合同。

He has drawn up a project for developing new market in Europe.
他起草了一个开发欧洲新市场的计划。

12. entertain　　v.　　招待

We intend to entertain guests with beef.
我们打算用牛肉来招待客人。

You should learn how to entertain yourself and enjoy your life.
你应该学会如何娱乐自己，享受你的生活。

13. reciprocate　　vt.　　报答；互换；互给
　　　　　　　　　vi.　　往复运动；互换；酬答；互给

I hope I can reciprocate your hospitality some time.
我希望下次能回报你的热情款待。

You have to do something first then others will do it too. You should perform a kind act first then others will reciprocate .
你必须先去做一件事情，别人才会跟着做。你先要对别人作出善意的举动，别人才会回报你。

14. a range of　　一系列；一些；一套
　　　a wide range of　　范围广泛的；一连串的；种类繁多；大范围的
　　　a broad range of　　　提供广泛的
　　　a remark range of　　大量的
　　　a complete range of specifications　　规格齐全
　　　a wide range of interest　　广泛的兴趣

Moreover, under normal circumstances, monetary policy can boost growth in a range of ways.
此外，在正常情况下，货币政策可以从很多方面促进增长。

Since then, melamine has been found in a range of products, including milk, eggs and fish feed.
其后，在一系列的产品中都发现了三聚氰胺，包括牛奶、鸡蛋和鱼饲料。

Unit 12 Agency

15. expand   *vt.*   扩张；使膨胀；详述
                   vi.   发展；张开，展开

     auto expand   自动扩展
     expand to   扩大为；扩展到
     expand employment   扩大就业面

     I hope to expand our exchanges and cooperation.
     我希望扩大我们彼此的交流与合作。

     In place of consumption and housing, the report says, business investment will expand.
     报告称，商业投资的扩张将取代消费和住房的扩张。

16. in particular   尤其，特别

     The risk is that Europe will get hit harder, in particular its financial system.
     风险在于，欧洲将遭受更严重的冲击，特别是欧洲的金融体系。

     There is also a big question about what happens if the Chinese market in particular goes into decline.
     还有一个大问题是，如果海外市场——特别是中国市场——出现下滑将会发生什么？

17. professional   *adj.*   专业的；职业的；职业性的
                       n.   专业人员；职业运动员

     You can, of course, get professional help, but I am not sure if I recommend it.
     当然，你还可以寻求专业帮助，但我拿不准自己是否该建议你这么做。

     Her ability to reach a large audience is the result of hard work and professional dedication.
     她所以能赢得大批观众，乃是刻苦工作和一心钻研业务的结果。

18. interval   *n.*   间隔；间距；幕间休息

     After a decent interval, he could then return to the Kremlin as president.
     一段时间之后，他又能以总统身份体面地回到克里姆林。

     "I love music," he told Bertha in interval.
     "我喜欢音乐。"幕间休息时他对伯莎说。

19. in the meantime   在……期间；同时

     In the meantime, one thing is getting harder.
     与此同时，有一件事变得更难了。

     In the mean time, US service exports to China also have recorded fast development.
     同时，美国对华服务贸易也在迅速发展。

Exercises

I. *Translate the following terms into English*:

1. 代理
2. 营销，买卖
3. 提议，建议
4. 资信状况
5. 委托，托付
6. 领土，版图，地域
7. 鉴于
8. 有利可图的

9. 佣金

10. 承担，担任，许诺，保证

II. Translate the following terms into Chinese:

1. principal
2. general agent
3. turnover
4. wholesaler
5. indenter
6. experienced and proficient in
7. the initial stage
8. draft an agreement
9. praiseworthy
10. heretofore

III. Choose the best answer to complete the following sentences:

1. We are _____ agents for a number of British publishers.
   A. acting   B. acting as   C. acting in   D. acting of

2. I am here today to _____ the sole agency of your products in our local market.
   A. ask for   B. apply for   C. propose   D. offer

3. We shall be glad to offer you _____ for the sale of our products in China.
   A. the sole agent   B. a sole agent   C. sole agency   D. a sole agency

4. We have decided to _____ the sole agency for our wooden toys in America.
   A. entrust you with   B. entrust you to
   C. give you of   D. give you for

5. Please advise us whether the attached Sole Agency Agreement _____ your approval.
   A. meets on   B. meets with   C. satisfied on   D. I satisfied with

6. _____ satisfactory terms could be arranged, I would _____ to guarantee payment of all amounts due on orders placed through me.
   A. Provided…prepare   B. Providing…prepare
   C. Provided…be prepared   D. Providing…be prepared

7. We are in a position to take good care of your import business as a _____.
   A. buy agency   B. buying agency
   C. buy agent   D. buying agent

8. When opportunity matures, we will consider _____ you our exclusive agent for the U.S.
   A. appoint   B. approving   C. making   D. proposing

9. We wonder whether we may _____ a long term agency contract with you.
   A. write   B. conclude   C. make   D. meet

10. The agency agreement was _____ with great care and we have found no loopholes in it.
    A. made out   B. signed   C. written   D. meet

IV. Fill in the following blanks of each sentence, pay attention to first letter of each word has been given:

1. With your excellent connections, we believe it will be possible to p_____ the sale of our products in your t_____.

2. We accept your terms and c_____ as set out in the d_____ agency agreement and

Unit 12 Agency

look forward to a happy and successful relationship with you.

3. We thank you for o_____ us the agency in China for your products and a_____ the confidence you have placed in us.

4. We should be glad if you would c_____ our a_____ to act as agents for the sale of your products.

5. There is a considerable d_____ for your products here, and we would do our utmost to push the sale on your behalf if you are disposed to entertain our c_____ rate proposal.

V. Translate the following sentences into Chinese:

6. We write to offer our services as your agent in China.

7. We wish to know if you could appoint us as your agent for the sale of your wooden toys.

8. If you could agree to our terms, we would appoint you as our sole agent.

9. Unless you increase the turnover we can hardly appoint you as our sole agent.

10. We usually work on a 5% commission.

VI. Translate the following sentences into English:

1. 我方写信是为请求做你方在中国的代理。
2. 感谢你方 5 月 5 日来函，欣知你方愿意做我方的独家代理。
3. 我们认为在目前这个阶段讨论代理事宜时机尚不成熟。
4. 我们保证不销售其他厂商的同类竞争产品。
5. 以上所开价格包括你方 5%的佣金。

VII. Simulated writing:

Write a letter on behalf of Bright Trading Co., to China National Import & Export Co., according to the following particulars:

敬启者：
　　我们很高兴从中国驻美国大使馆参赞处获悉贵公司的名称和地址，现冒昧去函介绍我方公司。
　　我们现在是独家代理商，专营家用装饰器皿我们一直与上海工艺品公司保持业务联系，至今已有 10 年，合作关系令双方十分满意。你们也可以向他们了解我们的情况。
　　我们非常希望成为贵公司瓷器商品在美国纽约的独家代理。
　　盼早日回复。

　　　　　　　　　　　　　　　　　　　　　　　　　　　　谨启

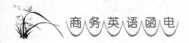

Dear Sirs,

Yours faithfully,

Supplementary Reading

销售代理协议书
Sales Agency Agreement

第一条 约因

1. Consideration

制造商姓名_____，其公司法定地址_____（简称制造商），同意将下列产品_____（简称产品）的独家代理权授予代理人（简称代理人），代理人姓名_____，其公司法定地址_____。

Name of the manufacturer_____, with its legal address at_____ (hereinafter called "Manufacturer"), agrees to appoint the exclusive agency of following products_____(hereinafter called "product") to the agent(hereinafter called "Agent") named_____ with his legal address at_____.

代理人优先在下列指定地区（简称地区）推销新产品：_____。

Agent has the priority to promote new products in the Territory herein defined (hereinafter called as "Territory"):_____.

第二条 代理人的职责

2. Duties of Agent

代理人应在该地区拓展用户，代理人应向制造商转送接收到的报价和订单。代理人无权代表制造商签订任何具有约束的合约。代理人应把制造商规定的销售条款（包括装运期和付款）对用户解释。制造商可不受任何约束的拒绝由代理人转送的任何询价及订单。

Agent shall develop customers in the Territory, and transmit offers and orders he receives to the manufacturer. The agent shall not be entitled to sign any binding contracts on behalf of the manufacturer. The agent shall explain sales provisions stipulated by the manufacturer to customers. And the manufacturer may at his own decision refuse any price inquiry or order transmitted by the agent.

第三条 代理业务的职责范围
3. Due Capacity of the Agent

代理人是_____市场的全权代理，应收集信息，争取用户，尽力促进产品的销售。代理人应精通所推销该产品的技术性能。代理所得佣金应包括为促成销售所需费用。

The agent is the general agent in _____, and shall collect information, obtain customers, and promote the sales of products at his best. The agent shall be expert at the technology and performance of the products in promotion. The agency commission shall include charges needed to promote sales.

第四条 广告和展览会
4. Advertisement and Exhibition

为促进产品在该地区的销售，代理人应刊登一切必要的广告并支付广告费用。凡参加展销会需经双方事先商议后办理。

In order to promote sales of the products in the Territory, the agent shall put on necessary advertisements at his own expense. And the attendance of any exhibition shall be conducted after mutual negotiation.

第五条 代理人对用户的财务责任
5. Financial Duties of the Agent to Customers

代理人应采取适当方式了解当地订货人的支付能力并协助制造商收回应付货款。通常的索款及协助收回应付货款的开支应由制造商负担。

未经同意，代理人无权也无义务以制造商的名义接受付款。

The agent shall get to know the local orderers' payment ability and help the manufacturer to collect due payment in proper manners. Charges rising out of claims and aid collection of payment usually shall be borne by the manufacturer.

The agent shall not be entitled and obliged to accept payment on behalf of the manufacturer without permission.

第六条 用户的意见、代理人的作用
6. Customer Complaint and the Function of the Agent

代理人有权接受用户对产品的意见和申诉，及时通知制造商并关注制造商的切身利益为宜。

The agent shall be entitled to accept customers' complaint on the products, immediately inform the manufacturer, and shall take care of vital interest of the manufacturer.

第七条 向制造商不断提供信息
7. Constant Information Supply to the Manufacturer

代理人应尽力向制造商提供商品的市场和竞争等方面的信息，每 4 个月需向制造商寄

送工作报告。

The agent shall supply information on the market and competition, etc. of the products to the manufacturer at his best and shall deliver working report to the manufacturer every four months.

第八条 保证不竞争
8. Guarantee of Non-competition

代理人不应与制造商或帮助他人与制造商竞争，代理人更不应制造代理产品或类似于代销的产品，也不应从与制造商竞争的任何企业中获利。同时，代理人不应代理或销售与代理产品相同或类似的（不论是新的或旧的）任何产品。

The agent shall not compete with or help others to compete with the manufacturer. And the agent shall not further manufacture product hereunder or those similar to product hereunder, nor benefit from any enterprise in competition with the manufacturer. Meanwhile, the agent shall not act as an agent of and sell any product the same with or similar to the product hereunder, whether new or old.

此合约一经生效，代理人应将与其他企业签订有约束性的协议告知制造商。代理人在进行其他活动时，决不能忽视其对制造商承担的义务而影响任务的完成。

Immediately after this contract comes into effect, the agent shall inform the manufacturer of binding contracts signed by and between the agent and any enterprise. When conducting other activities, the agent shall not neglect his duty to the manufacturer and be prevented from completing his task.

本协议规定在此协议终止后的 5 年内，代理人不能生产和销售同类产品予以竞争，本协议终止后的 1 年内，代理人也不能代理其他类似产品，予以竞争。

This contract stipulates that within 5 years after the termination of this contract, the agent shall not manufacturer and sell products of the same kind with the product hereunder for competition. Within 1 year after the termination of this contract, the agent shall not act as agent of other similar products in competition.

所有产品设计和说明均属制造商所有，代理人应在协议终止时归还给制造商。

All of the designs and specifications of the product hereunder shall be the sole properties of the manufacturer, and the agent shall return them to the manufacturer after the termination of this contract.

第九条 保密
9. Secrecy

代理人在协议有效期内或协议终止后，不得泄露制造商的商业机密，也不得将该机密超越协议范围使用。

In the duration of this contract or after the termination of contract, this the agent shall not let out the manufacturer's commercial secret and shall not use the commercial secret beyond the contracted scope.

第十条 分包代理
10. Sub-agent

代理人事先经制造商同意后可聘用分包代理人，代理人应对该分包代理人的活动负全部责任。

The agent may employ a sub-agent after approved by the manufacturer and shall be responsible for all the activities of the said sub-agent.

第十一条　工业产权的侵犯
11. Infringement of Industrial Property Rights

代理人应视察市场，如发现第三方侵犯制造商的工业产权或有损于制造商利益的任何非法行为，代理人应据实向制造商报告。代理人应尽最大努力并按照制造商的指示，帮助制造商使其不受这类行为的侵害，制造商将承担正常代理活动以外的此类费用。

The agent shall inspect the market and shall report the fact to the manufacturer in case of any infringement by the third party of the manufacturer's industrial property rights or any illegal act impairing the manufacturing interest. The agent shall at his best help to indemnify and hold the manufacturer harmless from said acts in accordance with the instruction of the manufacturer, and charges thus occurred excluding those for the normal agent activities shall be borne by the manufacturer.

第十二条　代理人独家销售权的范围
12. Scope of the Agent's Exclusive Sales Rights

制造商不得同意他人在该地区取得代理或销售协议产品的权力。制造商应把其收到的直接来自该地区用户的订单通知代理人。代理人有权按第十五条规定获得该订单的佣金。

The manufacturer shall not permit any other person to obtain the right of acting as agent for or selling the contracted products in the Territory. The manufacturer shall inform the agent of the orders he receives directly from the customers in the Territory. The agent shall be entitled to the commission of these orders under Article 15.

第十三条　向代理人不断提供信息
13. Constant Information Supply to the Agent

为促进代理活动，制造商应向代理人提供包括销售情况、价目表、技术文件和广告资料等一切必要的信息。制造商应将产品价格、销售情况或付款方式的任何变化及时通知代理人。

In order to promote agency, the manufacturer shall supply the agent with any and all necessary information including sales condition, price list, technical documents, advertising materials and so on. The manufacturer shall notify the agent in time of any change in price, sales condition or terms of payment.

第十四条　技术帮助
14. Technical Assistance

制造商应帮助代理人的雇员获得代理产品的技术知识。代理人应支付其雇员往返交通费及工资，制造商应提供食宿。

The manufacturer shall help employees of the agent to obtain technical knowledge of the products hereunder. The agent shall pay his employeestransportation fees and salaries and the manufacturer shall provide accommodations.

第十五条　佣金额
15. Commission Rate

代理人的佣金以每次售出并签字的协议产品为基础，其收佣百分比如下：
_____美元按_____%收佣
_____美元按_____%收佣

Commission for the agent shall be calculated on the basis of the sold products hereunder with signature per time at a commission rate as follows:
_____% Commission rate for_____ USD
_____% Commission rate for_____ USD

第十六条　平分佣金
16. Equal Division of Commission

两个不同地区的两个代理人为争取订单都作出极大努力，当订单于某一代理人所在地，而供货之制造厂位于另一代理人所在地时，则佣金由两个代理人平均分配。

Commission shall be divided equally between agents of two different territories provided that both agents have made great efforts in striving for orders, and that the order is made out in one territory in question while the supplying manufacturer plant is located in the other territory in question.

第十七条　计算佣金的方法
17. Calculating Method of Commission

佣金以发票金额计算，任何附加费用如包装费、运输费、保险费、海关税或由进口国家征收的关税等应另开发票。

Commission shall be calculated based on the invoice value. And additional invoices shall be drawn for any additional charges such as packing fees, transportation fees, insurance fees, duty and tax levied by the import country.

第十八条　佣金的索取权
18. Claim for Commission

代理人有权根据每次用户购货所支付的货款按比例收取佣金。如用户没有支付全部货款，则根据制造商实收货款按比例收取佣金，若由于制造商的原因用户拒付货款，则不在此限。

The agent shall be entitled to commission proportionally in accordance with payment by customers each time. If customers do not make the whole payment, commission shall be charged proportionally in accordance with the real payment collected by the manufacturer, excluding to the extent that customers refuse to pay due to the manufacturer.

第十九条　支付佣金的时间
19. Time for Paying Commission

制造商每季度应向代理人说明佣金数额和支付佣金，制造商在收到货款后，应在30天内支付佣金。

The manufacturer shall specify the amount of commission and pay such commission to the agent. And the manufacturer shall pay commission within 30 days after the receipt of payment by customers.

第二十条 支付佣金的货币
20. Currency of Commission

佣金按成交的货币来计算和支付。

Commission shall be calculated and paid in the currency of bargain.

第二十一条 排除其他报酬
21. Exclusion of Other Remuneration

代理人在完成本协议之义务时所发生的全部费用,除非另有允诺,应按第十九条之规定支付佣金。

As to charges arising out of the performance of the duties of this contract by the agent, commission shall be paid in accordance with provisions as stipulated in Article 19 unless otherwise promised.

第二十二条 协议期限
22. Duration of Contract

本协议在双方签字后生效,协议执行1年后,一方提前3个月通知可终止协议。如协议不在该日终止,可提前3个月通知,于下1年的12月30日终止。

This contract shall come into effect after both parties have their hands hereupon, may be terminated by any party with a notice three months in advance one year after the execution of this contract, failing which the contract may be terminated on December 30 of the following year with a notice three months in advance.

第二十三条 提前终止
23. Termination in Advance

如第二十二条规定,任何一方都无权提前终止本协议。除非遵照适用的_____法律具有充分说服力的理由方能终止本协议。

Neither party shall be entitled to terminate this contract in advance as stipulated in Article 22, unless otherwise the party has convincing reasons for termination in accordance with the applying law of _____.

第二十四条 文件的归还
24. Return of Documents

协议期满时,代理人应将第十三条中所述及的由制造商提供的全部广告资料及所有文件归还给制造商。

Upon the expiry of this contract, the agent shall return to the manufacturer all the advertising materials and documents supplied by the manufacturer as mentioned in Article 13.

第二十五条　存货的退回
25. Return of Stock

协议期满时，代理人若储有代理产品和备件，应按制造商指示退回，费用由制造商负担。

Upon the expiry of this contract, the agent shall return the products and spare parts, if any at stock, to the manufacturer in accordance with the manufacturer's instruction at the manufacturer's expense.

第二十六条　未完之商务
26. Unfinished Business

协议到期时，由代理人提出终止但在协议期满后又执行协议，应按第十五款支付代理人佣金。代理人届时仍应承担履行协议义务之职责。

Commission shall be paid to the agent in accordance with Article 15. Upon the expiry of this contract in case the agent applies for termination upon the expiry of this contract but continues to perform this contract after its expiry. The agent shall still undertake duties to perform this contract.

第二十七条　赔偿
27. Compensations

协议因一方违约而终止外，由于协议终止或未能重新签约，则不予赔偿。

Compensations shall not be paid due to the termination hereof or failure to renew a contract except for termination due to the breach of contract by one party hereof.

第二十八条　适用法律
28. Applicable Laws

本协议适用于制造商总部＿＿＿＿＿＿＿＿＿＿＿＿所在国之现行法律。

This contract shall apply to the existing laws of the country where the manufacturer's head office locates.

第二十九条　仲裁
29. Arbitration

因执行本协议而发生的任何争执应根据＿＿＿＿＿＿的法律＿＿＿＿＿＿仲裁解决。投诉方和被投诉方应各指定一名仲裁员，双方应提名一位公证人。

如两名仲裁员在30天内未能就提名一位主席达成协议，仲裁应有权提名第三名仲裁员为主席。仲裁所作出的裁决是终局的，对双方均有约束力。

Any and all disputes arising out of the execution of this contract shall be settled through ＿＿＿＿＿＿arbitration in accordance with laws of ＿＿＿＿＿. Both the complainant and respondent shall designate one arbitrator respectively and one notary mutually.

If two arbitrators hereof cannot reach an agreement on the nomination of a president within 30 days, the arbitration shall be entitled to nominate a third party as president. The award made by arbitration shall be final and binding upon both parties.

第三十条　变更
30. Modifications

本协议的变更或附加条款，应以书面形式为准。

Any modification or addition to this contract shall be valid in written form.

第三十一条　禁止转让
31. Non-transfer

本协议未经事先协商不得转让。

This contract shall not be transferred without prior negotiation.

第三十二条　留置权
32. Lien

代理人对制造商的财产无留置权。

The agent shall not be entitled to lien upon the property of the manufacturer.

第三十三条　无效条款
33. Void and Null

如协议中的一条或一条以上的条款无效，协议其余条款仍然有效。

In case one or more articles hereof are void and null, the other articles shall remain valid.

本协议一式二份，双方各执一份。

This contract is made out in duplicated and each party holds one copy.

制造商：	代理人：
签署地：_____	签署地：_____
日期：_____	日期：_____
董事长：_____	总裁：_____
Manufacturer:	Agent:
Signed at:_____	Signed at:_____
Date:_____	Date:_____
Chairman of Board:_____	President:_____

After-Class Study

Well-known Banks in the World

阿比国民银行　　　Abbey National　　英国
巴克莱银行　　　Barclays Bank PLC.　　英国

巴黎国民银行　　Banque Nationale de Paris　　法国
巴西银行　　Banco Do Brasil　　巴西
大和银行　　Daiwa Bank　　日本
大通曼哈顿银行　　Chase Manhattan Bank　　美国
德累斯顿银行　　Dresdner Bank　　德国
德意志银行　　Deutsche Bank　　德国
第一劝业银行　　Dai-Ichi Kangyo Bank　　日本
第一洲际银行　　First Interstate Bancorp　　美国
东海银行　　Tokai Bank　　日本
东京银行　　Bank of Tokyo　　日本
都灵圣保罗银行　　Istituto Bancario SanPaolo Di Torino　　意大利
多伦多自治领银行　　Toronto-Dominion Bank　　加拿大
富士银行　　Fuji Bank　　日本
国民劳动银行　　Banca Nazionale del Lavoro　　意大利
国民西敏寺银行　　National Westminster Bank PLC.　　英国
荷兰农业合作社中央银行　　Cooperatieve Centrale Raifferssen-Boerenleenbank　　荷兰
荷兰通用银行　　Algemene Bank Nederland　　荷兰
花旗银行　　Citibank　　美国
汉华实业银行　　Manufacturers Hanover Corp.　　美国
汇丰银行　　Hongkong and Shanghai Banking Corp.　　中国香港地区
加拿大帝国商业银行　　Canadian Imperial Bank of Commerce　　加拿大
加拿大皇家银行　　Royal Bank of Canada　　加拿大
劳埃德银行　　Lloyds Bank PLC.　　英国
里昂信贷银行　　Credit Lyonnais　　法国
伦巴省储蓄银行　　Cassa Di Risparmio Delle Provincie Lombarde　　意大利
梅隆国民银行　　Mellon National Corp.　　美国
美洲银行（全称"美洲银行国民信托储蓄会"）
Bank America Corp("Bank of America National Trust and Savings Associations")　　美国
米兰银行　　Midland Bank　　英国
摩根保证信托银行　　Morgan Guaranty Trust Corp. of New York　　美国
纽约化学银行　　Chemical New York Corp.　　美国
纽约银行家信托公司　　Bankers Trust New York Corp.　　美国
农业信贷国民银行　　de Caisse Nationale Credit Agricole　　法国
日本兴业银行　　Industrial Bank of Japan　　日本
瑞士联合银行　　Union Bank of Switzerland　　瑞士
瑞士信贷银行　　Credit Suisse　　瑞士
瑞士银行公司　　Swiss Bank Corp.　　瑞士
三和银行　　Sanwa Bank　　日本

三井银行	Mitsui Bank	日本
三菱银行	Mitsubishi Bank	日本
太平洋安全银行	Security Pacific Corp	美国
西德意志地方银行	Westdeutsche Landesbank Girozentrale	德国
西太平洋银行公司	Westpac Banking Corp.	澳大利亚
西亚那银行	Monte Dei Paschi Di Siena	意大利
意大利商业银行	Banca Commerciale Italiana	意大利
意大利信贷银行	Credito Italiano	意大利
芝加哥第一国民银行	First Chicago Corp.	美国
中国银行	Bank of China	中国
住友信托银行	Sumitomo Trust & Banking	日本

Chinese Version of Specimen Letters

<例信 1> 请求担任独家代理

敬启者：

本公司担任多家厂家的独家代理，专营精制棉织品，包括各类家用亚麻制品，行销中东。与贵公司向有事务联系，互利合作。贵公司纺织部亦十分了解有关事务合作的情况。

盼能成为贵公司独家代理，促销在巴林市场的货品。

上述建议，烦请早日赐复，以便进一步联系合作。

谨启

<例信 2> 拒绝对方担任独家代理

敬启者：

9月5日有关建议担任家用亚麻制品独家代理的来信收妥，谨致衷心谢意。

目前时机尚未成熟，不能应允该安排，深感抱歉。

然而，本公司乐意与贵公司先试行合作，为今后合作打下基础。

为证明担任独家代理的能力，贵公司宜就上述货品做市场调查，研究是否可扩大现有营业额。

随函奉上该货品报价单，敬希查照。专此候复。

谨启

<例信 3> 同意对方担任独家代理

敬启者：

5月18日建议担任办公室器具之独家代理来信已经收妥。

　　过去双方合作皆互利互助,能获您的眷愿做我公司于加拿大的独家代理,殊感荣幸。

　　现随函附上协议草稿,烦请查实各项条款,惠复是盼。

　　双方能加强业务,甚感欣喜。前次到访多伦多,蒙盛情款待,不胜感激。祈盼您莅临上海时,容我一尽地主之谊。

谨启

<例信 4> 物色代理商

敬启者:

　　本公司生产的一系列印刷机,获 20 多个国家的公司采用。

　　随函附上产品规格说明书,谨供参考。现为该产品开拓新市场,希望得知贵地区从事印刷工业的代理商资料。

　　如蒙贵公司协助,将不胜感激。如能拨冗寄来数个符合上述要求代理商商号,则感激不尽。

　　本公司将与其联系,研究能否建立互惠互利折业务关系。如蒙惠告,不胜感激!

谨启

<例信 5> 欢迎新代理商

敬启者:

　　欢迎加入本公司成为我们的一分子。相信您也会以本公司的产品为荣。欧洲销售代理安东尼·格林会定期与您联络,遇有问题可与他商讨。若有其他需要,欢迎向我提出。下月我将赴法国一游,期望能与您会面。谨祝产品销量节节上升。

谨启

Key to Exercises

Unit One Introduction of Business Letters

I. Look at the following letter, which breaks some of the rules we have just mentioned above. Identify each of the mistakes, and then rewrite the letter.

```
                    Business International Co., Ltd.
        68 Xingfu Street, Chongwen District, Beijing 100032, P. R. China
                  Tel: 86-10-67554422  Fax: 86-10-67554424

September 8, 2012
Purchase Manager
ABC Company
New York 66783
USA
Dear Sir or Madam,
                              Subject:
```

II. Design an envelope and fill it with the address in the above letter.

```
                                                    ┌─────────┐
                                                    │  Stamp  │
                                                    └─────────┘
68 Xingfu Street
Chongwen District
Beijing 100032
P. R. China
                        Purchase Manager
                        ABC Company
                        New York 66783
                        USA

By Air
```

Unit 2 Establishment of Business Relations

I. Translate the following terms into English:

1. commercial counselor's office
2. quote / quotation
3. order
4. chamber of commerce

5. handle, deal in
6. under separate cover
7. usual practice
8. catalogue
9. potential customers
10. pricelist

II. Translate the following terms into Chinese:

1. 建立业务关系
2. 业务范围
3. 进口商
4. 出口商
5. 欲购，想买
6. 贸易行名录
7. 专营
8. 总公司，总部，总店
9. 参考样品
10. 原样

III. Choose the best answer to complete the following sentences:

1. B　2. B　3. A　4. B　5. D
6. A　7. B　8. A　9. C　10. D

IV. Read the following sentences and try to find out the mistakes and make corrections. There is one mistake in each sentence.

1. We have obtained your name and address <u>to</u> Singapore Chamber of Commerce.
   (to → from)

2. We are in the market <u>on</u> Groundnuts.
   (on → for)

3. We are a state-operated corporation <u>dealing with</u> both the import and export of textiles.
   (dealing with → handling)

4. We wish to enter ∧ business relations with your corporation for the supply of light industrial products.
   (enter → enter into / enter → establish)

5. We are sending you catalog <u>in</u> separate cover.
   (in → by)

6. Would you please let us have a copy of your sample book so that we may acquaint ourselves <u>in</u> your business line?
   (in → with)

7. Should any of the items be <u>in</u> interest to you, please let us know
   (in → of)

8. Our mutual understanding and cooperation will certainly result <u>from</u> important business in the future.
   (from → in)

9. We have the pleasure of writing to contact <s>with</s> you in the hope of doing business with you.
   (contact with → contact)

10. In order to acquaint you with the chemical products we handle, we take pleasure in sending you <u>on</u> air our latest catalogue for your reference.
    (on → by)

Key to Exercises

V. Translate the following sentences into Chinese:

1. 我公司经营轻工产品已有 20 年。
2. 我们从商会得知你公司有意购买大量红茶。
3. 如果你认为我方的价格合理，请与我方联系。
4. 我们将非常乐意收到你方寄来的最新商品目录。
5. 我们从互联网上得知贵公司的名称和地址。

VI. Translate the following sentences into English:

1. We are willing to enter into business relations with your firm on the basis of equality, mutual benefit and exchanging what one has for what one needs.

2. Being specialized in the export of Chinese art and craft goods, we express our desire to trade with you in this line.

3. In order to promote business between us, we are airmailing you samples under separate cover for your reference.

4. If you are interested in our line of business, we would be happy to send you our company catalogue.

5. We foresee a bright prospect for your products in your market. We look forward to hearing from you and assure you of close cooperation at all times.

VII. Simulated writing:

Dear Sirs,

Your firm has been recommended to us by Golden Sun Trading Co., Ltd. with whom we have done business for many years.

We specialize in the exportation of Longquan Celadon, which have enjoyed great popularity in world market. Now we enclose a copy of our catalogue for your reference and hope you would contact us immediately if any item is interesting to you.

We hope you will give us an early reply.

Yours faithfully,

Unit 3 Enquiries and Replies

I. Translate the following terms into English:

1. commission
2. reasonable in price
3. by separate cover / post
4. for your reference
5. out of stock
6. latest catalogue
7. quote
8. terms of payment
9. specific enquiry
10. be in the market for

II. Translate the following terms into Chinese:

1. 样品
2. 建立业务关系
3. 折扣
4. 品质优良

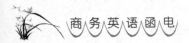

5. 一般询盘
7. 引起……的兴趣
9. 质量上乘
6. 立即回复
8. 业务范围
10. 插图目录（图解目录）

III. Choose the best answer to complete the following sentences:

1. B   2. D   3. A   4. D   5. A
6. B   7. D   8. A   9. C   10. D

IV. Fill in the following blanks with the words and expressions in the box, change the form when necessary:

1. quoted /on
3. available
5. for
7. interest
2. declining/acceptance
4. commission
6. to
8. appreciate

V. Translate the following sentences into Chinese:

1. 请向我方报椅子最低的汉堡港到岸价。
2. 如你的报价具有竞争性且交货期合适，我们将很高兴向你方订货。
3. 我们希望能向贵方再次订购，同时相信贵方能尽力满足我们的特殊要求。
4. 请通过传真方式向我方发来最优惠报盘，同时指明包装、规格、可供数量以及最早的交货期。
5. 若你们（产品）价格具有竞争力，我们相信能在我们当地市场上大量销售。

VI. Translate the following sentences into English:

1. Could you please quote us your lowest price on FOB Liverpool?
2. Samples and the most favorable quotation will be immediately sent to you upon receipt of your specific enquiry.
3. There is no possibility of getting business done unless you reduce your price by 5%.
4. We're very interested in importing your goods, could you please send us your catalogue, price list and samples if possible.
5. We shall appreciate it if you will send us the sample cutting by air immediately.

VII. Simulated writing:

Dear Sirs,

　　We learn from Sparking Co., Ltd., Chicago that you a leading exporter of hardware accessories in China. We are very interested in importing your goods and shall appreciate it if you can send us your latest illustrated catalogue and price list.

　　Please give us the detailed export information such as CIF New York, discount, packing and terms of payment etc.

　　We sincerely hope this will be a good start for our long-term business relationship between us and look forward to your early reply.

　　　　　　　　　　　　　　　　　　　　　　　　　　Yours sincerely,

Key to Exercises

Unit 4 Offers, Counter-offers and Acceptances

I. Translate the following terms into English:

1. offeror
2. offeree
3. specification
4. terms of payment
5. commission
6. preferential offer
7. duration of an offer / validity of an offer
8. confirmation of offer / confirming an offer
9. revocable offer
10. offer subject to prior sale

II. Translate the following terms into Chinese:

1. 新加坡成本加运费价
2. 简介说明
3. 大宗订单
4. 缺货子
5. 优惠价格
6. 原发盘
7. 虚盘
8. 报价
9. 撤回发盘
10. 根据，按照

III. Choose the best answer to complete the following sentences:

1. C   2. B   3. D   4. B   5. C
6. C   7. C   8. A   9. B   10. A

IV. Fill in the following blanks with the words and expressions in the box, change the form when necessary:

1. opportunity   2. recommend   3. purchase   4. quoting   5. various
6. substantial   7. subject   8. major   9. regularly   10. freight

V. Translate the following sentences into Chinese:

1. 上述报盘无约束力，以我方最后确认为准。
2. 感谢贵方昨日报盘，但因交货期过长，我方抱歉不能就此进行操作。在我方询价信中，已经说明交货期至关重要。
3. 我们希望能按比美国同类产品低10%的价格成交。
4. 现报盘如下，（此盘）以你方在9月24日前答复有效。
5. 你方还盘价格与现行市场价不符。

VI. Translate the following sentences into English:

1. We regret that your counter-offer is not acceptable to us as the price we quoted is quite realistic.
2. While you can reduce your offer by 2%, it is not acceptable to us.
3. From the present indications, the market will continue to be weak.
4. We might add here that, owing to heavy demand, our offer remains firm until January 10 and that there is little likelihood of the goods remaining unsold once this particular offer has lapsed.
5. There's no possibility of getting business done unless you reduce your price by 3%.

VII. Simulated writing:

Dear Sirs,

　　This is to acknowledge with thanks receipt of your letter of June 18.

　　As the price of our Cotton Table-cloth is reasonably fixed we regret we are not in a position to allow any discount.

　　Regarding terms of payment, we wish to point out that L/C is the usual practice with all customers in your country, and therefore we cannot make an exception in your case.

　　Since considerable business has been done with other buyers on our prevailing price an terms, we hope you will reconsider them and let us know your acceptance before long.

　　We await your prompt reply.

Yours faithfully,

Unit 5　Sales Promotion

I. Translate the following terms into English:

1. specialize in / be specialized in
2. moderate in price
3. enjoy fast sale / sell fast / sell well
4. supply from stock
5. out of stock
6. meet with warm reception
7. knock-out product
8. superior in quality
9. circular
10. give/offer/grant a 10% discount

II. Translate the following terms into Chinese:

1. 设计新颖
2. 性能稳定
3. 畜产品
4. 带有插图的产品目录
5. 特殊优惠
6. 工艺精湛
7. 迅速作决定
8. 比……要好
9. 以……为准
10. 售后服务

III. Choose the best answer to complete the following sentences:

1. B　　2. A　　3. C　　4. D　　5. A
6. D　　7. C　　8. C　　9. B　　10. D

IV. Fill in the following blanks of each sentence, pay attention to first letter of each word has been given:

1. quality / price / ready
2. design / reception
3. place / allow / discount
4. recommend / work / stock
5. purchase / specialized / after-sale

Key to Exercises

V. Translate the following sentences into Chinese:

1. 凭此优惠券你在"聪明孩子"玩具品店购买商品可以享受9折优惠；购物满300港币，可获赠精美礼品一份。

2. 我们18K珠宝饰品质量上乘，工艺精湛，所以很受东南亚地区用户的青睐。

3. 为了能够使你方对我们产品有更进一步的了解，我们另邮产品插图目录及一套相关的产品说明书供你方参考。

4. 虽然我们的MP3产品在价格上要比韩国产的高10%，但在产品质量和性能方面我们比他们的要好。

5. 我们打算清仓，若你方购买500套以上，我方可给你们打7折。

VI. Translate the following sentences into English:

1. We take this opportunity to introduce our sports apparatus herewith the catalogue and price list.

2. We have 15 years of experience selling overseas. Our factory produces 600,000 men's shirts per month, all for export.

3. In view of our long-term business relationship, we are willing to offer you a discount of 20% off.

4. In the past 10 years, we have built a reputation of honesty and integrity that is well known in business and financial circles, our products are popular with customers.

5. Our company is one of the leading tea suppliers in China and can supply various types of tea, our tea sells well, so we recommend you to place an order with us.

VII. Simulated writing:

Dear Sirs,

    We are glad to owe your name and address to the Commercial Counselor's Office of the Chinese Embassy in Canada. Now we take the liberty of introducing GPS navigators, our main products for export.

    We are the largest manufacturer specializing in GPS navigator products in China with a history of 12 years and enjoy good reputation in domestic and overseas markets. Our products are superior in quality, reasonable in price, easy in operation and novel in design, therefore they meet with warm reception in different countries and regions throughout the world.

    Now we enclose the price list and illustrated catalogue for your reference. We deem it to your advantage to push the sale of our products in your local market. We are prepared to give you a 10% discount if your first order exceeds 1,000 pieces.

    In view of the great demand for our products, we advise you to work fast and place an order with us as soon as possible.

    We are looking forward to receiving your reply.

                                                    Yours sincerely,

Unit 6　Orders and Acknowledgements

I. Translate the following terms into English:

1. place a trial order
2. sample
3. Sales Confirmation
4. Sales Contract
5. Proforma Invoice
6. counter-signature
7. discount
8. unit price
9. stock
10. terms of payment

II. Translate the following terms into Chinese:

1. 确认
2. 定期订单
3. 续订订单；续订的货物
4. 执行订单
5. 以你方为受益人
6. 安排装运
7. 30 天期限的付款交单
8. 供……存档
9. 一式三份
10. 放心

III. Choose the best answer to complete the following sentences:

1. A　2. A　3. C　4. B　5. C
6. C　7. D　8. B　9. B　10. C

IV. Fill in the following blanks of each sentence, pay attention to first letter of each word has been given:

1. best
2. sign, file
3. made, draft
4. order, requirements
5. open, favor

V. Translate the following sentences into Chinese:

1. 我方已接受你方第 13E 号订单订购 60 吨葡萄柚。请按照合同规定的条款开立以我方为受益人的信用证。
2. 我们认为贵公司的产品质量和价格都合意，并很高兴以现货现价为条件订购下列货物。
3. 由于我们双方都已在合同上签名，因此合同是有效的并对双方有约束力。
4. 抱歉你方所要的货物没有现货。
5. 很遗憾，鉴于你方第 FL34 号订单项下部分商品不属于我方经营范围，我方仅能部分接受你方订单。

VI. Translate the following sentences into English:

1. If you find everything is correct, please sign and return one copy of the contract to us for our file.
2. We are pleased to place an order with you for 1,500 DVD players, enclosing the order No.WL120.

3. We wish to infirm you that the relative L/C has been opened by the Bank of China.
4. We have enclosed Sales Confirmation No. DM-56 in duplicate to you.
5. We are glad to have concluded this deal with you.

VII. Simulated writing:

Dear Sirs,

　　Thank you for your quotation and the sample delivered on 6 June.

　　We are satisfied with the quality and price you offered. We take pleasure in enclosing our Order No. LB120 for your blouses, 20 dozen for each size (i.e. small, medium and large).

　　We hope you can supply these items from stock and make delivery by the end of July.

　　As the ordered goods are urgently needed by our customers, we would like you to arrange shipment as soon as possible.

　　Look forward to your early reply.

　　　　　　　　　　　　　　　　　　　　　　　　　　　　　　　　Yours truly,

Unit 7　Terms of Payment

I. Translate the following terms into English:

1. terms of payment / payment terms　　2. conclude business / transaction
3. sight L/C　　4. 30 days' L/C
5. confirmed, irrevocable L/C　　6. commercial invoice
7. pay on delivery　　8. pay in/by installment
9. telegraphic transfer　　10. mail transfer

II. Translate the following terms into Chinese:

1. 与……一致　　2. 期满，到期
3. 兹谈及，关于　　4. 履行合同
5. 开立信用证　　6. 规定
7. 按要求　　8. 以……为受益人 / 抬头
9. 背书，赞同　　10. 合法持有人

III. Choose the best answer to complete the following sentences:

1. B　2. D　3. C　4. B　5. D
6. B　7. B　8. C　9. C　10. C

IV. Fill in the following blanks with the words and expressions in the box, change the form when necessary:

(1) requesting　(2) to your request　(3) clear　(4) transactions　(5) amount
(6) equivalent　(7) exceed　(8) payment　(9) accommodation　(10) light

V. Translate the following sentences into Chinese:

1. 由于这笔交易的金额很小，对这批货物的货款我们准备接受即期付款交单。

2. 我们很遗憾，你方订单中规定的付款方式，我方无法接受。

3. 因为这一订单货款较少，我们相信你会同意我方在收到货运单据后通过信汇付款。

4. 因为这是一个很大的订单，机器要按你方规格制造，我们只能在即期信用证的基础上接受你方订单。

5. 非常抱歉，我们不能同意在装运货物前付款。

6. 我们不认为贵方会有任何困难开立以我方为受益人的保兑的不可撤销的信用证，来支付你方目前的这张订单，这样，我们可以预期在一个肯定的日期收到货款。

7. 按照你方要求，我方例外地接受即期付款交单，但这不应被看做是先例。

8. 我们很抱歉不得不谢绝贵方一切 D/P 付款。对于这些传统货物，我们一般的贸易支付方法是信用证付款。

9. 我方建议开立以我方为抬头的见票 60 天付款的汇票支付货款，请回复是否同意。

10. 按你方要求，我们破例接受即期付款交单，但只此一次，下不为例。

VI. Translate the following sentences into English:

1. In order to pave the way for your pushing the sale of our products in your market, we will accept payment by D/P at sight as a special accommodation.

2. We ask for payment by confirmed, irrevocable letter of credit in our favour, available by draft at sight, reaching us one month ahead of the stipulated time of shipment, remaining valid for negotiation in China until the 15th day after the time of shipment, and allowing transhipment and partial shipments.

3. Owing to the high expense for the opening of L/C here, we suggest that you draw on us a sight draft for collection through your bank against the shipping documents. We assure you that as soon as the draft is presented we will make payment.

4. For this transaction, we exceptionally agree to make payment by L/C but for future transactions, we would ask for more favorable payment terms, i. e. D/P.

5. In view of the long business relations between us, we will, as an exception, accept payment terms by D/P 30 days for your present trial order and hope you will accept our terms.

6. It has been our usual practice to do business with payment by D/P at sight instead of by L/C. We should, therefore, like you to accept D/P terms for this transaction and future ones.

7. Your request for payment by D/P has been taken into consideration. In view of the small amount of this transaction, we are prepared to effect shipment on this (D/P) basis.

8. While thanking you for your order for 50 reams of Glass paper, we regret being unable to agree to payment by D/A as it is our usual practice to accept payment by L/C only and you cannot be regarded as an exception.

9. Your proposal for payment by time draft for Order No. 1156 is acceptable to us, and we shall draw on you at 60 days' sight after the goods have been shipped. Please honour our draft when it falls due.

10. Our usual mode of payment is by confirmed, irrevocable letter of credit, available by draft at sight for the full amount of the invoice value to be established in our favour through a bank acceptable to us.

VII. Simulated writing:

Dear Sirs,

We have received your L/C No. 20110908 issued by the Bank of China, Shanxi Branch, for the amount of $30,000 covering 800 bag of women's down jackets. On perusal, we find that transshipment and partial shipment are not allowed.

As direct steamers to your port are few and far between, we have to ship via Hong Kong more often than not. As to partial shipment, it would be to our mutual benefit because we could ship immediately whatever we have on hand instead of waiting for the whole lot to be completed. Therefore, we are faxing this afternoon, asking you to amend the L/C to read: "TRANSHIPMENT AND PARTSHIPMENT ALLOWED".

We shall be glad if you will see to it that amendment is faxed without delay, as our goods have been packed ready for shipment for quite some time.

Yours faithfully,

Unit 8 Packing

I. Translate the following terms into English:

1. packing list
2. metal strapping
3. indicative marks
4. bulk cargo
5. crate
6. consignee
7. inflammable liquid
8. polythene sheet
9. use no hook
10. gross weight

II. Translate the following terms into Chinese:

1. 货运代理人
2. 原产国
3. 辐射性的
4. 平均搭配
5. 集合外包装
6. 集装袋
7. 海运包装
8. 中性包装
9. 波纹瓦楞纸盒
10. 易碎品

III. Choose the best answer to complete the following sentences:

1. C   2. A   3. B   4. B   5. D
6. A   7. D   8. C   9. A   10. B

IV. Fill in the following blanks with the words and expressions in the box, change the form when necessary:

1. put up with   2. facilitate   3. secured   4. ensures   5. accepted
6. observed   7. customary   8. novel   9. covering   10. comparatively

V. Translate the following sentences into Chinese:

1. 20 英尺标箱长 5.69 米，宽 2.13 米，高 2.18 米，因此一个 20 英尺标箱的体积约为

26.42 立方米。

2. 泡沫塑料用来防止挤压。

3. 我们同意关于包装和运输唛头的条款。

4. 请速向我们寄送一式三份的装箱单，并注明每箱的毛重、净重、长度、高度、宽度及箱子总数。

5. 既然丝绸服装在运输过程中易受潮损或雨淋，因此有必要采取预防措施。

VI. Translate the following sentences into English:

1. The packing must be seaworthy and strong enough to endure rough handling.

2. All the cartons should be lined with shockproof corrugated cardboard and are wrapped up with kraft paper.

3. Writing brushes are packed in wooden box, 5 pieces to one box.

4. Please see to it that warning marks like "FRAGILE"、"HANDLE WITH CARE"、"USE NO HOOK"should be stenciled on the outer packing.

5. The new packing adopted by us is not only easy to handle but also suitable for window display.

VII. Simulated writing:

Dear Sirs,

  We are in receipt of your initial order No. TK-223 for 5,000 pieces of GPS navigators on Oct. 13. We are in a position to supply them from stock due to the sufficient supply. Now, we'd like to inform you the packing details for the export commodities:

  All the navigators are packed in cardboard box lined with shock-proof plastic foam, 100 pieces to one carton sealed with polythene sheet. The gross weight of each carton is 70 kilos. In addition, we have stenciled the shipping marks with an ellipse, inside it is the initials "ETC" of consignee, under it is the port of destination (Vancouver), package number and country of origin. Meanwhile, warning marks like "HANDLE WITH CARE", "USE NO HOOK" are also stenciled.

  We enclose the following shipping documents:

  Packing List in duplicate; Certificate of Origin and Commercial Invoice in triplicate respectively.

  We hope the goods will be in good condition when received.

Yours faithfully,

Unit 9 Insurance

I. Translate the following terms into English:

1. invoice value
2. Ocean Marine Cargo Clauses
3. Institute Cargo Clauses (ICC)
4. FPA (Free from Particular Average)
5. WPA (With Particular Average)
6. All Risks
7. to cover insurance (to effect insurance)
8. coverage
9. premium
10. insurer (underwriter, insurance broker)

Key to Exercises

II. Translate the following terms into Chinese:

1. 保险金额
2. 保险单
3. 保险凭证
4. 借记通知
5. 全部损失
6. 保险条款
7. 海损
8. 部分损失
9. 保险范围
10. 保险批单

III. Choose the best answer to complete the following sentences:

1. C 2. C 3. D 4. B 5. A
6. A 7. C 8. B 9. D 10. B

IV. Fill in the following blanks with the words and expressions in the box, change the form when necessary:

(1) covering (2) refer (3) insurance (4) cover (5) additional
(6) insured (7) stated (8) franchise (9) lower (10) forward

V. Translate the following sentences into Chinese:

1. 我们已根据总保额为 50,000 美元的预约保单的规定，对今后启运你方制造的每批手工工具办理从我方的天津货仓至你方汉堡货仓的保险。如果货物的价值超过此金额，我们将作出相应的调整。

2. 我方客户希望贵方报纽约 CIF 价，因为他们认为你方安排投保较为简便。他们希望了解投保的险别、数额及由何人承保。

3. 我方通常以发票面额 110%价值投保一切险，如果你方对投保数额或范围有特别要求，请通知我方，可尽所能满足你方要求，但额外费用记在你方账目。

4. 请务必将上述船货按发票金额的 120%投保一切险。我们知道按照你们惯例，你们只按发票金额另加 10%投保。因此，额外的保险费将由我方承担。

5. 由于保险经纪人一般对保险业务的技术问题比普通的商人更熟悉，因此，后者通常使用前者的服务来取得保险单。

6. 如果你方希望成本加运费价，而不是如我方所报的成本、保险加运费价，你可以从报价中减去 0.3%；那么，结果的价格就是你方要求的成本加运费价。

7. 货物保险将由我方按照 CIF 金额的 110%投保，如需加保其他险别，其费用由买方负担。

8. 如果货物发生损失或损坏，你方可以货物到达你方 60 天内根据查验报告，保险单，索赔声明和其他有关单据向我们保险公司在你方当地的代理商提出索赔。

9. 请为我方订购的货物投保金额高于发票金 30%，以便万一事故发生能负担部分可能的支付。

10. 中国人民保险公司在世界各地都有调查和代理人员，如果你方货物发生任何损失或灭失，可在你方得到索赔。

VI. Translate the following sentences into English:

1. Please see to it that the above-mentioned goods should be shipped before the 15th July

and the goods should be covered for 130% of invoice value against All Risks. We know that according to your usual practice, you insure the goods only for 10% above invoice value, therefore the extra premium will be for our account.

2. Please let us know immediately the detailed risks you wish to insure against for your shipment in question. In the absence of definite instructions from our clients, we usually cover W.A. and war risk.

3. Since the cause of the damage is within the coverage of the insurance policy, you should claim compensation from the insurance company concerned.

4. In accordance with your cable instructions, we have today arranged insurance as usual with an approved underwriter.

5. We have insured your Order No. 55 for the invoice cost plus 15% up to the port of destination.

6. Claim on damaged goods usually involves three parties, i. e. the insured, the carrier and the insurer.

7. The goods under Contract No. 66 are ready for shipment. Please let us know immediately the details of the insurance you wish to cover for the consignment.

8. Insurance policy issued by insurance Company should be covered against W.P.A. for 10% above the full invoice value.

VII. Simulated writing:

August 30, 2011

Mr. Jones
J. B. Samson & Company
2816 St. Susan Street
Los Angeles, CA 030012
U.S.A.

Dear Mr. Jones,

Many thanks for your telex of Aug. 29, requesting us to effect insurance for your account on the captioned shipment sold on the CFR basis.

We are pleased to inform you that we have covered on the goods with PICC Shanghai Branch, against All Risks for USD 650,000. The relevant insurance policy is now enclosed together with our debit note for the premium.

Your cargo is expected to arrive at New York around October 20, on the M. V. Shenfeng, which will sail from Shanghai on or before September 15. We will advise you of the exact shipment time by fax.

Yours sincerely,

Enclose: (1) Insurance Policy
   (2) Debit Note

Unit 10 Shipment

I. Translate the following terms into English:

1. effect / arrange shipment
2. be ready for shipment
3. port of loading
4. port of destination
5. book shipping space
6. freight
7. bulk cargo
8. partial shipment
9. transshipment
10. prompt shipment

II. Translate the following terms into Chinese:

1. 装运指示
2. 装运通知
3. 裸装货
4. 航空运单
5. 预抵期
6. 机动轮
7. 预离期
8. 蒸汽轮
9. 一式两份
10. 装运单据

III. Choose the best answer to complete the following sentences:

1. B 2. C 3. C 4. A 5. C
6. B 7. B 8. C 9. D 10. A

IV. Fill in the following blanks with the words and expressions in the box, change the form when necessary:

1. overdue   2. punctual   3. utmost   4. assurance   5. sets
6. facilitate   7. proceed   8. consignment   9. obliged   10. dispatched

V. Translate the following sentences into Chinese:

1. 非常抱歉我们不能接受推迟装运，因为我们的客户急需这些货物，所以货物的迟交将使我们处于很被动的境地。

2. 为了赶上销售旺季，请收到我们的信用证后就安排装船，并电告我们装船通知。

3. 我方客户急需该批货物，希望你方能由六月提前到五月发货。

4. 很高兴通知你们 7246 号订单今天已经由"阳光号"直达轮发出，到达你方港口时间为 12 月 12 日。

5. 船公司通知我们，因为到你方的直达班轮和非定期轮船都很少，到 11 月底为止的船仓位都已经被订完。

VI. Translate the following sentences into English:

1. The goods are ready for shipment for a long time. Please inform us of the name, the voyage number and the E.T.A. of the vessel so as to enable us to effect shipment in time.

2. The goods will be shipped by M.V. "East Wind" Voyage No. 183, which is due to arrive at Copenhagen on October 31. Please book the shipping space immediately and confirm that the goods will be ready in time.

3. Something unexpected compels us to seek your cooperation by advancing shipment of the goods under Contract No. 123 from August to July.

4. We understand your position, but we are sorry to tell you that we can not advance shipment since our factory is booked with heavy orders.

5. This is to notify you that we have shipped you today 200 cartons of alarm clocks by M.V. "Yellow River" Voyage No. 029. They are to be transshipped at Singapore and are expected to reach your port early next month..

VII. Simulated writing:

Dear Sirs,

　　We have 50 cases of chemical reagents at the above address ready for dispatch to any European main port, and shall be glad if you will arrange for your shipping container to collect them. Each case weighs 60 kilograms.

　　As our client requires us to ship the goods not later than July 15, please quote us for a shipping container from Hong Kong to the above mentioned port before the deadline.

　　Your early quotation will be highly appreciated..

Yours faithfully,

Unit 11　Complaints and Claims

I. Translate the following terms into English:

1. short weight 　　　　2. look into / investigate
3. settle the claim 　　　4. lodge a claim
5. compensate for / make up for 　6. inferior quality
7. breach of contract 　　8. delay in delivery
9. survey report 　　　　10. dispute

II. Translate the following terms into Chinese:

1. 接受索赔 　　　2. 与……相符
3. 疏忽 　　　　　4. 替代品
5. 色差 　　　　　6. 次品
7. 要求赔偿 　　　8. 受损方
9. 差错，不符 　　10. 不可抗力

III. Choose the best answer to complete the following sentences:

1. C　2. B　3. A　4. D　5. A
6. B　7. C　8. B　9. B　10. D

IV. Fill in the following blanks with the words and expressions in the box, change the form when necessary:

1. claim　　2. inconvenience　　3. re-inspection　　4. report　　5. investigation

242

Key to Exercises

V. Translate the following sentences into Chinese:

1. 我方对于您未能收到 10 套 6 马力航海牌船尾发动机一事感到十分抱歉，但是我方认为我们双方都难辞其咎。

2. 我们非常遗憾地告知你方，你们的索赔不能被受理，因为它已远远超过了合同规定的索赔期限。

3. 由于这批货物质量低劣，我方将会把 100 箱全部退回，并务必请你方更换这些商品。

4. 如合同所示，轻微色差是允许的。故此，你提出的问题依然属于正常现象。

5. 对于此次货物损坏，唯一合理的解释是纸箱在转运港由于粗鲁搬运被挤坏。

VI. Translate the following sentences into English:

1. On checking, we find there is a shortage of 100 kilos.

2. Please return the 10 defective printers at your expense.

3. We hope you will try your best to make up for the loss we sustained.

4. We have no choice but to lodge a claim against you.

5. We will make effort to ensure that similar errors do not occur again.

VII. Simulated writing:

CLAIM FOR SHORT DELIVERY

Dear Sirs,

GPS navigators under the order No.TK-223 have been shipped to Vancouver by M.V. "YONGFENG" on 3 December. When taking the delivery, 10 cartons have been found missing. We were told by the shipping company that only 40 cartons had been shipped on board.

Because the short delivery is in large, please make up a deficiency of 10 cartons of the GPS navigators when you deliver the last three items. You are kindly requested to check whether these 50 cartons of GPS navigators were loaded on ship in whole at the port of loading.

Please reply by cable as soon as possible.

Yours sincerely,

Unit 12   Agency

I. Translate the following terms into English:

1. represent
2. marketing
3. proposal
4. financial standing
5. entrust
6. territory
7. in view of
8. profitable
9. commission
10. undertake

II. Translate the following terms into Chinese:

1. 委托人
2. 总代理

3. 营业额
4. 批发商
5. 委托代购人，订货客户
6. 在……方面有经验且熟练
7. 在起始阶段
8. 起草协议
9. 值得称赞的
10. 到现在为止，在此以前

III. Choose the best answer to complete the following sentences:

1. B   2. B   3. C   4. A   5. B
6. C   7. D   8. A   9. B   10. B

IV. Fill in the following blanks of each sentence, pay attention to first letter of each word has been given:

1. promote / territory
2. conditions / draft
3. offering / appreciate
4. consider / application
5. demand / commission

V. Translate the following sentences into Chinese:

1. 我方写信为你方提供在中国的代理业务。
2. 我方想知道，你方能否指定我方为你方木制玩具销售代理商。
3. 如你方能接受我方的条件，我方将指定你方为独家代理商。
4. 除非你方提高销售额，否则我方很难指定你方为独家代理商。
5. 我方通常接受 5%的佣金。

VI. Translate the following sentences into English:

1. We write to offer our services as your agents in China.
2. We thank you for your letter of 5th May and are favorably impressed by your proposal for a sole agency.
3. We think it premature for us to discuss the question of agency at the present stage..
4. We undertake not to sell the similar or competing of sales of other manufactures.
5. The above price includes your 5% commission.

VII. Simulated writing:

Dear Sirs,

　　We are glad to owe your name and address to the Commercial Counselor's Office of the Chinese Embassy in the USA. Now we take the liberty of introducing our company.

　　We specialize in the trade of household decorative wares. We have been in trading with Shanghai Arts and Crafts Corporation for more than ten years and our relations have proved mutually satisfactory. You may refer to them for any information concerning our firm.

We are very much interested in entering into an exclusive arrangement with your corporation for the promotion of sales of your enamelware in New York.

We are looking forward to receiving your reply.

Yours respectfully,

Bibliography
（参 考 文 献）

[1] 魏莉霞，周峰．国际商务函电[M]．北京：北京大学出版社，2006．

[2] 冯祥春，李敬梅．外经贸英语函电句型与写作一本通[M]．第二版．北京：中国商务出版社，2004．

[3] 方宁，王维平．商务英语函电[M]．杭州：浙江大学出版社，2004．

[4] 关国才．外贸英文函电[M]．北京：清华大学出版社，北京交通大学出版社，2010．

[5] 侯雁慧．外贸英语实务[M]．大连：大连理工大学出版社，2008．

[6] 檀文茹，徐静珍．外贸函电[M]．北京：中国人民大学出版社，2004．

[7] 甘鸿．外经贸英语函电[M]．上海：上海科学技术文献出版社，1996．

[8] 戚云方．新编外经贸英语函电与谈判[M]．杭州：浙江大学出版社，2002．

[9] 李宏波．国际商务英语等级考试教程[M]．中级．北京：科学技术文献出版社，2007．

[10] 袁永友．全国外销员统考外贸英语全真试题评析[M]．北京：中国对外经济贸易出版社，2003．

[11] 刘法公．国际贸易实务英语[M]．杭州：浙江大学出版社，2002．

[12] 方春祥．外贸函电[M]．北京：中国人民大学出版社，2005．

[13] 隋思忠．外经贸英语[M]．修订本．北京：中国对外经济贸易出版社，2002．

[14] 兰天．外贸英语函电[M]．第四版．大连：东北财经大学出版社，2004．

[15] 赵银德．外贸函电[M]．北京：机械工业出版社，2006．

[16] 中国国际贸易学会商务专业培训考试办公室．外贸业务员英语[M]．北京：中国商务出版社，2008．

[17] 黄丽威．外贸函电与单证[M]．北京：高等教育出版社，2006．

[18] 刘杰英．函电与单证[M]．第二版．大连：大连理工大学出版社，2007．

[19] 罗凤翔，杜清萍．国际商务英语模拟实训教程[M]．2008版．北京：中国商务出版社，2008．

[20] 王虹，耿伟．外贸英语函电[M]．北京：清华大学出版社，2009．

[21] 葛平，周维家．外贸英语函电[M]．第二版．上海：复旦大学出版社，2010．